WALLACE
STEVENS

WALLACE STEVENS

A MYTHOLOGY
OF SELF

Milton J. Bates

University of California Press
Berkeley
Los Angeles
London

University of California Press
Berkeley and Los Angeles, California

University of California Press, Ltd.
London, England

© 1985 by
The Regents of the University of California

Printed in the United States of America
1 2 3 4 5 6 7 8 9

Library of Congress Cataloging in Publication Data

Bates, Milton J.
    Wallace Stevens : a mythology of self.

    Bibliography: p.
    Includes indexes.
    1. Stevens, Wallace, 1879–1955. 2. Self in literature.
3. Poets, American—20th century—Biography.
I. Title.
PS3537.T4753Z592   1985   811'.52   [B]   84–8468
ISBN 0–520–04909–8

for Puck

Contents

Preface

What counts is the mythology of self.
"FROM THE JOURNAL OF CRISPIN"

There must have been such a moment—repeated how many times since?—when the thinking animal, stooping to drink from a pool of water, stopped instead to drink in the mystery of his own image. Pondering that outwardness of the inward thing and the inwardness of that outward thing, he became Plato, Paul of Tarsus, Hume, Nietzsche, Freud, and the latest post-structuralist critic. He survived Narcissus to invent the myth of Narcissus and those countless myths of self whose book has yet to be written.

This is not that book; neither is it biography. Rather, I suggest how one poet transcended biography by transforming it into fables of identity—what he called "mythology of self." Beginning with his adolescent years, when he first understood that he might in some measure create the self he would become, I follow him through his subsequent choices and makings until he arrived at the mature Wallace Stevens who regards us from the last pages of his *Collected Poems*. As poet, he enjoyed the godlike prerogative of continually refashioning himself in his poetry. His was not, however, a *creatio ex nihilo*: at each phase of his career, he had perforce to shape his image and likeness from materials that lay ready to hand, and his hand was to some extent subdued to what it worked in. I have therefore thought it useful to trace the genealogy of the selves that figure most prominently in his work. Concentrating on these, I have had to forgo cataloguing the many nonce personae that flit through his poems and to ignore seductive notions of self whose appeal was apparently lost on him.

My approach, then, is chiefly historical. Though I have benefited from recent criticism which suggests how Stevens' work anticipated—indeed, helped to generate—our current inquiries into the nature of the self, language, and reality, I have tried not to make this sophisticated poet any more sophisticated than he was. I generally proceed as though the meaning of the poems can be determined, and without elaborate theoretical apparatus. I do not forget, however, that fictive things wink as they will, wink most (to misquote Stevens) when critics wince.

As for my intended audience: I trust that this study will afford the Stevens specialist a fresh perspective on the poet and his most important work; but I particularly address these pages to students in and out of the university whose interest and good will have been balked by the difficulties of Stevens' poetry and the sometimes more formidable difficulties of Stevens criticism. For their benefit, I have avoided clogging the text with references to the body of Stevens scholarship and criticism that lies behind this book. My footnotes testify to this indebtedness; were there twice as many, they would not give credit to all of the books and essays that have shaped my understanding of Stevens and his poetry. I should like, however, to single out four persons whose work has proven indispensable to me: Holly Stevens, for her editions of her father's letters and journal; Samuel French Morse, for his edition of the uncollected poetry and prose; J. M. Edelstein, for his monumental bibliography; and Thomas F. Walsh, for his concordance to the poetry. I am further indebted to Holly Stevens for the specific information she has cheerfully and conscientiously supplied over the years, in our correspondence and conversations.

I take special pleasure in setting down here the names of the persons and institutions that have helped me bring this project to completion. It began as a thesis scrivened in delight under the direction of Alex Zwerdling, whose counsel and encouragement have sustained me through the seven years of its subsequent evolution. A. Walton Litz provided the kind of support for which he has become legendary among younger scholars, not all of them so young any more. I consider myself fortunate to have spent eighteen of the happiest months of my life doing research in the Wallace Stevens Collection at the Henry E. Huntington Library. To the staff, research associates, and readers at this remarkable place I am indebted for more than scholarly assistance; they and their spouses made the Huntington truly a home for my family and me. In addition to two summer stipends from the Huntington, my work was subsidized by fellowships from the Danforth Foundation and the American Council of Learned Societies, the latter with the help of funding from the National Endowment for the Humanities. On its way into print, the manuscript passed through the skillful hands of my editors at the University of California Press, Doris Kretschmer and Phyllis Killen, and those who assisted in other phases of its preparation: Mary Charrey, Donna Chenail, Natalie Hahn, David Howard, and Sally Serafim.

Second to none as a nurturing presence behind these pages is my wife. To Puck, the paramour blessedly exterior, I dedicate the book.

The reader can assume, unless a footnote tells him otherwise, that unpublished manuscripts and letters which belonged to the Stevens family, as well as their books, are in the Wallace Stevens Collection at the Huntington Library; I use these with the permission of the Huntington. For permission to use materials in other collections, I am grateful to Holly Stevens and the following institutions: the Department of Special Collections, University of Chicago Library (cited parenthetically as "Chicago" in the notes); Special Collections, University of Maryland Libraries (Maryland); Special Collections and Rare Books, University of Massachusetts/Amherst Library (Massachusetts); the Princeton University Library (Princeton); the Poetry/Rare Books Collection of the University Libraries, State University of New York at Buffalo (Buffalo); and the Collection of American Literature, the Beinecke Rare Book and Manuscript Library, Yale University (Yale). The Pennsylvania State University Library and the Reading (Pennsylvania) Public Library provided me with copies of items from the *Reading Eagle*. The Hartford Insurance Group supplied a copy of Stevens' "Insurance and Social Change" from the *Hartford Agent*. I am grateful, finally, to Richard Eberhart for allowing me to quote from his letter to Conrad Aiken, and to Arthur P. Laws for allowing me to quote from Judge Arthur Powell's letter to Stevens.

A Note on Texts and Dates

Except where otherwise noted, I use *The Collected Poems of Wallace Stevens* (1955) for the text of the poems. Poems in this volume can be readily located by means of the title index, though I sometimes supply a page number parenthetically in my text, following the abbreviation *CP*. I routinely supply page numbers for work published in the *Opus Posthumous* (1957, abbreviated *OP*), ed. Samuel French Morse; *The Necessary Angel: Essays on Reality and the Imagination* (1951, *NA*); the *Letters of Wallace Stevens* (1966, *L*), *The Palm at the End of the Mind* (1971, *PEM*), and *Souvenirs and Prophecies: The Young Wallace Stevens* (1977, *SP*), ed. Holly Stevens. I quote from these copyrighted works with the permission of Holly Stevens and the publisher, Alfred A. Knopf.

Dates assigned to poems and essays indicate year of first publication; those to lectures, year of delivery; those to plays, year of first performance. For the poems "Anecdote of the Abnormal" and "A Mythology Reflects Its Region" I accept the approximate dates of composition suggested by Morse in the *Opus Posthumous*.

· 1 ·

Selecting One's Parents

When Wallace Stevens' sister Elizabeth turned twenty-two,
she received from their father a letter studded with the
kind of wisdom J. Alfred Prufrock might have called "high
sentence." One piece of advice, otherwise unexception-
able, must have struck her as a trifle belated. "The first
step in the road to success," Garrett Barcalow Stevens
wrote, "requires a child to be mighty careful in the selection of its parents."[1] Fortunately for the Stevens children,
they had all chosen well. Wallace, by some criteria the most
successful of the five, showed uncommon discretion, assuming that he had planned from all eternity to be the man
and poet he was. Besides Garrett and Margaretha Catharine Zeller Stevens, he had other parents in the extended—
he might have said "French"—sense of the word (CP 303).
His hometown, Harvard College, George Santayana,
newspaper journalism, and New York City all helped to
shape his character and sensibility. But the road to success
led Wallace back to Garrett Stevens at a critical juncture in
his career, a Peniel where he wrestled with his father as
with an angel of vocation. He emerged from the experience
not yet a poet, but already the man who divided his life
between the world of business and the world of imagination.

The adult Wallace Stevens tended, in retrospect, to assign his mother a subordinate role in his personal devel-

1. Letter written ca. 1907.

opment. He recalled that Kate Stevens "just kept house and ran the family,"[2] and her extant letters do evoke a life largely taken up with cooking, laundry, and the peregrinations of her children. If the word "just" seems an ungrateful fillip, it is offset by Wallace's journal entries lauding the care and energy with which she performed these duties (*SP* 253–55). It is further offset by certain details in the admittedly sketchy portrait we have of this self-effacing woman. For example, though Kate Stevens' father was a shoemaker and the family poor, she traced her ancestry back to an officer in the Revolutionary army and so qualified as a Daughter of the American Revolution. Wallace was amused, as a young man, at her pride in family (*SP* 208) but came to share it himself. He not only featured members of his mother's family in his poems, but also borrowed words and phrases from their speech, the Pennsylvania Dutch dialect he had heard his mother use when speaking to farmers' wives at the market (*L* 417).

Wallace once remarked that, of the five Stevens children who survived infancy, he and his sister Mary Katharine most resembled their mother (*L* 213–14). He may have been thinking of his mother's religious piety, which he shared after his fashion, and her interest in poetry. A schoolteacher before she married Garrett Stevens in 1876, Kate had been involved professionally as well as personally with literature. Around 1869, she edited or helped to edit a literary publication of the annual Berks County Teachers' Institute.[3] When Garrett wanted to present her with a

2. Quoted in Jerald E. Hatfield, "More about Legend," *Trinity Review* 8 (1954): 30.

3. At the Huntington Library is a notebook into which Kate Stevens entered an editorial preface, a poem identified as "original," popular verse and verse parodies from published sources, and a selection of aphorisms, verse quotations, and humor. The preface suggests that this was the final manuscript copy of an organ published around 1869 by one of the institutes for the improvement of teaching in the public schools. Those for Berks County were held annually in Reading beginning in 1867. I am grateful to Paul M. Zall for help in identifying the popular verse in the notebook.

Christmas gift in 1871, he chose a collection of Alexander Pope's poems.[4] Kate fostered Wallace's interest in writing as the sympathetic reader of his lively teenage letters from Ephrata and Ivyland and later of his college verses (*L* 5–10, 23). She also presented him with two of the works he consulted often in college—a twelve-volume set of Emerson and Ernest Rhys's *The Prelude to Poetry*, an anthology of criticism by major English poets.[5]

We know more about the parent who played the dominant role in Wallace's development. Garrett Stevens might be defined—superficially, at least—by the question he placed before all others in his catechism for American youth: "*Starting with nothing, how shall I sustain myself and perhaps a wife and family—and send my boys to College and* live comfortably in my old age [?]"[6] Garrett was sixteen or seventeen years old when he confronted that question himself, though probably not in exactly these terms. He answered it by leaving the family farm in Feasterville, Pennsylvania, to become a schoolteacher. But the classroom could not long detain this ambitious young man who had memorized the U.S. Constitution by the time he was fifteen and who had been deeply moved by the notion of constitutional government (*SP* 17). Law was his destiny, and with ten cents more than nothing in his pocket, he came to Reading around 1870 to begin his clerkship.[7]

Admitted to practice in Berks County two years later, he quickly gained a reputation as an energetic and eloquent lawyer with a pleasing personality.[8] He continued to fur-

4. *The Poetical Works of Alexander Pope*, ed. Rev. H. F. Cary (London: Routledge, [1870?]).
5. Emerson, [*Works*], 12 vols. (Boston: Houghton, 1896–98); and Rhys, ed., *The Prelude to Poetry: The English Poets in the Defence and Praise of Their Own Art*, 2nd ed. (London: Dent, 1897). Kate Stevens inscribed both of these, dating the former Christmas 1898 and the latter 9 Oct. 1899.
6. Letter from Garrett to Wallace, 13 Nov. 1898; cf. *SP* 71.
7. Garrett recalls the ten cents in a letter to Wallace, 5 Dec. 1898.
8. Most of the information in this paragraph derives from articles in the *Reading Eagle*, 14 July 1911, p. 1; and 18 July 1911, p. 8.

ther the cause of education, in this case adult education, as a member of the Reading Lyceum. He was active in local politics and served for a time as associate editor of the *Spirit of Berks*, a Democratic organ published weekly. He had to find time for these civic interests in a life devoted primarily to making a living, for within a decade of his arrival in Reading he had a wife and three sons to support; another decade, and there were also two daughters to feed, clothe, and educate. He was a resourceful provider. At one time in the eighteen nineties, he was the senior partner in the law firm of Stevens and Stevens (W. Kerper Stevens, his partner, was not a relative), an officer of the Reading Hardware Company, and the owner of a bicycle factory and a steel plant.

This was the raw material of Garrett Stevens' success story. As he told and retold it to his children, it took shape in their minds as the myth of the self-made man. He had learned, and did not shrink from suggesting that others might learn from him, "the best lesson—a knowledge of the pleasure of real independence by Self Support."[9] His sons were thoroughly schooled in this lesson by the time they went to college. As a high-school senior, Wallace won an oratorical contest with a rhapsody on the topic "Greatest Need of the Age." That need was, in a word, opportunity, and there was scarcely a word dearer to his father's heart. Given the opportunity available in a democratic republic, a man might become the hero eulogized by the young orator:

> There is one triumph of a republic, one attainment of Catholicism, one grand result of Democracy, which feudalism, which caste, and which monarchy, can never know—the self-made man. We cannot help but admire the man, who with indomitable and irrepressible energy breasting the wave of conditions, grows to become the concentration of power and worth.[10]

9. Letter to Wallace, 2 May 1898.
10. Quoted in the *Reading Eagle*, 23 Dec. 1896, p. 5, col. 2.

If Garrett Stevens was among those who heard this performance, his pride may have been qualified by a sense of irony. His older son and namesake had, as the next day's newspaper noted, won this very contest two years previously. But Garrett Jr. had learned that opportunity is not enough; he had flunked out of Yale after only four months (*SP* 12). Though he had then enrolled at Dickinson College, closer to home, he continued to disappoint his father by running up debts and taking football and campus social life more seriously than his studies. This may have prompted the father to redouble his efforts with his younger sons, both of whom entered college in the fall of 1897. John, though he too played football, was a methodical and conscientious student who soon gave his father little reason to doubt that he would succeed at the University of Pennsylvania.

Wallace was a doubtful quantity. "I am solicitous about your success," his father wrote him after his first term at Harvard, "and knowing that you are in dead earnest and fully appreciate your opportunity."[11] That Wallace was able and determined there was no reason to doubt, for his first-year grades ran unfashionably to As and Bs in the day of the gentleman's C (*L* 17n); apparently on the strength of this showing, Harvard awarded him a scholarship the following year.[12] Garrett Stevens himself allowed that his son might be suited for a professorial chair—but for "eccentricities" in his genius (*L* 16). The father had apparently remarked that streak of hedonism, that appetite for the beautiful, which underlay Wallace's self-discipline. Taking this into account, Garrett judiciously served up his tidbits of Poor Richard with a piquant sauce from Pater, on the theory that his "work and study, study and work" would go down more easily with "Catch the reflected sun-rays, get pleasurable emotions—instead of stings and tears" (*L*

11. Letter of 1 Feb. 1898.
12. *Harvard College Class of 1901: Secretary's First Report* (Cambridge, Mass.: Class of 1901, 1903), p. 32.

Margaretha Catharine Zeller Stevens
(Courtesy of the Huntington Library)

Garrett Barcalow Stevens
(Courtesy of the Huntington Library)

14–15). He felt he could commend, too, his son's "power of painting pictures in words" so long as the poetic "afflatus" did not interfere with serious study (*L* 14, 23).

Even as Garrett Stevens urged his sons to take full advantage of their opportunities and ready themselves for the battle of life, he was beginning to register fatigue from his own campaigns. Early in 1898, he took on the Building Association case, a notoriously complicated lawsuit involving millions of dollars. His partner refused to master the intricacies of the case, so he worked at it virtually alone from eight o'clock in the morning till as late as ten in the evening.[13] Scarcely had he recovered from these exertions when, early that spring, his bicycle factory burned down.[14] He recovered much of his loss through insurance and rebuilt the factory, hoping to sell it as soon as he could make a profit. But in the fall he advised Wallace, then starting his second year at Harvard, "Every abatement in the general expenditure is appreciated for I have not yet disposed of either of the 'White Elephants' that came into my care while attempting to assist others[.] I refer to the Steel plant & the Bike plant both of which are costing me much money to hold and yet are things I cannot sell without great loss."[15] Contributing to Garrett Stevens' professional and fiscal anxieties was chronic worry over his prodigal eldest son. "I dont know what to make of this fellow," he wrote after Garrett Jr. left college to enlist for duty in the Spanish-American War; "—it takes him a long time to sow his wild oats—and he must reap a big crop of regrets. . . . He tires me out with his want of purpose—and succeeds at nothing. . . ."[16]

Garrett Jr., discharged from the army for a physical dis-

13. Letters from Garrett to Wallace, 21 Jan. and 22 Feb. 1898.
14. Garrett first mentions this loss to Wallace in his letter of 7 Apr. 1898.
15. Letter of 10 Oct. 1898.
16. Letter to Wallace, 20 May 1898.

ability a few weeks later, eventually resumed his studies and passed the bar examination. The Building Association case was settled and the white elephants apparently ambled off to new owners. But these afflictions and probably others we know nothing about had taken their toll on Garrett Stevens. Around 1901 he suffered a nervous breakdown, and John took him to the Adirondacks to recuperate (L 454). When he returned to his practice a half-year later, he appeared publicly as prosperous as before. The 1909 edition of Montgomery's *Annals of Berks County* described him as "eminent among the members of his profession in Reading, both for his attainments and his success."[17] When he died two years later, at the age of sixty-three, a colleague reported, "His career was successful in the highest sense. His comforting thought in later years was that he had been able to give his sons an education that fitted them for the Bar and that they were now self-sustaining."[18]

But things were not altogether as they seemed, for around 1901 some crucial spring had been broken or stretched beyond its capacity to recoil. It was all Garrett Stevens could do to "keep even" when his breakdown was followed within a few years by liver trouble and a financial setback in the panic of 1907.[19] Kerper Stevens sketched a grim picture of his partner at this period, remarking that for the last six years of his life he was "merely existing."[20] Neither was Garrett satisfied with himself as provider. The will he drafted in 1905 ends on a note of defeat. ". . . I am sorry," he wrote regarding the distribution of his estate among his wife and children, "that I am not able to solve the problem of subsistence for them more amply."[21] To his

17. Morton L. Montgomery, comp., *Historical and Biographical Annals of Berks County, Pennsylvania* . . . (Chicago: J. H. Beers, 1909), I: 782.
18. Joseph R. Dickinson, quoted in the *Reading Eagle*, 18 July 1911, p. 8, col. 3.
19. Letters from Garrett to Wallace, 17 Nov. 1907 and 22 Mar. 1908.
20. Quoted in the *Reading Eagle*, 18 July 1911, p. 8, col. 4.
21. Carbon typescript of will dated 2 Aug. 1905.

older daughter Elizabeth, who attended the Drexel Institute in Philadelphia, he sent a more circumstantial apology
around 1907; it reads in part,

> I slammed myself into debt, to the horror of my other
> farmer boy acquaintances who never heard of such a thing, in
> sending the three boys through college in the hope that at 21
> they would take the bit in their teeth, and make the wheels go
> round—but the only bit, they take, they get at home, and thus
> my dream of Vassar for you went to nought. . . . and all [the
> boys] save good soberfaced serious square John—were more
> or less a nuisance and as Romantic as Cinderella[.]

Wallace later found it painful to contemplate his father's
last years. He was particularly disturbed by a photograph
taken in 1910, which shows an overweight Garrett Stevens
gazing abstractedly at a point above and to one side of the
camera. The son had this picture before him in 1943, when
he wrote to his niece,

> When I think of my father's pride and of all the anxiety that
> he must have felt, and then look at this last picture of him in
> which he seems so completely defeated, the feeling isn't any-
> thing that I want to renew. I very much prefer to look at him
> and think of him in his prime. The truth is that I rather think
> that, seeing him as a whole, I understand him better perhaps
> than he understood himself, and that I can really look into his
> heart in which he must have concealed so many things.(L 458)

Wallace had not always been able to regard his father as a
whole. "When I was younger," he once recalled, "I always
used to think that I got my practical side from my father,
and my imagination from my mother."[22] Garrett Stevens
was then exclusively the self-made man—an inspiration to
high-school orators, perhaps, but little more than a lay figure, tricked out with gauds from Horatio Alger and the
Beadle Dime Novels. The mature Wallace better understood his father partly because he had become better acquainted with someone very like the man—himself.

22. Hatfield, p. 30.

Garrett Barcalow Stevens in 1910
(Courtesy of the Huntington Library)

Indeed, one cannot describe the father as a whole without to some extent describing the son. Garrett Stevens' friends and colleagues remembered him as an imposing person, both physically and morally. Though never showy, he carried himself with a dignity that some found intimidating. "On the outside his demeanor was cold and forbidding—like the cottage with its thatched roof, its outside rough and mean," recalled a fellow member of the bar, "but all within was wondrous neat and clean."[23] Those admitted to the cottage testified to his friendliness and generosity. Those who remained outside his circle of intimate friends could still respect his professional integrity and a sense of justice that transcended the interests of any one client.

Garrett Stevens spent the greater part of his life in his law office, where he could, as his second son put it, "create a life of his own" (*L* 454). At home he was apt to remain aloof and patriarchal, preferring to read rather than converse or take recreation with his family (*SP* 4–5). Even in later years, a meeting between Garrett and one of his sons could be a frosty affair. "Father was in town two days ago," Wallace wrote in his journal the year he worked as a reporter in New York. "I took luncheon with him at the Astor House—baked shad, asparagus, etc. We remarked that we looked well" (*SP* 97). Laconic and reserved in person, Garrett could be warmly affectionate in the letters he sent weekly to his offspring after they left home. Moreover, he urged family members to apply pen to paper when any of the Stevenses was ill or down on his luck. His sense of family solidarity extended beyond the living to those long dead. He was still in his early twenties when General W. W. H. Davis, then compiling a history of Bucks County, sought his assistance in tracing the origin of his mother's family, the Barcalows.[24] Though Garrett was unable to re-

23. Walter B. Craig, quoted in the *Reading Eagle*, 18 July 1911, p. 8, col. 3.

24. Garrett Stevens mentions his work for Davis in a letter to "Aunt Ann," 15 Aug. 1873. Davis' *The History of Bucks County, Pennsylvania, from*

construct even this line to his satisfaction, he pursued his genealogical research energetically for several years prior to his marriage.

Garrett Stevens may have "lived alone" among the members of his family, as Wallace later recalled (*L* 454). But he did enjoy hunting and fishing, walking and taking drives in the Reading countryside with friends like Kerper Stevens, Lewis Kershner, and Tom Zimmerman, editor of the *Reading Times*. These excursions provided the matter for several of the poems and he published anonymously in the *Times* and the *Reading Eagle*.[25] One of these, "Along the Drive," records an occasion when he and a companion stopped to watch a young girl plowing a field. To compare these lines with Wordsworth's "The Solitary Reaper" or, for that matter, with Wallace's "The Idea of Order at Key West," is to appreciate what Garrett Stevens meant when he spoke of his "unromantic sieve" (*L* 24):

> Sly little thing, she felt our eyes were following her,
> She heard us say to Colonel, our nag, "Wait and see her
>   make the turn."
> I think she grew an inch before she reached the end,
> And then, like a brawny boy, she jerked that plow about and
> Kept her traces clear, and in a voice to be like papa said:
> "Gee, Bill! Gee there, Tom;" and those kind beasts 'thout
>   guide or line,
> Sure winked at us as they proudly made the turn.
>
> Now see her raise the stilts and sink deep her share
> In the rich loam; hear her coarse "Get along there,"
> And as we passed slowly on I saw the little bonnet turn
> Just far enough to shoot a smile at us that seemed to say:
> "I'm glad you saw me, sirs," and we raised our hats to her.

There is nothing remote or picturesque about this Pennsylvania farm girl. Her voice evokes, not a supernal music,

---

the Discovery of the Delaware to the Present Time (Doylestown, Pa.: Democrat Book and Job Office Print) was published in 1876.

25. After Garrett Stevens' death, seven of his poems were reprinted with credit in the *Reading Eagle* for 30 July 1911; another appeared in the same newspaper on 13 Aug. 1911. All but one of these were again re-

but the huskier accents of her father. Rather than lifting her audience to an unfamiliar sphere or a new perception of reality, she struggles to meet their standards for handling team and plow. The charm and humor of the episode proceed from the wordless dialogue between men and girl, between man and beast, on a subject all know intimately.

Life was clearly an affair of people for Garrett Stevens, even as it was primarily an affair of places for his son (*OP* 158). His longest extant poem, "A Foosganger's Evening," celebrates a particularly convivial evening spent at Kuechler's Roost, a resort on the slope of Mount Penn. The hero of the poem is the host, Louis Kuechler, who regales his guests with roast pheasant, a rare wine, and his rarer blend of English and Pennsylvania Dutch. This high-spirited romp ends on an elegiac note, for Kuechler had already joined the "Foosgangers Blest" when the poem was written. Garrett also composed a full-length elegy for Kuechler, entitled "The Hermit's Burial." In this, his most ambitious poem, he represents the "Schwartze Geist" or black ghost of the forest leading a troupe of woodland elves and fairies to witness the burial of Kuechler's mortal remains. After a perfunctory Christian ceremony, Kuechler's spirit is apotheosized as the tutelary genius of Mount Penn. "And even now," the final stanza reads,

> And until the eastern hills are again alight,
>   This spirit still abides on mountain side,
> And with each elfin friend holds converse fond
>   And all that Nature's God has vitalized is loved;
> And all who hallow and not desecrate this sanctuary
>   Can there in peace repose. But woe betide
> The luckless lout or heated dame,
>   Who will on pleasure bent the sacred hills profane,
> For demons and imps, real devils, too,
>   Are spirits in his train—to work dire ill
> To those who will their host disdain.

---

printed in the *Eagle* for 20 July 1924, p. 14, together with four more poems. In quoting from the poems, I use the 1924 text.

"The Hermit's Burial" is marred by stock poetic diction and inversions of syntax. Despite its relatively free metrical form, the lines are stiff, as though each had been made to lie in a different Procrustean bed. There are nice touches, as when natural objects quicken into elves and sprites: "Each senseless / Stone, each shapeless root, turns to a / Moving thing." The poem moves from a sense of anticipation to its climax by nice degrees and arrives at a rounded conclusion just before the final sentence. That final sentence, however, reveals Garrett Stevens' besetting weakness as a poet: most of his pieces are simply didactic tales or sermons set to verse.[26] They offer to teach us, for example, that a dishonest lawyer is no better than a thief; that a miser receives a miserly reward; that one may as well try to banish the world as banish evil; that one is duty-bound to do one's share of the world's work; that colleges too often educate their students in sloth and opportunism.

Garrett Stevens' aesthetic sensitivity appears to better advantage in his letters, where he generally heeds his own advice to "[p]aint truth but not always in drab clothes" (*L* 14). Except on business trips to Philadelphia, Garrett had few opportunities to enjoy fine works of graphic or plastic art; yet his letters are graced with appreciations of these media. "Glad to see you admire the de milo in cold stone . . . ," he wrote Wallace in 1897, and went on to define the superiority of the original to castings: "the refinement in Sculpture is not mere outline, pose, proportion + such— but the delicacy or courage of the artist who picks with pin point or pounds with a sledge . . ." (*L* 15).

Wallace's father was, then, a man of many parts and many moods. He was businessman and poet, politician

---

26. Wallace wrote a prose eulogy for Kuechler which resembles his father's poem in some particulars. Wallace speaks of Kuechler's "Geiste" and calls him "the genius of the mountain woods"; he likewise concludes with a gibe at "the mere pleasure-seeking idler." Garrett sent Wallace's piece to Tom Zimmerman, who ran it in the *Reading Times*, 7 Jan. 1904, p. 2, col. 6.

and recluse, a civic leader most at home in the woods, an independent spirit who was also emotionally vulnerable, a success in life who sometimes thought himself a failure. He parceled out his qualities and his fate unequally among the three sons. Wallace, though named after a politician,[27] received none of the enthusiasm for party politics that went to Garrett Jr. and John, and they were not troubled with his weakness for a well-turned metaphor. Yet Wallace would seem to have been the son best able to understand the father, if understanding proceeds from shared interests and sensibility. He inherited not only his father's aesthetic sensitivity, but also his feeling for nature, especially the natural beauty of the hills and woods around Reading. Like his father, he was a conscientious lawyer who relied on intelligence rather than an aggressive or ostentatious manner.[28] Those who shared a table with him in the Florida Keys or at the Canoe Club in East Hartford discovered a companion every bit as congenial as Garrett's friends had known at Kuechler's Roost. His poem "A Fish-Scale Sunrise" (1934), which immortalizes the morning after a night on the town, is very much in the genre if not the style of "A Foosganger's Evening."[29] Those who encountered Wallace under less convivial circumstances were typically awed by his imposing physique or put off by his aloof, sometimes brusque manner. Shyness must take some of the blame for the latter impression, for he could be most cordial in correspondence with people he had never met. He went into agonies of remorse when he thought he might actually have offended someone whose friendship he valued.

27. In a letter of 1 May 1944, Wallace told Lila James Roney that he had been named after Wallace De La Mater (i.e., Delamater), a politician prominent in eastern Pennsylvania about the time he was born.

28. Stevens told Pitts Sanborn in a letter of 17 Feb. 1941 that he felt there was "something phoney" about the "relentless" type of lawyer.

29. For the occasion that inspired "A Fish-Scale Sunrise," see Peter Brazeau, *Parts of a World: Wallace Stevens Remembered* (New York: Random, 1983), p. 90.

The office was Wallace's refuge, as it had been his father's. It was his monk's cell, though this monk not only recollected himself there but also wrote letters to friends and trafficked in wares from Paris and Peking. Especially in later years, he corresponded with members of his extended family, showing a lively interest in their well-being and assisting some of them financially. His genealogical studies were carried forward with the help of relatives and might be regarded as his scholarly profession of family feeling. Wallace did not nourish himself on extramural friendships, as he admitted to Barbara Church (L 795). Like his father he did nevertheless require "discreet affection" and was hurt when he did not receive it. On one rare occasion in 1954, he allowed a good friend to glimpse his wounded feelings. "[Y]ou complained," Barbara Church reminded him later,

> yes a little, that many people do not love you. I should have said: but my husband did, I do, I am sure Marianne Moore does and also Tom [McGreevy]. I saw Holly look at you, also Mrs. Stevens the rare times we were together—it is already quite a number and I am sure—you could easily have a crowd if you yourself were willing.[30]

But he was not so much unwilling as he was temperamentally unable to impose himself on others. Even in this instance, he apologized to Church for having introduced a "dash of blue" into their conversation.[31] At home, his daughter remembers, the Stevenses "held off from each other" just as they had done the previous generation (SP 4). He and his wife rarely traveled or entertained, and he further secured his privacy by keeping to his study evenings and weekends.

As a Reading schoolboy and again as an established lawyer in Hartford, Wallace was unmistakably his father's son.

30. Letter of 19 Mar. 1954. Though Church apparently suspected a breach between Stevens and his wife (see Brazeau, pp. 223, 225), she may not have realized its extent.
31. Letter of 22 Mar.

Yet he was not the same son early and late. The nature of his mature filial piety is suggested by "Recitation after Dinner" (1945), a poem originally entitled "Tradition." After dismissing several quasi-official concepts of tradition in the opening stanzas, he settles on the familiar image of "the son who bears upon his back / The father that he loves . . ." (*OP* 87). The father, Anchises, survives by grace of his son's affection and reverence for him. Like the past he represents, he is only as vital as Aeneas allows him to be. Hence the final stanza stresses his limited tenure in present consciousness:

> The father keeps on living in the son, the world
> Of the father keeps on living in the world
> Of the son. These survivals out of time and space
> Come to us every day. And yet they are
> Merely parts of the general fiction of the mind:
> Survivals of a good that we have loved,
> Made eminent in a reflected seeming-so.

Garrett Stevens survived, somewhat altered, in Wallace's professional and social life. He survived considerably altered in his son's imaginative life, as their very different poems indicate. Thus Wallace could maintain that his father's "survivals" were merely part and not the whole of the "general fiction" of his mind. Other parts of that fiction were begotten and nurtured by other parents. Harvard College was one such parent, an alma mater whose influence can be seen in Wallace's undergraduate verse. To comprehend his later departures—physical as well as intellectual and emotional—from his father and fatherland, one must understand certain things about Harvard in the late eighteen nineties.

Wallace entered Harvard at an awkward phase of its development.[32] The College was growing like an adolescent

32. This account of Harvard in the nineties is indebted to Samuel Eliot Morison, *Three Centuries of Harvard, 1636–1936* (Cambridge, Mass.: Harvard University Press, 1946), pp. 400–438; Edward S. Martin, "Undergraduate Life at Harvard," *Scribner's Magazine* 21 (1897): 531–53; Daniel

and trying to resolve an adolescent crisis of identity in a family that included graduate and professional schools. "Class spirit" was much discussed, chiefly because it seemed to be in shorter supply than ever before, despite efforts to contrive it artificially by means of intercollegiate athletics. Over four hundred freshmen entered the College with Wallace in 1897, and not more than half of these could have met him before he left Cambridge three years later.[33] A growing number of Harvard students completed the B.A. in three years or, like Wallace, went on to professional schools without taking a degree.

President Eliot's controversial elective system further obscured class identity. Rather than taking most of his courses with other members of his class, a freshman in the nineties often found himself in a lecture hall with upperclassmen and even graduate students. Wallace, since he was not a degree candidate, appreciated the opportunity to tailor his course of study to his needs. "The Harvard System keeps one closer to the aims of life and therefore to life itself . . . ," he penciled in the margins of a college book. "Freedom of choice gives liberality to learning[.]"[34] His college transcript declares his interests and one of his aims, for he concentrated his study in English, French, and German literature (L 17n, 23n, 33–34n).

A fraction of each Harvard class found camaraderie, though scarcely class spirit, in the exclusive social clubs. The process of social selection—and exclusion—began as soon as a young man entered college. If he came from one of the preparatory schools that traditionally sent their

---

Gregory Mason, "At Harvard in the Nineties," *New England Quarterly* 9 (1936): 43–70; and "Harvard Class of 1901: History of Class Activities," in *Harvard Class of 1901, June 1951: Twelfth Report* (Cambridge, Mass.: Class of 1901, 1951), pp. 215–44.

33. The Class of 1901 was the largest that had entered Harvard College up to 1897, numbering 401 freshmen and 63 special students.

34. Notes in Stevens' copy of the *Select Essays of Dr. Johnson*, ed. George B. Hill (London: Dent, 1889), I: 230–31, signed and dated 10 Mar. 1899 on the flyleaf.

graduates to Harvard; if he had family or friends in Boston society; if he distinguished himself in some college activity, especially sports; if he made himself agreeable to upper-classmen without appearing to "swipe" or cultivate them; then he had a good chance of being initiated into the first ten of the D.K.E. ("Dickey") at the end of his freshman year. As a member of this sophomore secret society, he might contrive to have his friends elected to the second and third tens of the Dickey and was virtually assured of admission into one of the better social clubs—the Porcellian, say, or the A.D. As a club member, he would associate with other young men more or less like himself in the club-rooms and private dormitories along the "Gold Coast" of Mount Auburn Street.

Although the Dickey and the social clubs never included more than a minority of Harvard students, they exerted an influence out of proportion to their numbers. A knowing graduate in Charles Macomb Flandrau's *Harvard Episodes* (1897) remarks to a friend that, whereas other colleges have societies, "Harvard unquestionably has Society." "I'm not a sociologist, and I don't pretend to know what constitutes society with a big S—" the graduate continues,

> . . . But there is such a thing here more than in any other college. An outsider, hearing me talk this way, would say I was making an unnecessarily large mountain out of a very ordinary molehill. But that's because he wouldn't understand that Society at Harvard is really the most important issue in under-graduate life.[35]

This is a large claim, and Flandrau, whose forte was the comedy of undergraduate manners, had an artistic motive for exaggerating the importance of society at Harvard. Still, the College's proximity to Boston rendered it more susceptible than Yale or Princeton to the blandishments of society for, as George Santayana observed, Harvard men from the best social sets across the Charles River felt obliged to determine which of their classmates were "so-

35. Boston: Copeland and Day, p. 23.

cially presentable" and might be invited home for the weekend.[36]

The presentable Harvard student, while not necessarily wealthy, did have the means to live with fellow club members on the Gold Coast and did not need to take time from his club activities to earn his tuition. Though not necessarily well-born himself, he knew how to behave in the company of the socially prominent. His demeanor was a nice balance of indifference—the famous "Harvard indifference"—and strenuousness. "Teach us to care and not to care" was his daily prayer long before a member of the class of 1910 actually wrote those words. He had to make himself conspicuous among his peers as a freshman, yet avoid certain kinds of distinction. It would not do, for example, to earn grades much above passing or be too conspicuously the artist or littérateur. Santayana unwittingly violated this code as a young instructor, when he invited his friend Trumbull Stickney to one of the poetry readings he held regularly in his room with a half-dozen "presentable" students.[37] A spokesman for the group later informed Santayana that Stickney, who had mentioned the sunset and called it "gorgeous," had been weighed and found "too literary and ladylike" for Harvard. Santayana concluded from the experience that Harvard social distinctions had to be "understood and respected" if his literary evenings were to succeed.

That Santayana, the intrepid critic of American culture, should so accommodate himself to undergraduate mores may seem odd; but this episode is of a piece with others in his long sojourn at Harvard. As an undergraduate, he had particularly enjoyed gatherings of the O.K. Club because its membership included not only literary types but also the "sound simple active heirs of the dominant class."[38] He believed that, in a commercial civilization, these young

36. Quoted in Morison, *Three Centuries of Harvard*, pp. 420–21.
37. Santayana, *Persons and Places: The Middle Span* (New York: Scribners, 1945), pp. 102–3.
38. *Middle Span*, p. 200.

men were likely to remain "*better beings*" than scholars or intellectuals. When a friend in New Haven invited him to visit Yale, Santayana was delighted to discover that he not only liked this "toy Sparta," he "*believed*" in it.[39] He thought Yale more conducive than the "toy Athens" in Cambridge to the creation of an integral American mind. When Santayana wanted to provide English visitors with reading that would "represent the winds blowing at Harvard" around the turn of the century, he settled on his own recently published *Interpretations of Poetry and Religion* and Flandrau's *Diary of a Freshman* (1900), a novel which climaxes with its protagonist's initiation into the Dickey.[40]

Had Santayana been less typical of Harvard poets in the nineties, and less influential among them, his condescending enthusiasm for the high-toned Babbitt might have done less damage. Between Santayana and his colleagues, however, there intervened a wall which he called professional jealousy and they called snobbery.[41] Whatever its name, it threw him back upon the more appreciative company of talented students and younger instructors. With William Vaughn Moody, Robert Morss Lovett, Norman Hapgood, and others he founded the Laodicean Club, pledged to "the idea that Paul was too hard on the church that was in Laodicea, when he attacked it for being neither hot nor cold, and that there was much to say for the balanced attitude of that seldom-praised institution."[42] The Laodiceans half-facetiously opposed the "general oversupply of strenuousness" they professed to see about them, in effect making a virtue of Harvard indifference. Though the club lasted only a year and was something of a lark, it helps to explain why the Harvard poets were fated to remain, like

39. *Middle Span*, p. 175.
40. *Middle Span*, p. 29.
41. See Santayana, *Middle Span*, p. 148; and Rollo Brown, *Harvard Yard in the Golden Age* (New York: Current Books, 1948), p. 45.
42. Norman Hapgood, *The Changing Years* (New York: Farrar and Rinehart, 1930), pp. 44–45.

heat lightning, all augury and no fulfillment.[43] They would have considered it a breach of good taste to depart radically from the "genteel tradition." When Santayana gave this tradition its name at Berkeley in 1911, he praised Walt Whitman as the only American writer who had managed to escape it completely.[44] But at Laodicean Harvard, one would sooner have been caught with egg on one's cravat than sound a barbaric yawp over the roofs of Cambridge.

If Harvard was not prepared to absorb Whitman as wholeheartedly as Whitman had absorbed America, it did sit down with a ready appetite to the feast spread by the French and English *fin de siècle*. Santayana's friend Pierre la Rose, who was suspected of displaying a crucifix in his room for aesthetic rather than religious reasons, accepted a position as instructor in English shortly after graduating in 1895 and promptly began to initiate his students and fellow members of the Signet Society into the mysteries of the new French poetry.[45] In the spring of 1900, the Cercle Français supplemented his informal instruction with a series of eight lectures by Henri de Régnier on Parnassian and Symbolist poetry. Undergraduates dined at Marliave's in Boston, where they could play at being abroad, and repeated the Decadent commonplace that all the poems had been written and all the paintings painted.[46] They recognized the temper of their times in the *Punch* cartoon

43. Larzer Ziff considers the careers of several Harvard poets in *The American 1890s: Life and Times of a Lost Generation* (New York: Viking, 1966), pp. 306–33.

44. Santayana's University of California lecture, "The Genteel Tradition in American Philosophy," is reprinted, somewhat revised, in *Winds of Doctrine: Studies in Contemporary Opinion* (New York: Scribners, 1913), pp. 186–215.

45. Mason recalls the crucifix in "Harvard in the Nineties," p. 43. Malcolm Cowley remembers la Rose's enthusiasm for French Symbolist poetry in —*And I Worked at the Writer's Trade: Chapters of Literary History, 1918–1978* (New York: Viking, 1978), p. 71.

46. Stevens recalled this commonplace in "The Irrational Element in Poetry" (*OP* 218), a lecture delivered at Harvard in 1936. Samuel French Morse attributes it to Professor Charles Eliot Norton in *Wallace Stevens: Poetry as Life* (New York: Pegasus, 1970), p. 45.

which Norman Hapgood could quote from memory many years later. Drawn by George Du Maurier, it featured two Oxford students sitting in their room, smoking cigarettes and drinking black coffee. "What would life be without coffee?" sighs one of these exquisites. "Yes," replies the other, "and what is life, even with coffee?"[47] The Harvard Aesthete survived well into the twentieth century, to become the object of satirical gibes by Malcolm Cowley and Ezra Pound. Pound's sketch in *Pavannes and Divisions* (1918), representing the aesthete's journey from Harvard to Oxford, recalls a familiar nursery rime:

> This little American went to Oxford. He rented Oscar's late rooms. He talked about the nature of the Beautiful. He swam in the wake of Santayana. He had a great cut glass bowl full of lilies. He believed in Sin. His life was immaculate. He was the last convert to Catholicism.[48]

This was the Harvard Wallace Stevens discovered in the fall of 1897, at the end of a long train ride from Reading. Coming from a distant small town and educated in public schools, he was at a distinct social disadvantage in Cambridge. Though he was elected to the Institute of 1770,[49] the sophomore society from which the smaller clubs traditionally chose their members, he apparently did not make the Dickey or any of the more exclusive social clubs, and stayed all three years at a rooming house on Garden Street. Yet he was not without connections in Cambridge, for Edwin Stanton Livingood, a Reading compatriot with whom he shared long walks and conversation ranging "from the sublime to the ridiculous" (*SP* 49), had preceded him to Harvard. Livingood had graduated with that remarkable class of 1895, which included, besides Flandrau and la Rose, the poets Stickney, George Cabot Lodge,

47. Hapgood, p. 74.
48. New York: Knopf, 1918, p. 46. Stevens' copy of *Pavannes and Divisions* is signed and dated 12 July 1918 in New York.
49. *Harvard College Class of 1901: Secretary's First Report*, p. 75.

and—as a special student—Edwin Arlington Robinson. It also included Daniel Gregory Mason—composer, music critic, and Boswell to several Harvard writers, including William Vaughn Moody. When Livingood returned to Harvard for graduate study in 1898, he would have renewed his acquaintance with la Rose and Mason, fellow members of the Dickey and Institute of 1770 who were then teaching in the English Department. It was probably Livingood who introduced Stevens to la Rose and la Rose who introduced him to Santayana. By 1900, at any rate, Stevens was sharing dinner and literary talk with la Rose and Santayana (*SP*68).

At the end of Stevens' second year at Harvard, he was elected to the first seven of the Signet Society and eventually became its secretary.[50] Though the Signet had a reputation as a literary club, it considered for membership all young men who, in la Rose's words, "are companionable and interesting, who have individual minds and a few enlightened tastes in common."[51] Founded in opposition to the social clubs, this junior society tried to steer a middle course between "sportiness" and "preciosity." Stevens went on, in his final semester at Harvard, to make Santayana's favorite club, the O.K., and to be chosen president of the *Harvard Advocate*.[52]

To the *Advocate* and its rival, the *Harvard Monthly*, Stevens contributed poems that reflect both his literary and social aspirations in college. Robert Buttel has traced Stevens' undergraduate efforts to their nineteenth-century sources, notably in Tennyson and the Pre-Raphaelites, Keats and Shelley.[53] He singles out "Ballade of the Pink Parasol" as the piece which most portends those in *Harmonium*. Written not long before Stevens left Cambridge,

50. *Harvard Graduates' Magazine* 8 (1899): 63; 8 (1900): 529.
51. "The Signet," *Harvard Graduates' Magazine* 10 (1902): 514.
52. *Harvard Graduates' Magazine* 8 (1900): 529; 9 (1900): 52.
53. *Wallace Stevens: The Making of* Harmonium (Princeton: Princeton University Press, 1967), pp. 3–45.

Wallace Stevens (*standing, center*) with the *Harvard Advocate* staff, about 1900 (Courtesy of the Harvard University Archives)

the poem is probably modeled on Austin Dobson's "On a Fan That Belonged to the Marquise de Pompadour," with an ear to the *ubi sunt* refrain in Fitzgerald's *Rubáiyát*[54] or Rossetti's "The Ballade of the Dead Ladies":

> I pray thee where is the old-time wig,
>   And where is the lofty hat?
> Where is the maid on the road in her gig,
>   And where is the fire-side cat?
> Never was sight more fair than that,
> Outshining, outreaching them all,
>   There in the night where the lovers sat—
> But where is the pink parasol?
>
> Where in the pack is the dark spadille
>   With scent of lavender sweet,
> That never was held in the mad quadrille.
>   And where are the slippered feet?
> Ah! we'd have given a pound to meet
> The card that wrought our fall,
>   The card none other of all could beat—
> But where is the pink parasol?
>
> Where is the roll of the old calash,
>   And the jog of the light sedan?
> Whence Chloe's diamond brooch would flash
>   And conquer poor peeping man.
> Answer me, where is the painted fan
> And the candles bright on the wall;
>   Where is the coat of yellow and tan—
> But where is the pink parasol?
>
> Prince, these baubles are far away,
>   In the ruin of palace and hall,
> Made dark by the shadow of yesterday—
> But where is the pink parasol?[55]

What distinguishes this poem from Stevens' other undergraduate verses is its wit and lightness of touch. Usually given to writing lugubrious sonnets, Stevens for

54. Stanza 9 of the *Rubáiyát* contains the couplet, "Each Morn a thousand Roses brings, you say; / Yes, but where leaves the Rose of Yesterday?" Stevens' copy of the *Rubáiyát* is signed and dated 1898.
55. *Harvard Advocate* 69 (1900): 82; reprinted in *SP* 66–67.

once found a speaker and subject matter sufficiently remote from his experience and a form sufficiently exotic to
call forth the rarer part of his poetic gift. Though he surely
knew less than Dobson about eighteenth-century England,
he had only to read Dobson or *The Rape of the Lock* to learn
how a card game might be made a dynastic struggle and
Chloe's brooch an awesome weapon. Following Dobson
and the Verlaine of *Fêtes galantes*, he hankers after an ac-
cessory rendered useless in a world "made dark" and so,
by synecdoche, after the age of elegance and artifice. The
pink parasol was like nothing else in Reading and little else
in Cambridge. Therein, precisely, lay its appeal.

Appropriate to the diction, setting, and subject matter
of "Ballade of the Pink Parasol" is its form. Théodore de
Banville's *Petit traité de poésie française*, published in 1872,
inspired a revival of the old French verse forms among
English poets of the late nineteenth century, notably Dobson, Swinburne, and William Ernest Henley. From these
the vogue spread to poets in American colleges, who laid
claim to English and Continental sophistication with a bar-
rage of ballades, rondeaux, and villanelles. Why should
they attempt, like Pound's Mauberley, to wring lilies from
acorns when lilies could be imported at small cost? The
author of "Ballade of the Pink Parasol" would not have
paid his laundry bill in British pounds or prefaced his
classroom queries with "I pray thee"; but he probably
would have joined his peers in wishing that he might do
so. Such, at least, was the insight which inspired one Harvard wit to lampoon both the ballade form and its Cambridge social equivalent in a piece called "Ballad of the
Afternoon Tea," whose *envoi* reads,

> Prince, if these verses perchance you flout,
>   Deeming I know not at what I hit,
> Go then yourself to that babbling bout
>   And its "giggle, gabble, gobble, and git!"[56]

56. *Harvard Lampoon*, 16 Dec. 1898, p. 74.

In "Ballade of the Pink Parasol," Stevens happened upon a poetic strategy he would have to relearn while writing the first poems of *Harmonium*. Then, too, he would return to the English Decadence and its French precursors for inspiration. During his college years, however, he was more vitally concerned with another legacy of the *fin de siècle*. "Anybody who studies the moods and thoughts of the Eighteen Nineties," Holbrook Jackson has written, "cannot fail to observe their central characteristic in a widespread concern for the correct—that is, the most effective, the most powerful, the most righteous—mode of living."[57] Over black coffee, the Harvard undergraduate of the nineties might ask "What is life?" and shrug his shoulders. That was the obligatory attitude. Privately, however, he asked the same question with greater urgency and hope of finding a correct answer. If he had a talent for art or literature, he was apt to frame both question and answer in terms of the everlasting debate between truth and beauty, art and life.

Stevens' sympathies, to judge from his college marginalia and journal entries, lay with beauty rather than truth, with life rather than art. On reading James Russell Lowell's *Letters*, he encountered a passage in which Lowell demands that poetry "reduce to the essence of a single line the vague philosophy which is floating in all men's minds."[58] Stevens protested in the margin,

> The whole New England school of poets were too hard thinkers. For them there was no pathos in the rose except as it went to point a moral or adorn a tale. I like my philosophy smothered in beauty and not the opposite. Beauty, romance, the rush of life and love are, after all, things that "prove themselves" to one's mind as completely as "the reduction of vague philosophy into single lines.["]

From the last sentence of this annotation, one might infer

57. *The Eighteen Nineties* (London: Grant Richards, 1913), p. 12.
58. *Letters of James Russell Lowell*, ed. Charles Eliot Norton (New York: Harper, 1894), I: 73. Stevens' copy is signed and dated 19 Nov. 1898.

that this little American, too, had gone off to Oxford to worship Beauty and collect refined sensations. Not so. The notes in Stevens' copy of Pater's *Appreciations* suggest rather the irate copy editor than the disciple. He attacked not only the legendary stylist's stylistic tics, but also his aesthetic program. He grew especially restive as he read Pater's sympathetic account of Flaubert's devotion to style, and finally could contain himself no longer. "Flaubert holds no higher place in Fr. Lit. than Pater in Eng. Lit," he burst out. "This should settle the matter."[59]

He pursued his quarrel with Pater—or what he apparently took to be Pater's view—in a journal entry written several months after he purchased *Appreciations*. "Art for art's sake," he began, recalling the motto which the English aesthetes had adopted from Gautier,

> is both indiscreet and worthless. . . . Beauty is strength. But art—art all alone, detached, sensuous for the sake of sensuousness, not to perpetuate inspiration or thought, art that is mere art—seems to me to be the most arrant as it is the most inexcuseable rubbish.
>
> Art must fit with other things; it must be part of the system of the world. And if it finds a place in that system it will likewise find a ministry and relation that are its proper adjuncts. (*SP* 38)

To "perpetuate inspiration or thought": one could hardly expect a college student to specify art's "ministry and relation" to life more precisely. When he tried again about forty years later, the result was more satisfactory: "The relation of art to life is of the first importance especially in a skeptical age since, in the absence of a belief in God, the mind turns to its own creations and examines them, not alone from the aesthetic point of view, but for what they reveal, for what they validate and invalidate, for the support that they give" (*OP* 159). These widely spaced re-

59. Stevens' note appears on p. 28 of his copy of Pater's *Appreciations, with an Essay on Style* (London: Macmillan, 1897), signed and dated 7 Nov. 1898 on the flyleaf.

marks betray, ironically, Stevens' deep and abiding sympathy with the very program he thought he was rejecting. The Parnassians and aesthetes, while professing to be interested in art for its own sake, had ultimately been intent on living artfully or using art to create a style of life. T. S. Eliot did not hesitate to call Pater himself a moralist, since he had justified art by its capacity for enlarging life.[60]

Stevens' concern for the effective life did not turn exclusively upon aesthetic questions. In much the same spirit that his fellow Pennsylvanian Ben Franklin had conceived programs for self-improvement, Stevens mined his books for nuggets of life-wisdom and drew up a list of virtues he hoped to acquire. It was a sentence in Matthew Arnold's *Essays in Criticism* which inspired the list. "How prevalent all round us is the want of balance of mind and urbanity of style!" Arnold exclaims in his essay on "The Literary Influence of Academies," which prompted Stevens to reflect in a penciled note,

> By not calling up some ideal such as urbanity etc. we never attain any, except by chance; and if there is anything noticeable among those I know and I wonder whether it is not the same with the world as a whole it is the lack of ideals.

Below this, he called up some of the ideals he hoped to attain: "Soul. Persuasion and all it implies. Temperateness. Self-Control Confidence Taste Reason[.]"[61]

During his years at Harvard, then, Stevens was preoccupied with the claims of art and life, with the moral utility of aphorisms and ideals. This would scarcely distinguish him from hundreds of other undergraduates around the turn of the century, except that in his case these preoccupations would inform the work of the mature poet and

60. "The Place of Pater," in *The Eighteen-Eighties*, ed. Walter de la Mare (London: Cambridge University Press, 1930), p. 101.
61. Arnold's observation appears on p. 69 of his *Essays in Criticism* (London: Macmillan, 1895). Stevens' copy is signed and dated 5 Oct. 1898, though a note indicates he read "The Literary Influence of Academies" on 15 Feb. 1900.

lecturer on poetic theory. As a young dog worrying the old *fin de siècle* bones of contention, Stevens was preparing to sink his teeth into the sinewy matter of imagination and reality. As a connoisseur of other writers' aphorisms, he was learning how to mint his own and eventually how to elaborate an adage into a poem.[62] As a conjurer of moral virtues, he was anticipating his later efforts to identify worthwhile ideals and project them in his poetry.

Stevens did not know this at the time, of course. As a college student, he was wondering how he might translate his ideals into a satisfying and remunerative mode of life. His ambitions tended to fall into two categories, which he regarded sometimes as antithetical, sometimes as complementary. On the one hand were those appropriate to the man of practical affairs; on the other, those suited to the contemplative onlooker. The first was best represented by Garrett Stevens, who advised his son in 1898 that "life is either a pastoral dream—the ideal of the tramp, or superannuated village farmer—Or it is the wild hurly burly activity of the fellows who make the world richer and better by their being in it . . ." (*SP* 17–18). Couched in these terms, the choice was easily made. Wallace endorsed his father's ideal, with one reservation, a year and a half later. "The only practical life of the world," he wrote in his journal,

> as a man of the world, not as a University Professor, a Retired Farmer or Citizen, a Philanthropist, a Preacher, a Poet or the like, but as a bustling merchant, a money-making lawyer, a soldier, a politician is to be if unavoidable a pseudo-villain in the drama, a decent person in private life. We *must* come down, we *must* use tooth and nail, it is the law of nature: "the survival of the fittest"; providing we maintain at the same time self-respect, integrity and fairness. I believe, as unhesitatingly as I believe anything, in the efficacy and necessity of fact meeting fact—with a background of the ideal.(*SP* 53–54)

62. Beverly Coyle shows how aphorism informs Stevens' poetry in *A Thought to be Rehearsed: Aphorism in Wallace Stevens's Poetry* (Ann Arbor: UMI Research Press, 1983).

Garrett Stevens had shown that one could be both a decent person in private life and—in good times—a money-making lawyer. A man of self-respect, integrity, and fairness, he nevertheless knew how to draw blood in the courtroom. As a man of the world, he would have been less than completely gratified had his son chosen to be a professor, preacher, or poet. But what of that "background of the ideal" which concludes the journal entry? With this stroke, Wallace withheld absolute allegiance to the practical life. Though the phrase seems almost an afterthought, it signals his preoccupation with the spiritually symmetric life. Belonging to that "background" are some of the things Stevens would have first encountered in college, such as Jowett's translation of Plato and the elegance symbolized by a pink parasol. It would also have included his list of classical virtues and his conversations with the man who epitomized most of them—George Santayana.

Santayana was not one for the "wild hurly burly" of life. He preferred to think of himself as one who stood on the bank or paddled around in the backwaters rather than swim against the current.[63] Certainly these were points of vantage for one who wanted to study the mainstream in a disinterested manner. He helped Americans to understand their own culture, yet refused to assimilate it himself. "Santayana," recalled his senior colleague George Herbert Palmer, "impressed us as an onlooker in the world more than a sharer in its struggle. With nothing in hasty and democratic America had he a part."[64] Santayana remained a foreigner with respect not only to America but also to the ordinary concerns of daily life. He neither married nor assumed the burden of property. Anticipating the poets-in-residence of a later epoch, he turned to college teaching as an expedient while devoting himself mainly to the busi-

63. *Persons and Places: The Background of My Life* (New York: Scribners, 1944), p. 201.
64. "Philosophy 1870–1929," in *The Development of Harvard University Since the Inauguration of President Eliot, 1869–1929*, ed. Samuel Eliot Morison (Cambridge, Mass.: Harvard University Press, 1930), p. 16.

ness of thinking and writing. He was as different as could be from Garrett Stevens, and therefore the more important to Wallace Stevens. "I always came away from my visits to him," Wallace later testified, "feeling that he made up in the most genuine way for many things that I needed" (*L* 482).

What kinds of needs did Santayana supply? Stevens was doubtless flattered when the author of *Sonnets and Other Verses* (1896) and *Lucifer: A Theological Tragedy* (1899) took an interest in him and his poetry. He was diffident about the quality of his own work, which does augur less of the mature poet than the Harvard verse of Edwin Arlington Robinson or T. S. Eliot, and had all but resigned himself to being a poet in "mute feeling" merely (*SP* 39). Santayana not only invited Stevens to read his poems, but took one of them seriously enough to write a sonnet in reply (*L* 482, 637). Stevens must have been charmed, too, by the urbane intelligence and wit of the older man, qualities which did not preclude a boyish delight in Sparklets, the cylinders of compressed carbon dioxide he used to charge water for highballs (*L* 482). Ultimately, however, Santayana "made up for" deficiencies in Stevens' adolescent ideal. The so-called man of the world is apt to be spiritually and intellectually provincial, whereas the detached, contemplative Santayana was worldly in the best sense of the word. To his young friend from Reading, he may have seemed the more sophisticated when he humored the whims of Boston society and the Cambridge social clubs.

In the best of worlds, Santayana and Garrett Stevens would have been one man. A recurrent American dream would have it so: in some remote Golden Age, the republic boasted citizens who were half Emerson, half Franklin. These were beings of heroic stature, whose strength lay in the virtue James Russell Lowell called "mystic-practicalism." At length, according to Santayana, Van Wyck Brooks, and other chroniclers of the American mind, this portmanteau ideal split along the weak hinge of its hyphen. The dream then turned into a nightmare, with the nation divided spiritually into the hemispheres of vacuous gentility and vulgar opportunism. If Santayana and Garrett Stevens could not be one man, they could still be—and were—cobegetters of the poet who spent a lifetime trying to restore these halves to their first integrity, surprising critics who thought the task impossible and dismaying those who thought it misguided.

Stevens had not yet acquired the knack when he left Cambridge. He was resolved, he told English instructor Charles Townsend Copeland (the legendary "Copey"), to be a poet.[65] But since he had also to make a living, he could not be a Poet of the upper-case variety, remote from the hurly-burly of the marketplace. For Stevens as for so many aspiring writers at the turn of the century, journalism was the market which seemed to blend literature with the entity they called "life" in the most favorable proportions. Stevens was by no means sure he could succeed as a journalist; he was not even sure he could manage his rival ideals. Hence the entry he inscribed in his journal shortly before his final examinations at Harvard is a masterpiece of detachment and ambivalence:

> I am going to New York, I think, to try my hand at journalism. If that does not pan out well, I am resolved to knock about the country—the world. Of course I am perfectly willing to do this—anxious, in fact. It seems to me to be the only way, directed as I am more or less strongly by the desires of my parents and myself, of realizing to the last degree any of the ambitions I have formed. I should be content to dream along to the end of my life—and opposing moralists be hanged. At the same time I should be quite as content to work and be practical—but I hate the conflict whether it "avails" or not. I want my powers to be put to their fullest use—to be exhausted when I am done with them. On the other hand I do not want to have to make a petty struggle for existence—physical or literary. I must try not to be a dilettante—half dream, half deed. I must be all dream or all deed. (*SP* 70–71)

65. So Witter Bynner recalled in a letter to Stevens, 11 Dec. 1954.

The cavalier attitude of those first two sentences was probably self-protective. Like a novice circus rider, Stevens took the precaution of spreading extra sawdust on the floor: if he fell from journalism, he could land unbruised in a phase of sentimental vagabondage, enacting the poems of Bliss Carman. Stevens may also have had second thoughts about trying to straddle two mounts. Here, at least, he hops desultorily from dreaming to the practical life and envisions a day when he will stand squarely on just one of these.

Journalism, besides being the standard route to authorship for aspiring novelists and poets, may have appealed to Stevens for other reasons. It was not an entirely unfamiliar pastime, for one thing. Like Thoreau, Stevens had been for some time reporter to a journal of no very wide circulation—his own. This, together with his experience writing editorials for the *Advocate*, assured him that he could turn out prose even when his poetic muse failed him. Moreover, journalism had his father's blessing, as long as it could provide a living. Garrett Stevens had not only supplied copy for local newspapers and helped to edit one, but had also offered to help Wallace secure a summer job on a Reading newspaper. He had even suggested that a large New York or Boston daily might not exceed his son's capacity (L 19).

Finally, college students had come to regard journalism as a glamorous career, perhaps the last in which heroism was still possible, during the very years Stevens spent in Cambridge. One can be still more precise as to its most auspicious hour. On June 22, 1898, two months after the United States declared war on Spain, Richard Harding Davis found himself aboard an American troop transport steaming toward shore near Santiago, Cuba.[66] The young

66. This account of Davis' role in the Spanish-American War is indebted to Fairfax Downey's *Richard Harding Davis: His Day* (New York: Scribners, 1933), pp. 144–63.

but battle-tested reporter pondered the contrast between soldiers of the regular army, in their blue woolen uniforms, and the Rough Riders in their khaki fatigues. The regular army was badly outfitted and, in Davis' opinion, badly commanded by the aging General Shafter, an unglamorous figure who weighed some three hundred pounds. The Rough Riders were an elite corps of volunteers led by two young officers, former White House physician Leonard Wood and former Assistant Secretary of the Navy Theodore Roosevelt. If they were not seasoned veterans, they at least looked the part. Consequently, when the transports hit the beach Davis left the regulars behind and set off to report the exploits of the Rough Riders. From that moment on, as far as readers of the *New York Herald* and *Scribner's Magazine* were concerned, it was the Rough Riders' war, and they reveled in this burst of poetry amid the prose of the McKinley years.

It was also Harvard's war, from both the military and journalistic points of view. Harvard had graduated the statesmen and soldiers most responsible for the declaration and conduct of the Spanish War—Senator Henry Cabot Lodge, Secretary of the Navy John D. Long, Theodore Roosevelt, and Leonard Wood. Harvard students, too, proved themselves surprisingly ready to trade their indifference for the strenuous life of soldier or sailor. Though Professors Norton, William James, and Barrett Wendell urged them not to enlist hastily, hundreds of students began soon after the declaration of hostilities to drill in the gymnasium and participate in practice skirmishes on Soldiers Field.[67] Over four hundred students and graduates eventually enlisted for service in the war, with the Rough Riders drawing more Harvard men than any other command.[68] The Rough Riders, and to some extent the war itself, were in turn creations of the press. Again it was a

67. *Harvard Graduates' Magazine* 6 (1898): 525; 7 (1898): 71.
68. *Harvard Graduates' Magazine* 7 (1898): 46; 8 (1899): 280.

Harvard man, William Randolph Hearst, who helped to sow the seeds of discord and who for a time engaged Richard Harding Davis to reap the harvest. Though Davis soon dissociated himself from the Hearst newspapers, he remained the cynosure of student writers at Harvard, particularly those who gathered about Copey.[69]

Davis, not himself a Harvard man or even a college graduate, epitomized much that literary Harvard was or wanted to be. He wrote stories in a manner more genteel than realistic about young men from Harvard, Yale, and Princeton. He was athletic and handsomely masculine—qualities not to be underestimated in the era of the Oscar Wilde trials; surely the man who appeared opposite the Gibson Girl in *Harper's* and *Scribner's* magazines was untainted by homosexuality. He lived in the world as though it were a club on Mount Auburn Street, gliding easily from Delmonico's to the Bowery, from the battlefield to the Czar's court in Russia. One of his critics captured the Davis style in this leaf from an imaginary calendar:

> A perfect day for Mr. Davis would consist of a morning's danger, taken as a matter of course. In the afternoon a little chivalry, equally a matter of course to a well-bred man, then a dash from hardship to some great city, a bath, a perfect dinner nobly planned. Shrapnel, chivalry, *sauce mousseline*, and so to work next morning on an article which presupposed in others virtues his code compelled him almost to ignore in himself. Richard Coeur-de-Leon would not have disliked such a day, once he was used to shrapnel.[70]

Stevens may have inaugurated his journalistic career on the *Reading Times* the very summer Davis was following the Rough Riders in Cuba. There is nothing to indicate that he hankered to join his older brother and classmates in the army, and he could not have enlisted without incurring the wrath of his father, who was moved to superlative heights

69. Van Wyck Brooks, *The Confident Years: 1885–1915* (New York: Dutton, 1952), p. 104.
70. Quoted in Downey, p. 2.

of sarcasm by the slogans and military posturing which followed the sinking of the *Maine*. Yet he could not have helped but notice that, due partly to the war, his prospective career had gained a notch in prestige. Newspaper reporting would not be all shrapnel, chivalry, and *sauce mousseline*, of course. But the tedious round of police stations and ward meetings might serve as the gritty stepping-stone to an authentic literary career.

This was the hope which the New York *Commercial Advertiser* extended to would-be authors after 1897, when Henry J. Wright, J. S. Seymour, Lincoln Steffens, and Norman Hapgood assumed control of the newspaper. This enlightened group set out to hire, not professional newspaper men, but aspiring poets, novelists, and essayists with "fresh staring eyes" and stylistic flair.[71] Steffens, the city editor, issued a call to the universities to send him such men, and eventually hired a reportorial staff composed mostly of Harvard graduates, among them Hutchins Hapgood and Carl Hovey. Steffens credited Harvard with teaching its students "that there is such a thing as the beautiful in this world and that there is an art in writing." He knew he could rely on Copey to send him applicants who were suited for newspaper work. In June 1900, Copey provided Wallace Stevens with a letter of introduction to Carl Hovey, who in turn introduced him to Steffens (*SP* 71).

Though Stevens took the trouble to prepare a writing sample for the *Commercial Advertiser*, he favored its rivals, the *Evening Post* and the *New York Tribune* (*SP* 72, 74). The day after meeting Steffens, he carried a letter from Barrett Wendell to Oswald Villard, editor of the *Evening Post* and a Harvard graduate. Wendell's letter begins,

> May I introduce to you Mr. Wallace Stevens, of the class of 1900. He has shown marked literary aptitude in college, and has been for some time in charge of the *Advocate*. He would

71. The quotations in this paragraph are from *The Autobiography of Lincoln Steffens* (New York: Harcourt, Brace, 1931), I: 315–16.

like, if possible, to engage in some occupation related to journalism or to literature. Any kindness you may show him, or any advice you may give him, I shall heartily appreciate.[72]

The young man of marked literary aptitude liked Villard's manner of conducting business—"nine to three, and everybody a gentleman!" (*SP* 73)—so went to work supplying the *Evening Post* with sample sketches bearing titles like "A Happy-Go-Lucky Irishman" and "Wharves and the Sea" (*SP* 74). These eventually elicited an offer from the *Evening Post*, but not before he had accepted a position on the *Tribune*. The latter kept less genteel hours, and Stevens often found himself staying up until four o'clock in the morning to file pieces on the political campaigns of 1900, the Jennie Bosscheiter murder trial, and Stephen Crane's rather shabby funeral. If he had ever thought journalism as glamorous as Richard Harding Davis made it seem, that illusion was soon laid to rest. Its epitaph might have been the one Stevens penned for Crane, himself a Davis admirer: "There are few hero-worshippers. Therefore, few heroes" (*SP* 79).

Perhaps, as Witter Bynner surmised, Stevens' journalistic experience was a salutary antidote to the "fastidious instruction" they had received at Harvard (*SP* 96). That instruction, in concert with the aesthetic literary tradition, placed a high premium on personal thought and expression. One of the first literary exercises Stevens set himself in New York was rewriting his sketch "Wharves and the Sea" in an "impersonal vein" (*SP* 75). So thoroughly did he master this lesson that a month later he criticized the flicker of Pater's hard, gem-like flame in the prose of Daniel Gregory Mason:

> Mason illustrates the effect of Harvard on a man's personality. The essay was written all through by a quaint & entertaining person. As a matter of good taste, it should have been written by nobody at all: it should have been absolutely impersonal.

72. Letter of 4 June 1900 (Massachusetts).

But Harvard feeds subjectivity, encourages an all consuming flame & that, in my mind, is an evil in so impersonal a world. Personality must be kept secret before the world. (*SP* 82)

Stevens was still trying to develop calluses against the "impersonality" of New York as he wrote this, which may account for some of its emphasis (*SP* 80). Yet, when one remembers that this is the same writer who would later insist upon the presence of a "determining personality" in works of art,[73] who would recommend that even the journalist look into his heart before writing (*L* 145), one can understand why he should have grown weary of newspaper reporting as he knew it. Under a Lincoln Steffens, he might have learned how to reveal a facet of his personality to "the world." As it was, he kept his secret for a more select and receptive audience.

As an experiment in self-support, Stevens' newspaper career was modestly successful by the miserable standards of the time. Before the *Tribune* put him on a weekly salary of fifteen dollars, he was paid as much as twenty-six dollars a week for the space he filled (*SP* 86–87). Since his rent came to only twenty dollars a month (*SP* 85), he was spared the embarrassment of having to write home for money. Besides his savings, however, he had little to show for the routine he ironically called his "literary life" (*SP* 100). Before six months had passed, he found his gainful employment "dull as dull can be" (*SP* 90). He felt too lethargic and fatigued to attempt outside journalistic writing, and his few efforts at poetry failed to satisfy him.

In fact, he had scarcely unpacked his trunk when the old diffidence and self-doubt returned to haunt him. He began to wonder whether he had not made a mistake. "Is literature really a profession?" he asked himself. "Can you single it out, or must you let it decide in you for itself?" (*SP* 74). There were moments when he thought his literary

73. So Stevens wrote in his commonplace book, *Sur Plusieurs Beaux Sujects* [sic], Cahier I, p. 17.

life but a pose, and would as soon have been a manufac-
turer of pants or the proprietor of a patent medicine store
(*SP* 90). There had to be other ways of combining literature
with the business of making a living, and he glimpsed one
of these in the career of Philip Henry Savage, who had
been something of a legend at Harvard. Before entering
college, Savage had traveled about New England and
Pennsylvania selling shoes to earn his tuition. He was also
a poet, and his friend Daniel Gregory Mason recalled that
he sent home "long letters in which news of the shoe business is oddly mingled with descriptive bits about sunsets
and red-winged blackbirds."[74] Stevens was offended by
Mason's superior tone when he read this memoir in the
Harvard Monthly. Whereas Mason considered Savage's en-
deavor "praiseworthy if quixotic," Stevens deemed it "the
summum bonum" (*SP* 83). It recalled his own college ideal:
"fact meeting fact—with a background of the ideal."

This was Wallace's frame of mind in early March 1901,
when he returned to Reading for a brief visit, much of it
spent conversing with—or listening to—his father on the
subject of a law career. Since the previous fall he had felt
"at constant strain" against the tether of his newspaper
routine, and had been itching to travel to Florida, California, Arizona, Mexico, England, or Paris (*SP* 90, 94, 97). He
had communicated this impulse to his father while home
for Christmas, and Garrett Stevens, not one to take vacations himself, had apparently divined the element of dis-
content in his son's wanderlust. Wallace at first resisted his
father's urging to take up law. The literary life—that is, a
career devoted to some kind or aspect of literature—had
always been his ambition, and he was reluctant to give up
after so short a trial. Before capitulating to his father he
looked into the publishing business, but was dismayed to
learn that the work was chiefly clerical and unlikely to pro-

74. "Philip Henry Savage," *Harvard Monthly* 30 (1900): 187. Stevens
misquotes Mason slightly in his journal; cf. *SP* 82.

vide a living wage (*SP* 100). As a desperate counterpro-
posal, he suggested to his father that he resign his post at
the *Tribune* to take up writing full-time, presumably with
the aid of a paternal subsidy (*SP* 101). When this bolt
missed its mark he quit the *Tribune* anyway, for a position
as assistant editor on the *World's Work*, a monthly published
by Doubleday, Page and Company.[75] From this magazine,
pledged to "the literature of action rather than the literature of sheer entertainment,"[76] it was but a step, philosophically speaking, to the New York Law School. Wallace
reluctantly took that step in the fall of 1901.

Years later, when he enjoyed the specious clarity of retrospective vision, Stevens saw his surrender as either a
foregone conclusion or a deliberate decision. He had become a lawyer, he once remarked, because his father was
a lawyer.[77] On another occasion he told a correspondent
that he had simply chosen not to starve in a garret, *à la
mode de bohème*, while inditing deathless lyrics. "[A] good
many years ago," he said then,

> when I really was a poet in the sense that I was all imagina-
> tion, and so on, I deliberately gave up writing poetry because,
> much as I loved it, there were too many other things I wanted
> not to make an effort to have them. I wanted to do everything
> that one wants to do at that age: live in a village in France, in
> a hut in Morocco, or in a piano box at Key West. But I didn't
> like the idea of being bedeviled all the time about money and
> I didn't for a moment like the idea of poverty, so I went to
> work like anybody else and kept at it for a good many years.
> (*L* 320)

But he was not so clairvoyant or calculating in 1901—neither then nor for some time to come. Until shortly before
he took his position with the Hartford Accident and Indemnity Company in 1916, he would be chronically bedev-
iled with the problem of making a living and the nicer

75. *Harvard Graduates' Magazine* 10 (1901): 128.
76. *World's Work* 1 (1901): 584.
77. Hatfield, p. 30.

problem of keeping body and soul together. Nicer, inasmuch as this body needed expensive cigars and wines as well as food and shelter, while this soul required its background of the ideal. Knowing that he could not keep the two together under all conditions, he surrendered to his father conditionally.

Though Wallace could not have specified his conditions fully in 1901, he acted upon one of them by remaining in New York to study and practice law. The city which had at first seemed impersonal and lacking in character, whose materialism and vanity had appalled him and prompted his resolve to buy a set of Jowett's[78] Plato "as a sort of buoy," gradually came to exert a hold upon his imagination stronger than the ties binding him to Reading (*SP* 72–73, 79, 80–81). As late as October 1900, he considered seeking a position on the *Reading Times* (*SP* 86). But he had already begun to like New York that August, liked it "heartily and sincerely" by January, and came to "adore" it two months later (*SP* 84, 96, 100). His hometown suffered by contrast. Next to the "electric town" he had adopted, it began to seem childish and weak, the "acme of dullness" (*SP* 84, 100). "I have about made up my mind," Stevens reported to his journal in January 1901, "never to settle down in Reading" (*SP* 96).

This decision is the more remarkable when one views it in the light of Stevens' deep attachment to Reading and particularly to the woods, hills, and rivers around the town. As a boy, he had swum and fished in the Schuylkill River, climbed the tower on Mount Penn to survey the Oley Valley, bicycled to Ephrata and other neighboring towns. Then he went to college, and his first year away from home made, he observed later, "an enormous difference in everything" (*L* 126). He returned to Reading the following summer with the Harvard accent and sophisti-

78. "Jowett's" resembles "Lowell's" in Stevens' handwriting, and is so transcribed in *SP* 79 and *L* 42.

cated manner that forever distinguished him from his old friends and neighbors (*SP* 16). At first, he clung the more tenaciously to his native earth as he felt it slipping from his grasp. During his second year at Harvard, he published in the *Advocate* a prose sketch which features a student very much like himself who dreams "of a certain hill in Pennsylvania, of a certain grove of maples, and of a certain house which he knew as home on vacations and in summer time. He also thought that now would be a good time to rest an hour and be himself again."[79]

Stevens had the opportunity to be himself, or one of his selves, the following summer, when he divided his time between Reading and that "certain house" in nearby Berkeley, where he stayed as a guest of John Wily and his family. During that golden summer of 1899 he walked, read, swam, fished, journalized, and loafed to his heart's content. At the end of the three months, he predicted that this period would surpass all others in his memory (*SP* 59). This was his valedictory salute, for he left Cambridge the following spring convinced that he was simultaneously leaving "Reading, Berkeley, the mountains—and perhaps the clouds" (*SP* 70).

The move to New York did not, of course, preclude physical return to his cherished corner of Pennsylvania. While working as a reporter and studying law he occasionally visited the Wilys and climbed to Kuechler's Roost. But something had changed. Describing a walk from Berkeley to Reading late in the summer of 1900, he wrote in his journal, "Along the road the apples were beginning to look red & indeed everything was there as usual—excepting myself" (*SP* 85). At such moments, this part of the country seemed not dull or weak but a veritable Eden, a paradise he was helpless to regain (*SP* 206, *L* 97). Since the angel with the flaming sword was as much his own greater so-

79. "A Day in February," *Harvard Advocate* 66 (1899): 135–36; reprinted in *SP* 26–27.

phistication as anything else, it is appropriate that he should have borrowed a phrase from Nietzsche to express his ambivalence: "Reading is too, too human and so sot [sic] in its ways. I cast my shoes at it and empty my wash-pot upon it. But blessed be its name!"[80]

This *odi et amo* typifies Stevens' attitude toward Reading after 1901. He could neither regard his hometown with indifference nor find a substitute for it. His vacation in the Canadian Rockies in 1903 introduced him to the first mountain wilderness he had known and the last he would seek to know. From New York, he took long weekend walks along the Palisades of the Hudson River, and even found an elfin grot where he could commune with nature (*SP* 109, 111). These outings were, however, too brief and infrequent to afford the contact he needed. "Tomorrow if the sun shines I shall go wayfaring all day long," he wrote on the eve of an excursion into New Jersey. "I *must* find a home in the country—a place to live in, not only to *be* in" (*SP* 103). He believed he had found such a place in 1905, when he moved across the river to East Orange. But a year and a half later he returned, still homeless, to New York.

Why, one wonders, did Stevens not look for a home in the obvious place? Had he returned to Reading, he might have worked in his father's office, as both of his brothers had done, or set up his own practice nearby. He admitted on one occasion that he would probably have advanced more quickly in his profession if he had stayed in Reading (*L* 170). Instead, he chose to endure periods of loneliness, financial distress, and unemployment rather than return. New York undoubtedly compensated for these discomforts with its fine restaurants, shops, theaters, and museums. Stevens gloried in being "an exacting gallery-god" when he could afford the price of admission to a new play, and found the "great ideas, great feelings, great deeds" of a large city stimulating (*SP* 129, *L* 106). But it was something

80. Letter to Elsie Stevens, 6 Sept. 1913.

else, something he could not have articulated at first, that kept him in New York. He found the words for it in the fall of 1902, upon his return from a visit to Reading. In his hometown, he had noticed,

> dreaming is an effort in itself and hard work is merely meritorious—not instructive, and the way of the world is neither fine nor false. Fate carves its images there in a tedious fashion, and neither beautifully nor well. And the very wings of Time hang limp in the still air. (*SP* 109–10)

He was happy to be back in New York, for there, as he put it, "I can polish myself with dreams, exert myself in hard work, live in a fine, false way. . . ." Reading was a place of unrelieved reality, part of a land he would one day characterize as "too ripe for enigmas, too serene" (*CP* 374). New York, by contrast, was both enigmatic and lively. It was, in short, a place of imagination. At some half-conscious level, Stevens was choosing the ambience congenial to the poetry he would write. Dwelling in imagination, he needed repeatedly to visit the reality he loved and loathed.

Until about 1908 that poetry was still, as Emerson remarked of American literature in his day, in the optative mood. During business hours Stevens doggedly applied himself to the law, hoping one day to have a practice of his own (*SP* 114).[81] Since he lacked real enthusiasm for the work, he frequently had to flog himself to greater effort with admonitions that echo those in his father's letters. "Ambition and energy keep a man young," he told himself on one page of his journal, only to bemoan his failing ambition and energy on subsequent pages (*SP* 128–30). Ideally, another self was to emerge promptly at six o'clock,

---

81. Stevens apparently learned by trial and error what his associates at the Hartford Accident and Indemnity Company would perceive at once—that he had not the temperament for dealing with clients as a practicing attorney. Once he found his proper niche he went on to become, in the estimate of a colleague, the "dean of surety-claims men in the whole country"; see Brazeau, pp. 30, 67, 77.

when he left his office. Sometimes it did, but it was as often tardy or truant. "There is no every-day Wallace, apart from the one at work," he complained one day, "—and that one is tedious" (*L* 121). The poetic self was there, however, nourished by his walks, reading, and journalizing, by his visits to theaters and art galleries. Like a New York poet of an earlier generation, Emerson's unruly protégé, he was simmering, simmering, simmering. He would be brought to a boil shortly by the warmth of his love for Elsie Viola Moll and the renewal of old Harvard friendships.

· 2 ·

The Woman Won, the Woman Lost

It was W. B. Yeats who put the question: "Does the imagination dwell the most / Upon a woman won or a woman lost?" Yeats's own imagination dwelt painfully upon his frustrated love for Maud Gonne, and comfortably within the reciprocated love of Georgie Hyde-Lees. Both relationships suggest that love was the condition and matter of his art in a way it could not have been for Wallace Stevens. Or so we assume. Yet Stevens' first postcollegiate poems, slight as they are, were addressed neither to the general public nor to an *avant-garde* coterie but to a young woman named Elsie, whom he married in 1909. Stevens' courtship itself, because it was as much an affair of imagination as it was of emotion, serves to bridge the gap in his poetic development between the Harvard verse of 1898–1900 and the poems he began to publish in 1914.

Henry Church may have been the first to see it. ". . . I am convinced," he wrote Stevens in 1943, "that Mrs. Stevens has had an important part in the poetry of Wallace Stevens."[1] This was the amiable thing to say after meeting, for the first time, the wife of a poet who was also a close friend. But few others would have been so generous or clairvoyant in the case of Elsie Stevens. She was a lovely woman who never stooped to folly, yet looked and felt chronically foolish. Her literary taste ran to Longfellow and short fiction in women's magazines, a disclosure that would have raised eyebrows among the New York literati

1. Letter of 27 Mar.

who met the Stevenses in Walter Arensberg's apartment.[2] It took few encounters with people like these to keep her at home playing the piano or, later, studying the flowers in her garden or the family tree in old books. After a cruise from New York to San Francisco in 1923, she rarely accompanied her husband on excursions from the big house on Westerly Terrace in Hartford. Yet Church was right, for all that. This rather prim and conventional woman was Wallace Stevens' muse and a pretext for his flights of imagination, both in the winning and in the losing.

The winning of Elsie required all the finesse Stevens later displayed in his poetry. Though a handsome woman—she modeled for the Liberty dime and half-dollar minted in 1916—she suffered all her life from what her daughter has called a "persecution complex" originating in childhood.[3] Born Elsie Viola Kachel a few months after her parents' marriage, she lost her father the following year. Seven years later, her mother married Lehman Moll, who never formally adopted his wife's first child. Even Elsie's fiancé was occasionally unsure which surname to use; he addressed his letters to "Miss Elsie V. Moll" but, after some lawyerly deliberation, had the initials "E.V.K." inscribed on her wedding ring.[4] The Moll family was hard-pressed financially, especially after the birth of another daughter, so Elsie was unable to complete a full year of high school. Instead, she sold sheet music in a department store and gave piano lessons at home. Perhaps more disabling than these financial and educational handicaps was the social one. She lived not only on the wrong side of Reading's railroad tracks but also, apparently, in the shadow of gossip about her dubious legitimacy.

2. Louis Heizmann recalls Stevens' chagrin at Elsie's taste for Longfellow in Michael Lafferty's "Wallace Stevens: A Man of Two Worlds," *Historical Review of Berks County* 24 (1959): 113. Elsie recommends a *Good Housekeeping* magazine story to her half sister Dorothy La Rue Moll in a letter of 30 Aug. 1921.
3. This paragraph is indebted to Holly Stevens' portrait of her mother in *SP* 137–38.
4. Letter from Stevens to Elsie, 9 Sept. 1909.

Elsie Stevens in Elizabeth Park, Hartford, about 1916
(Courtesy of the Huntington Library)

Elsie had turned eighteen shortly before that summer evening in 1904 when she first met Wallace Stevens. He was almost twenty-six and the son of a popular Reading attorney and businessman; he had attended Harvard College, had recently been admitted to the bar in New York City, and enjoyed a local reputation as a poet. He evinced but one weakness, and that was for the young woman he considered the prettiest girl in Reading.[5] During their courtship, he did everything in his power to bolster her pride in her family and herself. Once, when Elsie's grandmother alluded to a washerwoman in his mother's family, he appreciated the joke at his mother's expense, remarking to Elsie,

> . . . I don't in the least mind what your grandmother said either about her relatives or mine. It is amusing to think of that washer-woman. Mother must be worried to death when she thinks of her. You know she is a Daughter of the Revolution and traces herself through two or three generations to an officer in the American army. You can imagine her crowding out the details. (*SP* 208)

He went on to draw the moral, "that individuals rise or fall on their own merits. Their families are nothing." Garrett Stevens, though he shared his son's amusement at Kate Stevens' social pretensions, was not prepared to have the family treated as nothing. That Wallace had misplaced his affections on someone beneath his social station was bad enough; that he neglected his own family on his visits home was too much. There was an angry confrontation between father and son in 1908, and the two were not to be reconciled during Garrett's lifetime.[6] Having cast his lot entirely with Elsie, Wallace asked her to be his wife and presented her with an engagement ring later that same year. He persuaded her that he could not only provide for

5. Stevens told his daughter that this was why he married Elsie; see Brazeau, p. 260n.
6. For details of the confrontation between Stevens and his father, see Brazeau, pp. 254–64.

her but also create a special, scarcely terrestrial world for them to inhabit.

Stevens received as much or more in return. His friends in high school and college had known an enthusiastic and companionable young man, despite the cynicism and "coldness" for which he reproached himself (*SP* 50).[7] His high spirits gradually evaporated, however, as he gave himself to the solitary business of making a living in New York. Except for infrequent evenings in the company of old friends from Reading or Harvard, he endured what he called the "terrible imprisonment" of boarding-house life (*SP* 103). "I wish a thousand times a day," he wrote in his journal in 1900, "that I had a wife—which I never shall have, and more's the pity for I am certainly a domestic creature, par excellence. It is brutal to oneself to live alone."[8] When Elsie appeared, he believed he had found both an ideal soulmate and vicarious contact with his native soil.

Like poetry, however, life with Elsie was a luxury to be deferred until he had established himself in his profession. Even before Stevens began to specialize in surety bonds, he had the insurance lawyer's horror of uncalculated risk. Writing to Elsie of a more adventuresome couple, he asked, "Don't you like the idea of people who give up everything wildly, as Sylvia and Hilton did? Instead of hanging on to dreary safety, they take a tremendous fling. That seems to be the New York idea."[9] That it was not his idea appears in the next sentence: "I'm glad some people do it though I shouldn't do it myself—nor recommend it."

7. Richard Ellmann regards Stevens' cynicism and its transformation from a source of guilt into a virtue as the matter of a significant intellectual crisis; see his "How Wallace Stevens Saw Himself," in *Wallace Stevens: A Celebration*, ed. Frank Doggett and Robert Buttel (Princeton: Princeton University Press, 1980), pp. 149–70.

8. Journal entry of 26 July 1900; cf. *SP* 81.

9. This passage appears on p. 18 of a notebook in which Elsie entered excerpts from Stevens' letters, some of which she later destroyed. Hereafter I cite this notebook simply as "Excerpts."

For five years, then, between 1904 and 1909, Stevens postponed marriage and lived at a distance from his fiancée. How Elsie regarded this arrangement we cannot be sure, for her side of their correspondence during these years is not extant; but Stevens' letters so often anticipate rebellion in the provinces that she cannot have been entirely complaisant. Though she later destroyed Stevens' letters of 1904–6, except for the excerpts she preserved in a stenographer's notebook, two of his 1907 letters suggest they had had to rebuild their relationship the previous spring, after some kind of falling out.[10] Elsie needed frequently to be assured that she was not risking spinsterhood by waiting beyond the eligible age of her friends in Reading; conceivably, her approaching twentieth birthday touched off the crisis of 1906. Stevens probably allayed her doubts then, as later, with a combination of soft words and hard facts. In his letter of April 14, 1907, for example, he assures Elsie that she is still young at twenty, then exhorts her to patience with a few pertinent figures:

> Need I speak of this now any more clearly than we needed to speak during our first summer? We do not understand each other the less, I hope, for not speaking. You know. I have a special dread of speaking of it to-night, because Mrs. Jackson had a piece of beef for dinner to-day that cost $2.25 and some asparagus, for salad, that cost .85 a bunch. Oysters are .15 and oranges .40 a dozen. It is frightful. Whenever the desire becomes so strong as to make me unreasonable, I find it a great help to inquire about the price of eggs and pine-apples and coal. . . . But you know my views. Meditate on the figures— and then put your right hand in my left and let us call down the wrath of heaven on all butchers, grocers, landlords, laundresses, tailors, seamstresses, and so on; and thank goodness that for the present we can be happy without them. You must not scold me for saying all this.

As late as August 4, 1909, Stevens sent his fiancée a newspaper clipping reporting the current egg prices, presum-

---

10. Letters to Elsie, 18 and 20 Mar.

ably to get her through the final weeks before their wedding on September 21.

These communications suggest, not that Stevens keyed his serenade to the commodities market, but that he sang most comfortably in the prescient light of day. His caution had one pleasurable consequence for all who enjoy his poetry: it forced him to write often and, in writing, to admit an audience to the deliberations of his mind and heart. The journal he kept between 1898 and 1904 is a private chamber, with himself the sole occupant. The love letters which began to supplant the journal after his meeting with Elsie are a kind of intimate theater. Perhaps "theater-in-the-making" would better describe these letters, for they continually dramatize the distinction he makes in a 1906 journal entry: "There is a perfect rout of characters in every man—and every man is like an actor's trunk, full of strange creatures, new & old. But an actor and his trunk are two different things" (*SP* 166). The actor, as one happens upon him backstage, is a rather lugubrious fellow who frets about the meaning of life, the validity of religious belief, his fiancée's loyalty, and the moral compromises to be made in getting a living. But he is scarcely glimpsed before he rummages through his trunk and comes up with a diverting costume or antic disposition.

This scenario is readily seen in his letter of December 8–9, 1908, which opens, "Dear Elsie:— Here I have been sitting for an hour writing 'The Book of Doubts and Fears.' Bang! I'm not a philosopher. —Besides, it did not seem desireable to disclose so much of my own spirit" (*L* 112). So he disguises his malaise, even in Elsie's presence, by offering "a list of Pleasant Things to drive dull care away, my lass, oh, to drive dull care away—and a jig, and a jig, and a jig, jig, jig. . . ." He salutes her the next evening with another "Rig-a-jig-jig," followed by a comic improvisation:

> Now, quick, for a change of masks—so that as you follow me around you only find—Tom Folio—a lazy-bones in an eighteenth-century pair of knee-breeches, with a long-tailed coat,

holding his large spectacles to the sun as he looks for dust on them. In one hand he has an umbrella, neatly rolled up, and under his arm is one of the early editions of nothing less than the never-ending "Book of Doubts and Fears." (L 113)

The rest of the letter is a crazy quilt of dialogue from a melodrama; a remark upon his fatigue after drawing up a legal document; the story of Our Lady's juggler; an onomatopoetic rendering of a tune with fiddle, saxophone, and flute; a sobering reflection from "The Book of Doubts and Fears"; and more jiggety-jigging. To read this and similar letters is to witness the rehearsals for Stevens' later comic productions, notably "The Comedian as the Letter C." Later, as here, he will rely upon fantastical characters and gaudy or nonsensical diction for comic effect. Later, too, the high spirits will often be contrived to drive dull care away.

Besides Tom Folio, the cast of characters in Stevens' love letters includes a number of would-be scholars and moralists, bearing names like "Scribe and Learned Hand" and "Old Prune."[11] These are ironic inversions of the Stevens who occasionally seizes the lectern to instruct or edify his younger and less educated fiancée. He wanted to be taken seriously, but not too seriously. The same impulse moved him to adopt the mask of Pierrot. Elsie had awakened in him an emotion whose value he could not overstate. "I should come to you clapping my hands," he exulted, "because you have made me feel so much the lover."[12] He enjoyed being in love, was half in love with love, and saw it as a phase of romance in the literary sense of the word. "'Romance is the taste for the extraordinary,'" he wrote Elsie, quoting Octave Feuillet. "'It is imagination in revolt against reason.'"[13] But it was not his nature to remain long

11. Letters to Elsie, 18 June and 19 Jan. 1909. Alex Zwerdling suggests that "Learned Hand" may be a playful allusion to the famous American jurist.
12. Excerpts, p. 12.
13. Excerpts, p. 49.

in a state of emotional deshabille, so he dressed up as Pierrot (the Pedrolino of the *commedia dell'arte*) and cast Elsie as his Columbine. "Columbine and Pierrot," he wrote her. "How aptly those two evanescent characters symbolize, in some aspects, ourselves!"[14]

Which aspects, we are left to wonder, typified their relationship? Perhaps Stevens saw in himself something of Laforgue's inept and cerebral Pierrot. Movie-goers who remember Jean-Louis Barrault as the Funambule Pierrot in *Les Enfants du paradis* (1945) have another clue: certainly Stevens idealized his fiancée and saw her as scarcely more corporeal than moonlight; she was his Good Angel, his *princesse lointaine* to be worshiped from afar.[15] She was also, it pleased and tormented him to reflect, sufficiently the coquette to attract any number of village Harlequins. Still another facet of Stevens' clown catches the light in a letter to Elsie:

> Pierrot was "pale, slender, dressed in white clothes, always hungry and always being beaten—the ancient slave, the modern member of the mob, the [pariah?], the creature, passive and disinherited who assists, gloomy and malign, at the orgies and frolics of his masters." That was all changed. Pierrot powdered his face with flour. He wore many disguises. As a marquis, "all in white satin"—made love to Columbine in other people's clothes, kissed her, "grew drunk with glory."[16]

Historically, Pierrot never quite lived down his past as the servile zany of Greek and Roman farce until nineteenth-century mimes like Jean-Gaspard Deburau ennobled and romanticized his character. Similarly, when Stevens felt himself a minion of the legal profession and resented "lending people the use of [his] bald-head" for the better part of the day (*L* 124), he found release in assuming a very

14. Excerpts, p. 44.
15. Excerpts, p. 38; *SP* 146.
16. Excerpts, p. 50; punctuation as shown. Stevens seems to be quoting another source, which I have been unable to identify, on the historical development of Pierrot's stage character.

different costume to woo Elsie. We see him figuratively changing clothes and entering the realm of romance—in both senses of the word—in his letter of February 28, 1909:

> Ought I not suddenly pull off my black wig and black gown and put on a white wig, full of powder, and a suit of motley— or maybe, the old costume of Pierrot? For when I sit at the window and write, I look out on real things and am a part of them; but with my lamp lighted and my shade down—there is nothing real, at least there need not be and I can whisk away to Arcady—or say Picardy. (L 134)

But why did Stevens choose to make love to Columbine in other people's clothes? Immediately following the passage on Pierrot and Columbine in Elsie's notebook is an excerpt which may provide the answer: "The plain truth is, no doubt, that I like to be anything but my plain self; and when I write a letter that does not satisfy me—why it seems like showing my plain self, too plainly."[17] Stevens hated to be his plain self, even—perhaps especially—in love. Though he looked forward to seeing Elsie on his visits to Reading, he dreaded the first minutes of each reunion because he thought himself then cast in the conventional role of "gentleman caller." Leave-takings were little better, and one in particular prompted a remorseful postscript the next evening:

> I have been worried to-day by the thought that, perhaps, I made a bad impression on you last night after we had reached home, and particularly while we were saying, "good-bye." I do not know just what it was: something vague. —You saw me thread-bare—for I *am* thread-bare when I stand beside you, dear, spouting those long sentences. You dont say much, but I don't believe the smallest thing escapes you. And I dont like to be seen thread-bare. —The purple robe must, of course, be laid aside now and then; but never, I hope, entirely lost sight of.[18]

Here Stevens is hankering for something more grandiose than Pierrot's white pajamas to clothe his threadbare self,

17. Excerpts, p. 50; L 109.
18. Letter to Elsie, 6 July 1909.

just as, in the poetry of the late thirties, he would try to cloak his comedian in the purple of the noble figure he called "major man." In both cases, he chose to weave his new garments—and so a new self—out of words. That was the advantage of courting Elsie on paper: he could, as he put it, "command" himself there (*L* 80).

Conveniently, he could also command Elsie there. After observing in his letter of March 10, 1907, that he and Elsie were more at ease in their correspondence than in person, Stevens concludes,

> It must be because you are more perfectly yourself to me when I am writing to you, and that makes me more perfectly myself to you. You know that I do with you as I like in my thoughts: I no sooner wish for your hand than I have it—no sooner wish for anything to be said or done than it *is* said or done; and none of the denials you make me are made there. You are *my* Elsie there. (*L* 96)

Though Stevens was surely aware that he ran the risk of self-delusion in trying thus to improve upon the actual Elsie, he must have thought this a legitimate, even a gallant distortion. Years later, in "Notes toward a Supreme Fiction" (1942), he would have Ozymandias tell Nanzia Nunzio that

> the spouse, the bride
> Is never naked. A fictive covering
> Weaves always glistening from the heart and mind.
> ("It Must Change," VIII)

Neither would Stevens have been disturbed by the element of narcissism in such weavings. In his letters to Elsie he frequently speaks of her as his second self or as an aspect of himself, hence he could properly describe his letter-writing as "self-communion" or "meditation."[19] Theoretically, this meant that he might dispense with Elsie herself so long as he possessed that which she represented. "Even if I did not know you," he speculates in one place, "I should always find myself in what you are. I

19. Excerpts, p. 5; *L* 123.

should be dreaming of some such—Elsie."[20] But this was purely hypothetical. As long as she could sustain his illusions, she was crucial to his psychic integrity. Without exaggeration he could tell her, "to have written last night was like recovering a part of myself that had been lost for a little."[21]

An especially valuable part of Stevens' self quickened to life when he fell in love with Elsie. None of his college verses had been written in the presence, even fictive, of another person; they were meant to be overheard by the world in general and so by no one in particular. Whether Elsie understood or even read the poems Stevens gave her on her birthday in 1908 and 1909 is immaterial. She was his first audience, and the theater of their love letters continued to inform his sense of the poet's ideal relationship with his public. In today's world, he wrote in 1940, poetry

has

To construct a new stage. It has to be on that stage
And, like an insatiable actor, slowly and
With meditation, speak words that in the ear,
In the delicatest ear of the mind, repeat,
Exactly, that which it wants to hear, at the sound
Of which, an invisible audience listens,
Not to the play, but to itself, expressed
In an emotion as of two people, as of two
Emotions becoming one.

("Of Modern Poetry")

One might go further, and say that Elsie was to the poems of 1908–9 what the "Interior Paramour" would be to his later work. Poetry, Stevens affirmed in a letter to Elsie, lies in the "remoter places" of the mind (L 131). In that interior of interiors, he embraced his second self, the creative anima, and celebrated those weddings of the soul in his poems.

Yet there is something curiously unsatisfactory about those first nuptial hymns, the forty poems which make up

20. Excerpts, p. 36.
21. Letter of 18 Mar. 1907.

the 1908 "Book of Verses" and the 1909 "Little June Book."
One is prepared to overlook, in apprentice work, the shop-
worn diction, predictable rimes, and arthritic rhythms. But
one comes away from these poems feeling dislocated. They
are neither here nor there, topographically speaking. In
this respect, they betray Stevens' precarious sense of locale
when he wrote them.

By the time Stevens began to court Elsie in 1904, his first
ardor for the "electric town" (SP 100) of New York had
cooled. He still took aesthetic pleasure in the Manhattan
and Washington Bridges, the architecture of Columbia
University and the panorama of city and river to be seen
from the Williamsburg Bridge.[22] He felt a special affinity
for downtown Manhattan around Washington Square,
where he had lived during his first months as a newspaper
reporter and where he supposed he and Elsie would begin
their life together.[23] Increasingly, however, he became prey
to that strain of *mal de la ville* he called "New York gloom,"
and would gladly have left the city, never to return (SP 150,
185, 226). New York lacked the one balm that might have
rendered its chafing tolerable. Stevens required "country"
but could not find the right sort within walking distance of
the city (SP 172). Only one kind would really serve the
purpose, and that was in a certain corner of Pennsylvania.
"I am not emotional," he wrote Elsie in 1909,

> but I am aware that I look at the country at home with emo-
> tion. The twenty years of life that are the simplest and the best
> were spent there. But I do not look at the country here with
> emotion. When it is beautiful I know that it is beautiful. When
> the country at home is beautiful, I don't only know it; I feel
> it—I rejoice in it, and I am proud. (L 148)

The love letters posted between New York and Reading
reminded Stevens almost daily of the region to which he
belonged emotionally. Reading claimed him practically

---

22. Letters from Stevens to Elsie, 22 Apr. 1907 (SP 178); 9 May and 18
June, 1909.
23. Letter to Elsie, 7 May 1909.

against his better judgment: it was dull and ugly and got on his nerves (*SP* 143, 159, 168). At the same time, he considered this spot of earth his Horatian *"fons Bandusiae"* and the best place in which to think life over (*SP* 143, 249). In college, he had been "rather furiously set up" by his visits home, but he found it progressively more difficult to make this Antaean connection after moving to New York (*L* 728, 108). He came to feel "very much of a stranger" in Reading and might have drifted away altogether, he admitted, were it not for Elsie (*L* 112, 126).

If Elsie touched the springs of romance in Stevens, she also touched his longing for a native land, the thing he would call "reality" in his later work. "Your voice comes out of an old world," he told her.

> It is the only true world for me. An old world, and yet it is a world that has no existence except in you. —It is as if I were in the proverbial far country and never knew how much I had become estranged from the actual reality of the things that are the real things of my heart, until the actual reality found a voice—you are the voice. . . . You are my—you know what I want to say—what in the fairy tales is called the genius. . . . (*L* 131)

Stevens'"genius" afforded him the occasion for many pilgrimages, both real and imaginary, to Reading. He planned, savored, and finally reminisced over their hikes and carriage rides in the Reading countryside. Ever in the background, however, was the certainty that marriage would bring this era to a close. They deluded themselves for a while with plans of returning one day to settle in Reading or at least buying a summer home nearby, with a suitably poetic name like "Phosphor Farm."[24] But by then something else would have been lost. Stevens alludes to it in a letter written two weeks before their wedding: "We shall probably not get back to [Reading] before Xmas—and then you will already be something of a New-Yorker, and

24. Letters from Stevens to Elsie, 9 and 16 June; 9 July 1909.

the little country girl you like to call yourself will have disappeared."[25]

Stevens underestimated Elsie's resolve to remain a little country girl. She had made it clear early in their courtship that she could not live happily in the city. Still, there must have been moments when Elsie believed she could be in New York without being of it. She would inhabit the world her fiancé had created for her in his letters and poems. That world was pleasant enough, as he described it:

> In Japan the ladies of the court are kept in a palace with many gardens, where they never see any of the wretchedness of life—the princesses. They do not know that there is anything in the world except cherry-trees, and poets, and things of pearl and silk and ivory.[26]

"As far as it is possible," he went on to assure her, "I should like to do that for you." The poems of 1908–9 promised much the same world, a kind of Japanese garden furnished with poets, picturesque trees, and precious *bibelots*. One vignette will serve to suggest the whole:

> Life is long in the desert,
> On the sea, and in the mountains.
> Ah! but how short it is
> By the radiant fountains,
>
> By the jubilant fountains,
> Of the rivers wide-sailing,
> Under emerald poplars,
> With round ivory paling.
>
> (*SP* 228)

One would gladly prolong one's life in these pleasant surroundings; in this sense, the garden is not proof against thoughts of mutability. But such thoughts never become so distinct as to ruffle the repose of the scene or the measure of the verse. Whether the "round ivory paling" is literally

25. Letter of 8 Sept. 1909.
26. Excerpts, p. 57.

an ivory fence or—as is more likely—an enchanted circle of moonlight, it effectively excludes the workaday world.

For Stevens, the dislocation of the 1908–9 poems was purposeful without necessarily being deliberate. He was simply exerting what he would later call the pressure of imagination against the reality of his daily routine and surroundings. He still required the world of dreaming and imagination which New York had once represented (*SP* 109–10). Consequently, when he began to find the city disagreeable, he transferred this need to foreign places like Paris, London, and Germany. Postcards from friends traveling in England and Europe moved him to fancy a similar journey with Elsie one day.[27] Except in imagination, he would never make that journey. While there were no doubt practical reasons for this, one suspects Stevens of that more perverse inhibition dramatized by Huysmans' Des Esseintes. This hero of the *fin de siècle*, once disappointed by a trip to Holland, chooses not to risk his illusions a second time by visiting the London he knew chiefly from Dickens' novels. For Stevens, Paris in particular would become a "precious fiction" (*L* 773) nurtured by a steady influx of French postcards, paintings, books, and periodicals. Gertrude Stein, the more intrepid expatriate, might have been describing Stevens when she observed that "writers have to have two countries, the one where they belong and the one in which they live really. The second one is romantic, it is separate from themselves, it is not real but it is really there."[28]

While Stevens was courting Elsie, however, he neither belonged to New York nor regarded Paris as anything but a place to visit. He could not bring himself to make poetry of the city, like Baudelaire, or to freight his poems with the memories of Reading which distinguish his most engaging letters. He chose instead to conjure up an idealized land-

---

27. Letters to Elsie, 26 Jan. and 24 June 1909; also *SP* 238.
28. *Paris France* (New York: Scribners, 1940), p. 2.

scape, owing something to Reading but more to books and paintings. There he could dwell all but physically, to judge from a letter he wrote to Elsie six weeks after he gave her the poem quoted above. "The pressure of Life is very great in great cities," he began on this occasion. So he invited her to come live with him in the land of radiant fountains:

> The wind has fallen. The moon has risen. We are where we have never been, listening to what we have never heard. We are in a dark place listening—contentedly, to—well, nightingales—why not? We are by a jubilant fountain, like the one in the forgotten "June Book," under emerald poplars, by a wide-sailing river—and we hear another fountain—a radiant fountain of sound rise from one of the dark green trees into the strange moon-light—rise and shimmer—from the tree of the nightingales. —And is it all on a stage? And can't you possibly close your eyes and, by imagination, feel that it is perfectly real—the dark circle of poplars, with the round moon among them, the air moving, the water falling, and that sweet outpouring of liquid sound—fountains and nightingales—fountains and nightingales—and Sylvie and the brooding shadow that would listen beside her so intently to fountains and nightingales and to her? (L 149–50)

Poetry might bring the nightingale to America and woodland Sylvie to the city; but could it assure their happiness once translated? It was too much to expect. Elsie arrived to find neither Japanese palace nor garden, but an upstairs apartment in a noisy city. Stevens, failing to find a suitable place around Washington Square, had taken an apartment on West Twenty-First Street, opposite the dark north wall of the General Theological Seminary. Though he proposed that they move to the suburbs after a year or two,[29] they were not to be dislodged until the move to Hartford seven years later. In the meantime, Stevens introduced Elsie to his friends and bought her a piano to help her pass her days; but he could not fill the place once occupied by Elsie's family and her social life in Reading. An acquaintance from these years remembers that she wanted

29. Letter to Elsie, 18 July 1909.

to have a child (*SP* 247). Apparently this too was a luxury to be deferred until Stevens felt he had a surer footing in his profession.

Given these circumstances, it seems less peculiar that Elsie should have returned to Reading not only that first Christmas but also late the following spring, for a stay of several weeks. This visit apparently caused a stir among the Molls' neighbors, who wondered if Elsie was being sufficiently "affectionate" to her husband.[30] Had anything been truly amiss in their relationship, Elsie would probably not have reported the gossip to Stevens and he would not have supplied her with an amusing rejoinder in his letter of June 10, 1910:

> And why should a girl not go home for two or three weeks and be at ease and think pleasant things in the Spring? Oh, because her lord and master cannot care for her if he gives her such liberty. But, ladies, the damsel is not my prisoner, nor my slave. Oh, because she ought to be busy with pots and pans, just as we are. Honorable ladies, there ain't no pots and pans—we live on strawberries etc. etc. etc. Then her lord should be with her. Most noble ladies, he is: he is in her heart, and therefore he does not fear to be out of her sight.

This philosophy served him well enough for the first couple of weeks, but after another twelve days he was begging Elsie to return (*SP* 250). When the pattern of Christmas and summer separations persisted the following year, Stevens decided to take stock of his career. Alone in July 1911, he wrote to Elsie: "I mean to spend my evenings at home reading and trying to *think* a way through the future, that will lead us all through pleasant places" (*SP* 251). Elsie must have suggested that Reading was a not unpleasant place, for Stevens' reply of August 6 dispels that dream once and for all: "If I were to come back, I should want to go into a business—and that requires capital and experience and a willingness to make money 1¾ cents at a time. I fully intend to continue along my present line—because

30. Letter from Stevens to Elsie, 10 June 1910.

it gives me a living and because it seems to offer possibilities" (*L* 170).

This course led Stevens eventually to a position in the main office of the Hartford Accident and Indemnity Company, and so solved the problem of keeping Elsie at home after 1916.[31] Meanwhile, between 1910 and 1915, he was restored to solitude for weeks at a time while Elsie spent her summers at various country resorts in Pennsylvania and New York. How Stevens felt about these absences, once he grew accustomed to them, appears in his letter of August 30, 1915:

> I've been lonely for you anyhow—that's the truth . . I think that it is not only my desire for solitude that suggests vacations to me. It appeals to my pride to be able to send you away. I have not made much progress as the world goes; but I forget that, when I can feel that you are away in the country, like everybody else, doing pleasant things. When New-York is empty and dull, I should feel as though I were of no account to have you here and be unable to make things pleasant for you.

Clearly, Stevens thought it important not only to be, but also to appear to be, a good provider. In later years, he would neglect few opportunities to *épater le bohème* with his businesslike manner and verbal assaults upon the stereotype of the poet as a loafer and man of "no account." But this passage indicates that he also appreciated the solitude—as opposed to the loneliness—of these summers. In fact, on this and at least one other occasion, he suggested that Elsie prolong her vacation in the country.[32] Though Stevens urged this partly from concern for Elsie's health, which was never robust, he had another reason for wanting to be alone during this period. He was having an affair, so to speak, with her rival.

31. "I miss New-York abominably," Stevens told Ferdinand Reyher shortly after the move, "but Mrs. Stevens, with murderous indifference, pretends that Hartford is sweet to her spirit" (letter of 3 June 1916; copy at Huntington Library).

32. Letter of 11 Aug. 1914.

"Rival" may not be quite the right word, for the Interior Paramour never became emotionally distinct from Elsie. For a while, at least, both lovers inhabited the inner chamber of Stevens' mind, a chamber which appears to have had a counterpart in the outer world. Addressing Elsie on August 16, 1911, from their apartment, Stevens remarked, "I am writing by candle-light. The electric light, you remember does not reach the table. . . . You would be surprised to find how pleasant a candle on this table makes the room. It gives such a quiet, uncertain light—very favorable to meditation, and the likes o' that."[33] Readers familiar with Stevens' "Final Soliloquy of the Interior Paramour" (1951) will recognize in this excerpt the décor of the "intensest rendezvous" recreated in that poem and also in an address before the Poetry Society of America written about the same time (see *OP* 243). It may be, too, an after-image of the candle at 441 West Twenty-First Street that flickers with an uncertain certainty in the prologue to "Notes toward a Supreme Fiction":

> And for what, except for you, do I feel love?
> Do I press the extremest book of the wisest man
> Close to me, hidden in me day and night?
> In the uncertain light of single, certain truth,
> Equal in living changingness to the light
> In which I meet you, in which we sit at rest,
> For a moment in the central of our being,
> The vivid transparence that you bring is peace.

Had Stevens taken his cue from classical invocations of the muse, he would have addressed his Interior Paramour with the reverence befitting a goddess. Conscious of her official role with respect to all practitioners of his art, he would not have presumed to monopolize her attention as he does. But Stevens' relationship with his Interior Paramour, based as it was on his relationship with Elsie, re-

---

33. Stevens had also mentioned writing by candlelight in his letter of 6 Aug. 1911 (*L* 171).

mained one of love and intense privacy. As a bridegroom, Stevens had resented even the intrusion of a public wedding ceremony into the "old-time secrecy" of his love affair.[34] As poet, he preserved that secrecy by admitting an audience to his private chamber only under the guise of his muse. Thus in 1941 he maintained that "all poets address themselves to someone and it is of the essence of that instinct, and it seems to amount to an instinct, that it should be to an elite, not to a drab but to a woman with the hair of a pythoness . . ." (*NA* 29).

This suggests something about the character of the poetic muse. Traditionally, she represents that mysterious phenomenon called "inspiration." Inspiration springs in turn from a happy agreement between the poet's personal resources and the requirements of his prospective audience, his "elite." No audience, no inspiration. Though Stevens sometimes insisted that he wrote only for himself, and that he would write whether or not his poems were read, he came nearer the truth of his own experience in a brief speech accepting the National Book Award for *The Auroras of Autumn* (1950). "There is about every poet," he observed on that occasion, "a vast world of other people from which he derives himself and through himself his poetry. What he derives from his generation he returns to his generation, as best he can. His poetry is theirs and theirs is his, because of the interaction between the poet and his time . . ." (*OP* 245). In this sense, he maintained, poetry must always be modern with a modernity free of modishness.

Where the birthday poems of 1908–9 were written primarily for Elsie, the later work presupposes an Interior Paramour who represented a larger and more sophisticated audience. Around 1913 she was, among other things, Stevens' awareness of a new ferment in the arts, signaled most conspicuously by the Armory Show of Post-

34. Letter to Elsie, 16 Sept. 1909.

Impressionist art. This source of inspiration might have proved too diffuse and remote to overcome his inertia had it not been transmitted and reinforced by more proximate sources, college friends who were active in New York artistic and literary circles. Stevens had maintained contact with two of these, Walter Arensberg and Witter Bynner, apparently from his first years in New York. But it was a third, Pitts Sanborn, who promoted him abruptly to the ranks of the *avant-garde*. Sanborn, then music editor of the New York *Globe*, joined the staff of *Trend* magazine in 1914 and proceeded to invite contributions from his wide literary acquaintance. That September, *Trend* carried items by seven Harvard men, including Arensberg, Bynner, and Stevens. It also carried a poem by Donald Evans and an advertisement for Claire Marie, the press Evans had founded to publish "Belles-Lettres for Exotic Tastes," including titles by Evans, Gertrude Stein, and Allen and Louise Norton.

For exotic tastes, too, was the first poem in "Carnet de Voyage," the sequence Stevens contributed to the issue:

> An odor from a star
> Comes to my fancy, slight,
> Tenderly spiced and gay,
> As if a seraph's hand
> Unloosed the fragrant silks
> Of some sultana, bright
> In her soft sky. And pure
> It is, and excellent,
> As if a seraph's blue
> Fell, as a shadow falls,
> And his warm body shed
> Sweet exhalations, void
> Of our despised decay.[35]

Superficially, the star in this poem resembles "the quiet star / Lighted beyond the half-seen trees" in one of Elsie's birthday poems (*SP* 195). But this orb demands a more complex

35. 7 (1914): 743; reprinted in *SP* 259.

response, for it is at once more transcendent and more earthly than its predecessor. It is in fact a Blessed Damozel, invested with the fainting eroticism of the Pre-Raphaelites. Though not markedly different from the other seven poems of "Carnet de Voyage," five of which were lifted from the "Little June Book" of 1909, this bit of celestial seduction would surely have offended Elsie. Stevens placed it first in the *Trend* sequence to catch the eye of another sort of reader.

He had not miscalculated. "Carnet de Voyage" piqued the interest of Carl Van Vechten, who asked for more of Stevens' work when he served temporarily as editor of *Trend*. He published two of Stevens' poems, one from the 1908 "Book of Verses," in the November issue and identified Stevens on the contributors' page as "one of the most gifted of the younger American poets."[36] Together with Donald Evans and Allen and Louise Norton, Van Vechten formed the literary circle Glen MacLeod has called the "Patagonians," after the group portrait Evans sketched in *Sonnets from the Patagonian* (1913).[37] Though loyal to the spirit of the *fin de siècle*, the Patagonians eagerly absorbed the modernist experiments of Gertrude Stein and, later, of the French expatriate artists who gathered at Arensberg's apartment on West Sixty-Seventh Street in New York. Once the two groups were brought together, probably by Pitts Sanborn, they proved oddly compatible and eventually combined forces to create the movement known as New York Dada, a more playful version of European Dada. They collaborated on two short-lived magazines, *Blindman* and *Rongwrong*, both published in 1917 under the direction of Marcel Duchamp. The Patagonians still possessed a distinct identity late in 1914, when Van Vechten, then hatch-

36. 8 (1914): ii.
37. For an illuminating account of Stevens' relationships with the Patagonians and the other artists mentioned in this paragraph, see MacLeod's *Wallace Stevens and Company: The Harmonium Years 1913–1923* (Ann Arbor: UMI Research Press, 1983), pp. 3–41.

ing plans for a "post-decadent" literary movement, conspired with Arensberg to bring Stevens into their circle of friends.[38] Realizing that they would have to win Elsie over before they could win her husband, they elaborately stage-managed a soirée for the Stevenses in December. They banished tobacco and strong waters from the Arensberg apartment and coached the company, which included Van Vechten's wife Fania Marinoff and the Nortons, in the dress and discourse likely to make a favorable impression on Mrs. Stevens.

Of the several poems Stevens read to the group that evening, one brilliantly fulfilled the promise of "An odor from a star. . . ." It was called "Cy Est Pourtraicte, Madame Ste Ursule, et Les Unze Mille Vierges":

Ursula, in a garden, found
A bed of radishes.
She kneeled upon the ground
And gathered them,
With flowers around,
Blue, gold, pink, and green.

She dressed in red and gold brocade
And in the grass an offering made
Of radishes and flowers.

She said, "My dear,
Upon your altars,
I have placed
The marguerite and coquelicot,
And roses
Frail as April snow;
But here," she said,
"Where none can see,
I make an offering, in the grass,
Of radishes and flowers."
And then she wept
For fear the Lord would not accept.

The good Lord in His garden sought
New leaf and shadowy tinct,

38. Van Vechten recounts the story of the "post-decadent" movement and the party at the Arensbergs' studio in "Rogue Elephant in Porcelain," *Yale University Library Gazette* 38 (1963): 41–50.

And they were all His thought.
He heard her low accord,
Half prayer and half ditty,
And He felt a subtle quiver,
That was not heavenly love,
Or pity.

This is not writ
In any book.[39]

Like "An odor from a star . . . ," this is a poem that selects its own audience. The title may have been taken from a fifteenth-century French translation of the *Legenda Aurea*, where it would have identified a simple woodcut depicting the martyrdom of Saint Ursula and her eleven thousand followers at the hands of the Huns.[40] Stevens' richly colored and carefully composed "portrait" illustrates an episode which has, as his footnote indicates, no previous written authority. Yet this pseudo-legend with its pseudo-antique diction is not out of keeping with Jacobus de Varagine's account of the princess who parlayed her virginity into a heavenly reward. Stevens manages, in the most discreet language, to lift the veil which obscures the subliminal side of religious piety. He also burlesques the more recently fashionable pieties of the *fin de siècle*, with his aesthete-God and his Pre-Raphaelite damozel. Des Esseintes, who also collected medieval saints' legends, would have been nearly as offended as Jacobus by this poem.

Van Vechten reports that all were delighted with "Cy Est Pourtraicte" when Stevens read it at the party. All save one: while the others applauded, Elsie professed distaste for the poem because it had been undertaken in a "mocking spirit."[41] In other company, Elsie might not have stood

39. *Rogue*, 15 Mar. 1915, p. 12; cf. *CP* 21–22.
40. Though there are several fifteenth-century editions of the *Legende dorée* with woodcuts of Saint Ursula and the eleven thousand virgins, I have been unable to find the one from which Stevens took his title. I suspect that he either came upon this caption in a book catalogue with a facsimile woodcut—he once remarked that editions of the *Legenda Aurea* were "constantly in catalogues" (*L* 216)—or invented a plausible caption of his own.
41. Van Vechten, p. 49.

alone. When Stevens sent his latest poems to *Poetry* magazine in Chicago, Harriet Monroe rejected them as "recondite, erudite, provocatively obscure, with a kind of modern-gargoyle grin in them—Aubrey-Beardsleyish in the making."[42] Though she had liked his previous submissions, the series of war poems entitled "Phases," she thought his new work "weirder" and advised him to "chase his mystically mirthful and mournful muse out of the nether darkness." About the time Stevens received this rejection notice, he also received a letter from Allen Norton, asking for the "poem about radishes, or which had radishes in it, or was somehow connected with radishes."[43] Norton was ready to launch *Rogue* magazine and assured Stevens that he would appear in "very select" company. When *Rogue* came out that March, "Cy Est Pourtraicte" mingled agreeably with prose by Gertrude Stein and distinctly Beardsleyish drawings by Robert Locher.

Stevens never felt at ease in the company of the self-styled post-decadents, and shortly before Arensberg moved to California in 1921 he had a falling-out with his old Harvard friend (*L* 850). But he gained by his association with the writers and artists who gathered at 33 West Sixty-Seventh Street, and his gain went beyond matters of technique and attitude. They provided him with the impetus he needed to start writing again. Not since the poems of 1908–9 had he enjoyed the sense of a distinct and appreciative audience. From the simmering of "Carnet de Voyage" he came rapidly to a boil, publishing over a hundred poems and plays over the next ten years. Elsie's birthday poems, chaste and earnest to a fault, gave way to the irreverent and risqué wit of "Cy Est Pourtraicte," "The Worms at Heaven's Gate" (1916), "Cortège for Rosenbloom" (1921), and "A High-Toned Old Christian Woman"(1922). The purely ideal landscapes of Elsie's poems made way for

42. Note to Stevens, 27 Jan. 1915.
43. Letter of Jan. or Feb. 1915.

American settings like Oklahoma, the Carolinas, Uncle Remus' plantation, Arkansas, Connecticut, Tennessee, and preëminently Florida. This is partly, no doubt, because Stevens began to travel extensively for the Hartford in 1916. But he had remained immune to the poetic possibilities of some of these same places while on the road in 1905, when Elsie had been his muse.

Not that Stevens deliberately withdrew from his first muse or deceived her about the nature of his new work. He apprised Elsie of his tentative return to poetry in the summer of 1913 and confided to her his anxiety over the publication of "Carnet de Voyage " (*L* 180, 165–66). But he may have neglected to tell her that among the pieces he submitted to *Trend* in 1914 were six of her birthday poems. When Elsie gained entry to the "central" of Stevens' being and helped him to discover the poetry there latent, she acquired something like a proprietary interest in all of his subsequent creations. It seemed only right that he should make her a clear gift of the birthday verses. Hence she felt profoundly betrayed, she later told her daughter, when these entered the public domain. Thereafter, she read little of her husband's poetry and seemed to resent the publication of his books (*SP* 227).[44] What she did read of his poetry after 1914 would only have confirmed her suspicion that she had been supplanted within the candle's golden aura.

If Stevens was hurt by Elsie's sulky response to his poetry, he kept his feelings to himself at first. In letters written while traveling, he continued to report not only on the day's work in court but also on the evening's work in his hotel room, writing poems. When his first collection ap-

44. In later years, Elsie became reconciled to Stevens' literary fame to the extent of acknowledging that his poems would probably outlive him. Stevens told Louis Martz in 1949 that he read parts of "An Ordinary Evening in New Haven" to Elsie before reading it to the Connecticut Academy of Arts and Sciences; however, I doubt that (as Martz also remembers him saying) he customarily tried out new work on his wife. See Brazeau, pp. 88, 175.

peared in 1923, it bore a dedication to his wife. But he gave
vent to a general sense of injury in a 1924 poem, "Red
Loves Kit."[45] The graffito title itself marks the distance he
and Elsie had come since they were Pierrot and Columbine. The poem opens in the aftermath of a domestic
quarrel:

> Your yes her no, your no her yes. The words
> Make little difference, for being wrong
> And wronging her, if only as she thinks,
> You never can be right. You are the man.
> You brought the incredible calm in ecstasy,
> Which, like a virgin visionary spent
> In this spent world, she must possess. The gift
> Came not from you. Shall the world be spent again,
> Wasted in what would be an ultimate waste,
> A deprivation muffled in eclipse,
> The final theft? That you are innocent
> And love her still, still leaves you in the wrong.
> Where is that calm and where that ecstasy?
> Her words accuse you of adulteries
> That sack the sun, though metaphysical.

This is obviously a partisan version of their tiff: the speaker
is innocent and his spouse only thinks she has been
wronged. Yet the stanza is less a complaint than a "consolation." We overhear the husband talking to himself
("you"), trying to probe to the source of their petty dis-
agreements and so make sense of them. It appears that,
while he had truly won her once, he had failed to keep on
winning her. He might protest that he had been merely the
occasion rather than the cause of her self-surrender, and
that so complete a surrender could never be repeated. But
he is "the man," the archetypal male, and she expects him
to restore her to that apocalyptic ecstasy. Short of this, he
commits adultery in all but the technical sense of the word.

This stanza doubtless had its origin in one of those
"blow-ups of the nerves" between the Stevenses, for which

45. *Measure*, no. 42 (1924), pp. 8–9. In *OP* 31, line 11 of Stanza II reads
"Impelled by a convulsive harmony."

he once apologized to his daughter (*L* 422). These were perhaps more frequent and less explicable during Elsie's pregnancy, when this poem was probably written. Yet Stevens may have been only partly right in assigning the motive of her disaffection. Though he neglects to mention it, the writing of poetry might have qualified in Elsie's eyes as metaphysical adultery. In any case, he counters her charge with one of his own in the next stanza:

> A beautiful thing, milord, is beautiful
> Not only in itself but in the things
> Around it. Thus it has a large expanse,
> As the moon has in its moonlight, worlds away,
> As the sea has in its coastal clamorings.
> So she, when in her mystic aureole
> She walks, triumphing humbly, should express
> Her beauty in your love. She should reflect
> Her glory in your passion and be proud.
> Her music should repeat itself in you,
> Impelled by a compulsive harmony.
> Milord, I ask you, though you will to sing,
> Does she will to be proud? True, you may love
> And she have beauty of a kind, but such
> Unhappy love reveals vast blemishes.

By substituting the word "milord" for "you," the speaker signals a change of tone from the querulous to the courtly. Courtly, too, is his notion of the ideal paramour. She should be proud and lofty in bearing, yet humbly derive her sense of importance from the passion and praise of her troubadour. When she neglects that dimension of beauty which is in the eye of the beholder, she remains less than perfectly beautiful, like a moon without moonlight. When she fails to behave as one loved, she effectively rejects her lover.

Those who knew Elsie personally would have had little difficulty unraveling the intricate metaphors of this stanza. Though beautiful and beloved of her husband, she was temperamentally incapable of basking in his love and praise—or anyone else's. In this sense, her beauty was

"blemished" and her love affair with Stevens "unhappy."
Indeed, it was because she declined the "mystic aureole"
that he crowned the Interior Paramour in 1922 with "A
band entwining, set with fatal stones" (*CP* 88). The final
stanza of "Red Loves Kit" offers meager consolation for the
marital bliss denied:

> Rest, crows, upon the edges of the moon,
> Cover the golden altar deepest black,
> Fly upward thick in numbers, fly across
> The blueness of the half-night, fill the air
> And darken it, make an unbroken mat
> Out of the whirl and denseness of your wings,
> Spread over heaven shutting out the light.
> Then turn your heads and let your spiral eyes
> Look backward. Let your swiftly-flying flocks
> Look suddenly downward with their shining eyes
> And move the night by their intelligent motes.
> Make a sidereal splendor as you fly.
> And you, good galliard, to enchant black thoughts
> Beseech them for an overpowering gloom.
> It will be fecund in rapt curios.

Picking up the image of the moon from the previous
stanza, the speaker here invokes a grotesque version of the
eclipse his wife had demanded in Stanza I. The only stars
in his heaven will be the eyes of crows. He braces for a
Satanic display of courage, saying in effect, "Bitterness, be
thou my love." But he will probably not write an epic vili-
fying the ways of maidens with men. Instead, he will play
the good galliard, the stalwart fellow who is also something of a jester, juggling balls and producing curios from
his sleeve to enchant not only the lords and ladies of the
court but also his own black thoughts.

We have seen this strategy in the love letters, where
Stevens turns abruptly from the "Book of Doubts and
Fears" to his comic Tom Folio, and we can only speculate
which of the baubles in *Harmonium* are rapt from a fecund
gloom. Like the letters, "Red Loves Kit" affords a rare peek
into Stevens' dressing room. Not to be twice glimpsed

without his cap and bells, he never republished the poem after it appeared in the *Measure* or included it in any of his collections. In fact, for six years after "Red Loves Kit" he adopted the perfect disguise of silence.

When he resumed his poetic career in the early thirties, he picked up the theme of unhappy love where he had left off in 1924. "Good Man, Bad Woman" and "The Woman Who Blamed Life on a Spaniard," both published in 1932 and not reprinted during Stevens' lifetime, find him still unreconciled to his fate. In the first poem, which may reflect his relationship with the Depression as well as with Elsie, he tries to ignore his companion's spite but finds that she can "corrode" his experience of the world, if not his inmost self (*OP* 33). In the second, he relinquishes hope that she will ever throw off her evil humor and shine forth like the full moon, "rounded in beneficence, / Pellucid love" (*OP* 34). He considers playing his role as Spaniard to the hilt and so winning her by sheer bravura; but he finally persuades himself that love is "blessedly beknown," not as Venus' dove merely, but as a fabulous composite of dove, goose, nightingale, parrot, and even eagle, "proud in venting lacerations."

During the thirties, Stevens was more circumspect than proud in venting his lacerations. Two years before "The Woman Who Blamed Life on a Spaniard" appeared in *Contempo*, he had sent a version of Stanza III to Harriet Monroe by way of a belated Christmas card, advising her that it was for herself alone (*L* 260). Similarly, around January 1935 he sent Ronald Lane Latimer a short poem for him to read but not to publish in his quarterly *Alcestis*:

> The cold wife lay with her husband after his death,
> His ashen reliquiae contained in gold
> Under her pillow, on which he had never slept.
>
> (*L* 274)

Stevens ventured no explanation of these lines, which he entitled simply "The Widow." But he may have provided a clue to their private meaning in the unusual word "reliquiae," which he used to describe some of his own poems in a letter written to Latimer about this time (*L* 272).

The cold wife reappears in Stevens' last treatment of unhappy love, "World without Peculiarity" (1950). Perhaps because he considered it more successful as a poem than his previous efforts in this vein, perhaps because he felt he had for once approximated the eagle's lofty stance, he admitted it to both *The Auroras of Autumn* and the *Collected Poems*. Its third stanza speaks movingly of the contrast between the season of year and the season of romance:

> The red ripeness of round leaves is thick
> With the spices of red summer.
> But she that he loved turns cold at his light touch.

By the end of the poem, however, its persona has achieved so perfect an accord with the earth and the earthly scheme of things that he is indifferent even to the "hating woman." One of Stevens' manuscript notebooks contains what may be another version of the title for "World without Peculiarity," and thereby hangs a lesson. The original or alternate title read "A Poet Without Peculiarity,"[46] which suggests that, like the man described in the poem, Stevens was occasionally able to rise above such "peculiarities" as rejection by his lover. It may also imply that disappointment in love is one of the poet's occupational hazards. Like Penelope in Stevens' "The World as Meditation" (1952), the writer is perpetually composing a self to embrace an imaginary lover or audience. With two variables and no constants, this equation must often fail of happy resolution. In the relationship between the Stevenses, as in algebra, there were gremlins but no villains. He was betrayed less

46. *From Pieces of Paper*, p. 6. This notebook has been edited by George S. Lensing, who presents the text and discusses its relation to Stevens' poetry in *"From Pieces of Paper*: A Wallace Stevens Notebook," *Southern Review* 15 (1979): 877–920.

by Elsie than by his own imagination; she was betrayed more by insecurity than by her spouse.

The Stevenses apparently coped with disillusionment in the fashion their generation approved—he by remaining a loyal husband, she by remaining a faithful wife. Did the arrangement entail strict sexual fidelity, as Stevens understood it? Though rumors of his extramarital activity persist, these might be attributed to a combination of things: his dissatisfaction with his marriage, known to many of his friends and colleagues; his eye for attractive young women; and his extended trips away from home for business and recreation. Anthony Sigmans, who accompanied Stevens on bachelor weekends in New England and upstate New York in the thirties, maintains that he never became romantically involved with women on their excursions.[47] The letters he wrote from Florida's more venereal soil offer a choice between equally conventional and non-venereal self-portraits: he is either the conscientious tourist or the vinolent reveler, depending on whether the letter is addressed to his wife or a male friend. What the catechism calls "near occasions of sin" were not wanting; a business associate once proposed "knocking round the country with a couple of girls" on a forthcoming trip to Florida."[48] But Stevens, in what seems to have been his characteristic gesture, vetoed the idea. "Puritanism has nothing to do with it," he explained; "I simply want to be myself as much in Florida as I am anywhere else."

Elsie's exacting household regimen, a source of amusement to Van Vechten, would have made it difficult for another man to be himself at home. If Stevens found it awkward to entertain guests at the front door or in the garden behind the house rather than risk inviting them into the mistress's domain, he had at least the satisfaction of knowing his own privacy would not be invaded; indeed, he may

47. Quoted in Brazeau, p. 79.
48. Letter to Philip S. May, 27 Jan. 1936 (copy at Huntington Library). Excerpts from this letter appear in L 307.

occasionally have used Elsie to excuse his own reclusiveness. Like Doctor Williams, the happy genius of a household in Rutherford, New Jersey, he embraced his loneliness—including the loneliness of his narrow bed—as though it were his true spouse. It was a solitude different from the kind he had known in the boarding houses of New York, and probably better.

In the last analysis, his and Elsie's is an unremarkable love story. But the years of courtship and early marriage were years of remarkable poetic growth for one of the lovers, which returns us to the question posed by Yeats: did Stevens dwell more upon the winning of Elsie, or upon the losing? Inasmuch as Stevens "lost" Elsie the year he published his first important work, his imagination dwelt upon loss. Emotional deprivation became to some extent the condition of his craft, the somber backdrop for the motley antics of *Harmonium*. In another sense, Elsie was no more lost to Stevens' imagination than the acorn is lost to the oak tree. The Interior Paramour was still Elsie, but Elsie firmly rooted and fully ramified. She remained both the genius of reality, calling him back to Reading, and the genius of imagination, inviting him to share her candle-lit chamber. What Stevens told her in his letter of March 18, 1907, has, then, the ring of prophecy: "You must be my poetess and sing me many songs. I shall hear them in strange places and repeat them afterwards as half my own."

· 3 ·

Burgher, Fop, and Clown

When the managing editor of the *Dial* magazine wrote Stevens in 1922 to request a brief biographical sketch to accompany a group of poems, the poet replied, "Do, please, excuse me from the biographical note. I am a lawyer and live in Hartford. But such facts are neither gay nor instructive" (*L* 227). Stevens might have embellished the facts in that second sentence almost indefinitely; but next to poems like "Bantams in Pine-Woods" and "The Emperor of Ice-Cream," such information would indeed have seemed deficient in gaiety. Far from enlightening *Dial* readers regarding the biographical context or inspiration of the poems, the note would have further reinforced the legend, already taking shape in 1922, of the "divided life" of Wallace Stevens.

According to the legend, Stevens lived during business hours the rigorously conventional life he described best himself, in an early version of "The Comedian as the Letter C":

> let the burgher say
> If he is burgher by his will. Burgher,
> He is, by will, but not his own. He dwells
> A part of wilful dwellings that impose
> Alike his morning and his evening prayer.
> His town exhales its mother breath for him
> And this he breathes, a candid bellows-boy,
> According to canon.[1]

---

1. "From the Journal of Crispin" is reprinted, with notes and an introduction by Louis L. Martz, in *Wallace Stevens: A Celebration*, pp. 3–45.

Stevens' burgher is the urban counterpart of Emerson's farmer, a specimen of humanity Emerson considered inferior to Man on the farm. Like Emerson's farmer, the burgher has no life he can call his own; he is the creature of his occupation and environment rather than free choice. Well might Stevens protest, as he does in one of his adages, that he had no life except in poetry (*OP* 175). "No doubt that would be true," he added ruefully, "if my whole life was free for poetry."

During the part of Stevens' day that was free for poetry he enjoyed—so legend would have it—a very different mode of life. Then he took that exhilarating "walk in space" he recommends in Section XXXII of "The Man with the Blue Guitar." To leave the "wilful dwellings" behind and enter the space of imagination is to throw away the "canons," to discard anything that might come between oneself and one's possible selves:

> How should you walk in that space and know
> Nothing of the madness of space,
>
> Nothing of its jocular procreations?
> Throw the lights away. Nothing must stand
>
> Between you and the shapes you take
> When the crust of shape has been destroyed.

The "you" of this poem, like the "we," "they," "he," and even "she" of other Stevens poems, is not entirely distinct from the "I" who committed the words to paper. Stevens lived a frequently jocular, occasionally melancholy, always thoughtful life in his "procreations," the poses and dramatis personae of his poetry. Whether one regards these as masks or alter egos, their use tends to reinforce the dichotomy of that 1906 journal entry already cited in connection with his letters to Elsie: "There is a perfect rout of characters in every man—and every man is like an actor's trunk, full of strange creatures, new & old. But an actor and his trunk are two different things" (*SP* 166).

How different, indeed? One might argue that an actor

cannot efface himself completely in his roles, try as he may. Even the strangest of those "strange creatures" dramatizes some aspect of himself—an aspect the more characteristic and revealing, perhaps, to the extent it appears "different." Hence to the acute and interested observer the actor's performances are always instructive and—depending on the role—may even be gay. Stevens legend has perpetuated a facile dichotomy between the businessman and the poet, one that should not survive a moment's introspection. Like most of us, he was simultaneously one and many, whether onstage or off. Let us consider him first as he appears onstage, in a role but slightly removed from the one he lived offstage. "The Weeping Burgher" (1919) is at once a prayer and a confession:

> It is with a strange malice
> That I distort the world.
>
> Ah! that ill humors
> Should mask as white girls.
> And ah! that Scaramouche
> Should have a black barouche.
>
> The sorry verities!
> Yet in excess, continual,
> There is cure of sorrow.
>
> Permit that if as ghost I come
> Among the people burning in me still,
> I come as belle design
> Of foppish line.
>
> And I, then, tortured for old speech,
> A white of wildly woven rings;
> I, weeping in a calcined heart,
> My hands such sharp, imagined things.

Two years after "The Weeping Burgher" appeared in *Poetry*, Genevieve Taggard told Stevens of the rumor that his poems were "hideous ghosts" of himself, to which he replied, "It may be" (*L* 222–23). The poem anticipates the rumor and improves upon it. Here the burgher, with his sober sense of reality, seems initially to regret all masquerade and pretense. It is a world of "sorry verities" where ill humors pass themselves off as innocent girls and a conniving servant affects the elegance of his betters. Yet the burgher can appreciate the therapeutic value of such "excess," and admits that he would like to transcend his own middle-class circumstances. The gods permitting, he would slough off his too solid flesh and join the creatures of his fancy, a ghost of "belle design" among imaginary peers.

Reviewing *Harmonium* in 1924, Louis Untermeyer characterized the book's author as a poet who "luxuriates in an ingeniously distorted world."[2] Untermeyer was right, inasmuch as the burgher's ghost haunts much of Stevens' early poetry, his sharp imaginary hands shaping old speech and foppish line into poems like "Ballade of the Pink Parasol" and "Cy Est Pourtraicte, Madame Ste Ursule, et Les Unze Mille Vierges." But surely it is significant that the burgher distorts his world from a compulsion avowedly strange and malicious. The very adjective "foppish" signals his detachment from the apotheosis of euphuism to which he aspires, and that detachment is apt to become outright mockery. The burgherly cast of mind which impelled Stevens to write "Bah—mere words" at the end of a journal entry describing a moonlit night in 1900 (*SP* 87) also surfaces in "Depression before Spring" (1918), whose daring metaphoric flight—

> The hair of my blonde
> Is dazzling,
> As the spittle of cows
> Threading the wind—

is brought abruptly to earth by a derisive "Ho! Ho!" Apparently the same spring Stevens wrote this poem, he sent William Carlos Williams a letter detailing the pleasures of the season in Nashville, where he was then staying. It was doubtless the burgher who got into the letter's conclusion:

2. "Five American Poets," *Yale Review* 14 (1924): 160.

"I spare you the whole-souled burblings in the park, the leaves, lilacs, tulips and so on. Such things are unmanly and non-Prussian and, of course, a fellow must pooh-pooh something, even if it happens to be something he rather fancies, you know."[3]

Offstage—that is, apart from such literary performances as poems, journal entries, and letters—Stevens similarly appeared now in the guise of burgher, now of fop. The former was doubtless the norm, due to a social prejudice Delmore Schwartz singled out in a eulogy written shortly after Stevens' death. "It is easy to forget," said Schwartz, "that when Stevens was a young man, the adult male who read a great deal was regarded as, at best, anti-social and probably literally addicted to secret vices: and the adult male, unless he was a foreigner, a gigolo, or a sissy, was supposed to suffer nausea or become comatose when forced by his wife to go to the opera."[4] Schwartz errs only in saying that this state of affairs is easy to forget, for the Prussian ideal of manliness has enjoyed a Prussian longevity. It was particularly vigorous among the Pennsylvania Dutch with whom Stevens spent his youth; and, despite his efforts to ennoble the poet's role, he could not quite rid himself of the feeling that writing poetry was a slightly absurd and possibly effeminate activity. When dissatisfied with his poems, he compared them to "the trifling designs one sees on fans" (L 171) or the French flowers the girl of "Explanation" (1917) embroiders on her Teutonic tunic.

Schwartz had attended Stevens' first public reading of his poems at Harvard in 1936. He remembered that after the performance Stevens turned to the member of the faculty who had introduced him and said, "I wonder what the boys at the office would think of this?"[5] They would

3. Letter dated ca. Apr. 1918 by Holly Stevens (Buffalo).

4. "Wallace Stevens—An Appreciation," *New Republic*, 22 Aug. 1955, p. 21.

5. "Wallace Stevens—An Appreciation," p. 21. Though Stevens later denied saying anything on this occasion that would have suggested a

hardly be more shocked, he supposed, to discover he was the head of an opium ring. Curiously, the business associates whom Stevens called "the boys"—Ralph Mullen, Anthony Sigmans, and Manning Heard, for example— would not have been shocked at all, for they already knew of his reputation as a poet.[6] It was rather for the literary world that Stevens posed as burgher, a role his physical size rendered convincing, perhaps inevitable. On the evidence of Stevens' exquisite miniature "Tea" (1915), Alfred Kreymborg had been led to expect a "slender, ethereal being, shy and sensitive."[7] The poet he actually met at a social gathering for *Rogue* contributors stood over six feet tall and weighed over two hundred pounds.

Though Stevens' diffident manner seemed at variance with his physique during those early years in New York, suggesting to Carl Van Vechten the image of a rogue elephant in porcelain, he could play the role of bluff executive to the hilt once he had drowned his shyness in distilled spirits. Winfield Townley Scott remembered him as a "steamroller" who drank quantities of undiluted Scotch as he maneuvered the 1952 National Book Award Committee around to his own way of thinking. "Stevens is big, ruddy, talkative, assertive," Scott observed on that occasion; "one beheld the insurance executive if not the poet."[8] Even during the thirties, when he was on a strict diet to control his

dichotomy between his poetic and business lives, he was apparently recalling his lecture rather than the "boys at the office" remark; see Brazeau, p. 163n.

6. The interviews which Peter Brazeau has assembled in Part I of *Parts of a World* (pp. 3–109) indicate that Stevens' colleagues in the home office of the Hartford knew he was a poet even before the publication of *Harmonium* and were later proud to have a famous poet as a senior officer in the company.

7. *Troubadour: An Autobiography* (New York: Boni and Liveright, 1925), p. 219.

8. Scott records these impressions in a letter to Horace Gregory, quoted in Scott Donaldson, *Poet in America: Winfield Townley Scott* (Austin: University of Texas Press, 1972), p. 249; and in *A Dirty Hand: The Literary Notebook of Winfield Townley Scott* (Austin: University of Texas Press, 1969), p. 38.

weight and blood pressure, he departed from his usual regimen on trips to Florida, with results ranging from theological discussion to the 1936 fistfight with Hemingway. Hard drinking was part of the pose, and sets the tone of the letter he sent to poet and novelist Ferdinand Reyher in 1922:

> I live like a turtle under a bush, and when I get away from town, believe me, I don't stay sober any longer than I must. The amount of talking that I have done about things of this sort [i.e., literary gossip] during the last year would probably boil down to a few syllables. I pride myself on being a member of the Long Key Fishing Club of Atlanta and of the Brown Derby Club of East Hartford, and I take damned little stock in conversation on philosophy, aesthetics, poetry, art, or blondes. Of course, I hanker for all those things as a fly hankers for fly paper. But experience has taught me that fly paper is one devil of a thing to get mixed up in.[9]

To anyone who had spent time in Stevens' company, this bit of middle-border roaring would have seemed superfluous. He carried himself with a natural dignity that suggested nothing of the gigolo or sissy. That he could not have been mistaken for a foreigner, despite his interest in things foreign, is clear from a letter Richard Eberhart sent to Conrad Aiken in 1950, shortly after being with Stevens and Eliot during their visits, just a day apart, to Harvard. "Stevens," Eberhart reported, "has something of the mountainous gruffness that we recognize in ourselves as American—the stamina, the powerful grain showing in a kind of indifference. Eliot showed the American at his most civilized, his most urbane, unselfish and worldly."[10]

Yet the burgher of coarse American grain was by no means the whole Stevens, even in public life. To his office at the Hartford there came, over the years, a staggering array of items of "belle design": paintings, prints, *catalogues raisonnés*, fine bindings, and French periodicals from

9. Letter of 6 Apr. (Maryland).
10. Letter of 1 Dec.

Paris; press books from England; necklaces, fans, saris, and a carved Buddha from Ceylon; wood and jade statuettes from Peking; classical dolls and a fossilwood pen stand from Japan; a Swedish tapestry and a rare eighteenth-century pottery lamp from New York. Far from concealing his taste for the finer things from business associates, Stevens enlisted their help in shopping for special items and making contacts abroad. Wilson Jainsen, also a senior officer at the Hartford, recalls that the arrival of a package from Paris—here one might substitute any of a half-dozen other ports of lading—was something of an event:

> Stevens always looked forward to receiving the package from Paris and this was one of the moments that he would share with his associates. He would receive them at the office by mail from Paris and would open them and would want you to enjoy them with him and then of course, he took them home and after that we don't know what he did with them except to enjoy them as his property.[11]

Jainsen was also struck by Stevens' meticulous attention to personal appearance; his expensive suits and ties accorded with an air of superiority, if not snobbery.[12] Jainsen would probably not have used the word "dandiacal" to characterize Stevens' appearance and bearing, but that was the epithet which always occurred to Carl Zigrosser, editor of the *Modern School*.[13] Stevens cultivated this pose, Zigrosser suspected, from a fear of being thought "bohemian." If so, his strategy succeeded. Though William Carlos Williams scarcely qualified as a bohemian, he spoke for the more casual element of the New York *avant-garde* when he recalled that Stevens always maintained a "distant man-

11. Quoted in "Perspective from Two Worlds: Wallace Stevens, Poet and Businessman," written and produced by Caroline Isber and Jean Shub, WGBH-FM Boston, 18 Jan. 1966.
12. "Perspective from Two Worlds."
13. The comments by Zigrosser in this paragraph are quoted in Morse, p. 71.

ner" among them: "He was always the well dressed one, diffident about letting down his hair. Precise when we were sloppy. Drank little."[14] Along with the formal appearance went a manner of speaking which Zigrosser called "precious" and "slightly affected." Alfred Kreymborg noticed that Stevens, more than any of the others he met at the *Rogue* gathering, cultivated an "indirect method of speech." Kreymborg, who would later parody Stevens' manner in the character of Fastidious in his comedy *At the Sign of the Thumb and Nose*, speculated that it betrayed "an aesthetic fastidiousness in the matter of living as well as of expressing art."[15]

These memoirs and anecdotes, most of them long a part of the Stevens legend, frustrate any attempt either to divide his life neatly between the roles of public burgher and private fop or to view it as the expression of a single, simple self. It was a caricature rather than a portrait William Carlos Williams achieved when he wrote, some months after Stevens' death, "He was a dandy at heart. You never saw Stevens in sloppy clothes. His poems are the result."[16] If Williams' statement begs to be challenged today, it might not have been accorded that much consideration in 1956, for it flies in the face of what was then the orthodox view of the poet's relation to his work. The poet's mind, Eliot had argued in his influential "Tradition and the Individual Talent," enters into his poems only as a catalyst enters into a chemical reaction: effecting the new combination, it remains itself unaffected. Though Eliot did not deny the role of personal experience and emotion in the making of poems (he would later record his admiration for Yeats's use of the personal), he insisted in his 1919 essay

14. Quoted in William Van O'Connor, *The Shaping Spirit: A Study of Wallace Stevens* (Chicago: Regnery, 1950), p. 15.

15. Kreymborg makes these observations in *Troubadour*, pp. 219–20. *At the Sign of the Thumb and Nose* appears in *Plays for Merry Andrews* (New York: Sunwise Turn, 1920), pp. 31–61.

16. *Poetry* 87 (1956): 236.

that good poetry is always, in his special sense of the word, "impersonal."

Stevens himself addressed the relation between poet and poem most explicitly in his 1943 lecture, "The Figure of the Youth as Virile Poet." Replying to Aristotle's precept that the poet should say very little *in propria persona*, Stevens agrees that the poet should not make himself the subject of his poems; but he maintains that the poems will disclose their author none the less.[17] "The chief characteristic of the mind," he affirms, quoting Henri Focillon, "is to be constantly describing *itself*" (*NA* 46). Poetry is a "process of the personality of the poet," reflecting "the physical and mental factors that condition him as an individual" (*NA* 48). Rather than belabor what must have seemed to him an obvious point, Stevens canceled the following passage in a late draft of his lecture:

> We take a man like Picasso, for instance, and assume that here is Picasso and there is his work. This is nonsense. Where the one is, the other is. This son of an intellectual and antiquarian, with his early imaginative periods, as inevitable in such a case as puberty, may sit in his studio, half-a-dozen men at once conversing together. They reach a conclusion and all of them go back into one of them who seats himself and begins to paint. Is it one of them within him that dominates and makes the design or rather could it be? Can Picasso choose? Free will does not go so far.[18]

Insofar as this passage represents Stevens' experience in writing poetry—and he had only his own experience on which to base the passage—it further complicates our sense of the relation between the man and his work. As the son of his parents and the product of a middle-class

17. In his own copy of *Aristotle's Art of Poetry: A Greek View of Poetry and Drama*, ed. W. Hamilton Fyfe (Oxford: Clarendon, 1940), Stevens has underlined the passage on p. 68 where Aristotle advises the poet against speaking in his own voice (Massachusetts).

18. This passage follows the sentence "Yet it is commonly thought that the artist is independent of his work" (see *NA* 48) in the holograph draft of the manuscript.

environment, he was undeniably the burgher. But his Harvard verse and letters to Elsie testify, early on, to the variety of selves conversing behind the burgherly façade. Throughout Stevens' career, these selves enter into preordained yet incalculable combinations to produce his poems. Nowhere can this be seen more clearly than in his first volume.

With few exceptions, early critics of *Harmonium* overlooked the burgher in favor of the volume's more flamboyant personae. The author of the poems was an aesthete and dandy, they agreed, but they disagreed whether these were terms of praise or censure. To Gorham Munson, Stevens was the first dandy of American letters, a dandy whose work suggested rather the "comfortable tranquillity" of baronial estates than the more tortured dandyism of Baudelaire or Eliot.[19] To Louis Untermeyer, however, he was a "conscious aesthete" whose war with reality conduced merely to "an amusing preciosity."[20] Untermeyer, who remained the incumbent critic of Stevens' aestheticism to the very end (as Yvor Winters was to remain the critic of his hedonism), had placed Stevens in the Decadent tradition four years before *Harmonium* appeared. In a famous exchange with Conrad Aiken, whom he regarded as an advocate of "art for art's sake," Untermeyer defined decadence as preoccupation with manner of expression; this preoccupation must, he argued, "lead inevitably to The Yellow Book, to the mere verbal legerdemain of the Pound-Stevens-Arensberg-Others."[21]

The "Pound" of this decadent constellation is doubtless the "E.P." whom Pound laid to rest in *Hugh Selwyn Mauberley* (1920), before taking up his fiscal and political causes. We have already had occasion to look at the Arensberg circle, with its "post-decadent" aspirations and enthusiasm for Stevens' "Aubrey Beardsleyish" poems. It was Ar-

19. "The Dandyism of Wallace Stevens," *Dial*, Nov. 1925, pp. 413–17.
20. "Five American Poets," p. 160.
21. "The Ivory Tower—II," *New Republic*, 10 May 1919, p. 61.

ensberg who provided Alfred Kreymborg with the financial means to found *Others*, perhaps the best of the poetry magazines published in New York between 1915 and 1919. Though less self-consciously decadent than the Nortons' *Rogue*, it hosted some of the same contributors and sported a binding in *Yellow Book* yellow. Untermeyer correctly associated Stevens with *Others*, for he published eighteen poems in the magazine during its brief span, plus a total of twenty-eight poems in the three *Others* anthologies. Granting Untermeyer's contention, that Stevens wrote a distinctly "decadent" poetry for an audience that appreciated this quality, we have yet to specify which elements of the Decadent tradition Stevens salvaged, and to what purpose.

The aesthetic dandyism which Stevens first came to know as a college student was a distinctly English translation of a French text. Gautier, for one, had crusaded on behalf of *l'art pour l'art* before Pater was even born; but it was the Oxford don who fathered aestheticism in England by means of his *Studies in the History of the Renaissance* (1873). Pervading the famous "Conclusion" to that book is Pater's conviction, announced in the epigraph from Heraclitus, that all things flow and nothing remains. Mirroring the flux of the physical world is the drift of passions, thoughts, and impressions through the human mind. Powerless to escape the current without and the current within, one may well grasp, says Pater, "at any exquisite passion, or any contribution to knowledge that seems, by a lifted horizon, to set the spirit free for a moment, or any stirring of the senses, strange dyes, strange flowers, and curious odours, or work of the artist's hands, or the face of one's friend."[22] Religious and philosophical ideas are useful only insofar as they enable one to capture sensations that would otherwise be lost. The wise man devotes him-

22. *Studies in the History of the Renaissance* (London: Macmillan, 1873), p. 211. I use this edition whenever quoting from Pater's "Conclusion."

self to the love of art for its own sake or, more precisely, for the moment's sake.

Pater's "Conclusion" was immediately taken up by a generation of young men, many of them still undergraduates at Oxford, who hankered for just this kind of advice. Though afflicted with nostalgia for religious belief and the trappings of religion, especially the liturgy and rich symbolism of the Roman Church, they were born too late for faith. Yet they could accommodate themselves neither to the bourgeois morality of Victorian society nor to the didacticism of its official art and literature. Pater at least offered them a way to improve the time: they would, as he advised, burn always with a "hard gem-like flame," transforming the Heraclitean fire of life into something as comely, substantial, and enduring as a work of art. Oscar Wilde set himself no trivial ideal when he tried to live up to his china.

Unfortunately, the gem-like flame succeeded better as metaphor than as moral paradigm. The young aesthete could not burn always without consuming either himself or his fuel. When the fuel was consumed first—the sort that lay near at hand—the aesthete ranged further afield, cultivating sensations stranger than those which occurred to Pater or the more feverish imagination of Des Esseintes. If he succeeded in gratifying his appetite for novel sensations, he was still apt to find himself *post delectamentum tristis*, awash in the malaise that follows satiety. This state was particularly galling to the aesthete, not only because it contrasted sharply with his aspirations, but also because he had jettisoned that sense of purposeful suffering which tides the believer and philosopher over such periods. The "moment" proved then to be the kind of rudderless boat Hugh Selwyn Mauberley rides to disaster, leaving as a warning to others his famous epitaph:

"I was
And I no more exist;

Here drifted
An hedonist."

Pound ascribes the demise of his castaway to a flaw in
the Paterian consciousness, which he calls

A consciousness disjunct,
Being but this overblotted
Series
Of intermittences. . . .

Pater invites this charge in his "Conclusion," where he describes the mind as a sort of universal solvent which breaks
up the external world into component impressions of color,
odor, and texture. Since the Paterian self is no more than
the sum of its impressions at a given moment, its integrity
is likewise resolved into a series of brilliant but discontin-
uous particles; the "passage and dissolution of impressions, images, sensations " is simultaneously the "contin-
ual vanishing away, that strange, perpetual weaving and
unweaving of ourselves." Wilde, for a time Pater's protégé,
dramatized this facet of Decadent psychology by retailing
a dazzling variety of selves to his contemporaries.[23]

Wilde's antics as "Professor of Aesthetics," the pose he
assumed while touring America in 1882 to promote Gilbert
and Sullivan's *Patience*, were reason enough for Pater to
want to put some distance between himself and his disciples. He omitted the "Conclusion" from the second edition of his book, entitled *The Renaissance*, then restored it
with some of the more sensitive passages revised in the
1888 edition. In *Marius the Epicurean* (1885), he recounted
the spiritual pilgrimage of a second-century aesthete who
learns the error of his ways and turns at last to Christianity.
Such precautions were unnecessary insofar as they pre-
supposed that the generation of the late eighties and nineties still hung on Pater's every word, for a new influence

23. For further discussion of the Decadent consciousness, see Barbara
Charlesworth's *Dark Passages: The Decadent Consciousness in Victorian Literature* (Madison: University of Wisconsin Press, 1965).

from the Continent had begun to absorb and supersede aestheticism.

French *Symbolisme* was not only a literary technique but, together with its corollary *dandysme*, a complete aesthetic, intellectual, and social philosophy. Its patron saint was, however, an Englishman: the Regency dandy Beau Brummell. Brummell had shed the elaborate finery of the eighteenth-century macaronis—which inspired even a backwoods Yankee named Doodle to stick a feather in his cap—in favor of a version of hunting garb smartened for town wear.[24] Had this dandy been merely the "Clothes-wearing man" Carlyle deemed him, he would have remained but a footnote to the history of fashion. Instead, George Brummell, gentleman, set himself up as arbiter of elegance for all classes of Regency society and won a place beside Napoleon and Lord Byron in Byron's admittedly biased list of the age's three great men.[25] The task of accounting for Brummell's magnetism was abruptly bequeathed to the French in 1816, when insolvency forced the Beau to flee England for Calais. French writers, remote from Almack's and other resorts where the English dandy clubbed and snubbed, were at liberty to fashion an ideal of the dandy unperplexed by firsthand observation.

In the hands of Barbey d'Aurevilly and Baudelaire, dandyism became a pose for the artist and intellectual in revolt. Barbey d'Aurevilly likened Regency dandies to the eighteenth-century *philosophes*, who had appealed to an obligation superior to the laws of the monarch—the superior law being, in the case of the dandy, solely his personal audacity.[26] In France, however, the encyclopedists

24. James Laver, *Dandies* (London: Weidenfeld and Nicolson, 1968), p. 85.

25. Ellen Moers cites Captain Jesse as the source of this anecdote concerning Byron in *The Dandy: Brummell to Beerbohm* (New York: Viking, 1960), p. 22. My discussion of dandyism is indebted to Moers' study at many points.

26. *Oeuvres romanesques complètes*, ed. Jacques Petit, II (Paris: Gallimard, 1966), 681–82.

had done their work so well that no monarchy remained
for the dandy to subvert; he therefore set himself against
the ascendant bourgeoisie. Like the bohemian of the Latin
Quarter, he regarded the artistic community as a class
apart; but where the bohemian sulked in the purlieus of
society, the dandy strode through its midst with superb
contempt. Flaunting his sartorial elegance as a symbol of
his "supériorité aristocratique"—the phrase is Baudelaire's[27]—he scorned both the dowdy burgher and the rum-
pled bohemian.

In art as in dress, the dandy was a formalist. Subscribing
to Gautier's *l'art pour l'art*, he played down the importance
of subject matter and discursive meaning, thus depriving
the public of its usual means of understanding and evaluating art. Whistler, among others, proclaimed his disre-
gard for subject by calling his paintings "symphonies,"
"harmonies," "arrangements," and "nocturnes." He re-
stricted his palette to a few colors—black, gray, silver, and
white being favorites—so as to concentrate on tonal effects. His technique was both a challenge to the viewer and
a taunt. When Ruskin accused him of "flinging a pot of
paint in the public's face," Whistler sued the critic for libel—less to clear himself of the charge, one suspects, than
to seize an opportunity for flinging more paint.

To Whistler must go much of the credit for translating
dandyism from Paris to London, where it had several features in common with English aestheticism. Dandy and
aesthete found a common enemy in the middle-class philistine, whom they tried to shock out of his complacency.
Both sought, as a sort of stopgap moral code, to make their
lives into works of art and to make art an absolute value.
Both occasionally tasted the wormwood of ennui, though
in this as in most things the dandy seemed the more heroic
figure. Sartre has convincingly portrayed Baudelaire as an

27. "Le Peintre de la vie moderne," *Oeuvres complètes*, ed. F. F. Gautier, IV (Paris: Nouvelle Revue Française, 1923), 242.

existentialist *avant la lettre*, and his spleen as "un sentiment métaphysique," a glimpse into the abyss of nothingness that threatened, but for the discipline of dandyism, to engulf him.[28] The dandy, who cultivated the bored, indifferent manner, required the aesthete's susceptibility to impressions to make him a better artist, while the aesthete needed to school himself in the dandy's wit and social *savoir-faire*.

Oscar Wilde, ever the telltale to a change of wind, took Whistler for mentor in the eighteen eighties and was soon embroiled in his own disastrous lawsuit. When the court determined that the Marquess of Queensberry's charge of sodomy was not libel but plain truth, aesthetic dandyism was effectively stigmatized and forced underground, for Wilde had called himself aesthete and dandy. Though Max Beerbohm and Virginia Woolf would write appreciations of the dandy for a later generation, aesthetic dandyism never recovered, in England, the prestige it enjoyed before 1895. In America, curiously, the English *fin de siècle* prolonged its Indian summer well into the new century. During the nineties, Richard Mansfield was immensely popular with New York audiences in the title role of *Beau Brummell*, a play written for him by Clyde Fitch, while a host of little magazines—among them the *Chap-Book*, *M'lle New York*, the *Lark*, and the *Philistine*—strove to emulate the *Yellow Book*. On the eve of World War I, Malcolm Cowley recalls, Harvard students were still trying, as they had in Stevens' day, to create in Cambridge "an after-image of Oxford in the 1890s."[29] After the war, Floyd Dell noted that the so-called "new literature" of Greenwich Village was actually a throwback to the *Yellow Book* period. "In our day," Dell said of the early twenties, "the Whistler influence was still powerful in literature."[30]

28. *Baudelaire* (Paris: Gallimard, 1947), pp. 32, 153–54.
29. *Exile's Return: A Narrative of Ideas* (New York: Norton, 1934), p. 37.
30. *Intellectual Vagabondage: An Apology for the Intelligentsia* (New York: George H. Doran, 1926), pp. 197–98, 241–42.

Aesthetic dandyism appealed to young Americans for many of the same reasons it appealed to young Britons: it was anti-Victorian, anti-philistine, anti-bourgeois, and anti-puritanical. In this country, it had the additional appeal of being anti-democratic, a sentiment H. L. Mencken traded upon in his very different way. To Americans, moreover, aesthetic dandyism seemed more exotic than it did to the English, and was therefore the more attractive. At the turn of the century, when American literature was still in the grips of gentility, this Anglo-French hybrid offered new possibilities in the way of subject matter, dramatis personae, tone, and even diction. Writers who wanted to escape a stale native literary tradition or what they took to be a hostile literary environment did not necessarily have to book passage for Paris or London, though many of them did just that. In fact, as Stevens and other members of the "Arensberg-Others" group demonstrated, they did not even have to travel as far downtown as Greenwich Village to make good their escape.

Stevens absorbed the poses and preoccupations of the English Decadence and transmitted them, refracted by the medium of his unique sensibility, in the poems of *Harmonium*. A handful of these, while they do not derive from particular antecedents in the nineties, have a distinct period flavor to them. "Mandolin and Liqueurs" (1923), the first of Stevens' poems to be published originally in England, is a typical instance:

> La-la! The cat is in the violets
> And the awnings are let down.
> The cat should not be where she is
> And the awnings are too brown,
> Emphatically so.

> If awnings were celeste and gay,
> Iris and orange, crimson and green,
> Blue and vermilion, purple and white,
> And not this tinsmith's galaxy,
> Things would be different.

The sun is gold, the moon is silver.
There must be a planet that is copper
And in whose light the roses
Would have a most singular appearance,
Or nearly so.

I love to sit and read the *Telegraph*,
That vast confect of telegrams,
And to find how much that really matters
Does not really matter
At all.[31]

One recognizes in this poem the aesthete's fondness for gay colors (the awnings are too brown), his fastidious sense of composition (the cat should not be where she is), and his malaise, here induced by the drab urban setting and the trivialities which pass for news. The speaker reads an English newspaper and is given to turns of phrase which strike one as English ("Emphatically so," "a most singular appearance"), not to mention Miltonic ("a vast confect").

The speaker of "Mandolin and Liqueurs" might well be the "Peter Parasol" of a poem Stevens had submitted to *Poetry* in 1919 (*OP* 20). In the earlier piece, Peter Parasol, whose name and manner recall Stevens' Harvard ballade, applies his discriminating taste to the order of divine rather than human creation. As in "Mandolin," he is conscious of a lapse in decorum: if bulls have horns and horses have hooves, if elephants have tusks and tigers a ferocious beauty, why should not all women be fair? As an argument, this is rather slight. Stevens, fearing that readers would overlook the element of pastiche in the poem and would judge it in terms of substance rather than style, tried to withdraw it from consideration (*L* 214).[32] Perhaps he had

31. *Chapbook*, no. 36 (1923), p. 15; reprinted in *OP* 28–29. Alfred Kreymborg was guest editor of this issue, which consists entirely of work by American poets.

32. Stevens inscribed the French lines which serve as the poem's epigraph above "Women's Gift" in his copy of Richard Aldington's *Greek Songs in the Manner of Anacreon* (London: Egoist, 1919), p. 17 (Massachu-

learned from "Gray Room" (1917), where he had deliberately sought substance rather than style, what can happen
when *fin de siècle* conventions are taxed beyond their capacity. The poem recalls Whistler's most famous painting:

> Although you sit in a room that is gray,
> Except for the silver
> Of the straw-paper,
> And pick
> At your pale white gown;
> Or lift one of the green beads
> Of your necklace,
> To let it fall;
> Or gaze at your green fan
> Printed with the red branches of a red willow;
> Or, with one finger,
> Move the leaf in the bowl—
> The leaf that has fallen from the branches of the forsythia
> Beside you . . .

Were the poem to end here (and it probably should), it
would gratify the expectations aroused by its title. However, this lengthy concessive clause anticipates the two
lines still remaining:

> What is all this?
> I know how furiously your heart is beating.
>   (*PEM* 23)

"Gray Room" invites us to feel the contrast between appearance and reality, between the cool formalism of the
setting and the intense feeling of the woman. But this turn
is too abrupt and too easy. So effectively does the first part
of the poem condition the reader to the emotional tenor of
the gray room that he is apt to find the last lines maladroit
and sentimental.

"Gray Room" suggests that the aesthetic dandy is least
himself when delving into furiously beating hearts. His
ideal subject is the sophisticated bit of good taste, as in

---

setts). Beneath them he wrote the single word "*Pléiade*," referring possibly
to a Pléiade edition or to the school of sixteenth-century poets who modeled their work on the Greek Anthology.

"Mandolin and Liqueurs" and "Peter Parasol." Two other pieces which seem at first to be in this mode are Kreymborg's favorite, "Tea," and "Floral Decorations for Bananas" (1923). These remind us, however, that there is a world beyond the artificial, indoor world where the dandy is most at home. By means of their "sea-shades and sky-shades," the lamplit pillows in "Tea" recall that extramural world and offer an appealing alternative to it now that autumn has overtaken the park. Similarly, the speaker of "Floral Decorations" protests that plums arranged with budding flowers in an eighteenth-century dish would complement, better than bananas, the ladies who will attend the dinner party. But the world evoked by the bananas captures his imagination in the end. Pile the bananas on planks, he contends, and they will transform the ladies of "primrose and purl" into native women; add a garnish of the appropriate leaves, "Plucked from the Carib trees, / Fibrous and dangling down," and the centerpiece will summon up the barbarous landscape to which these women belong.

Though the aesthete might occasionally dabble in the barbaric and primitive in order to secure novel sensations, he usually sought pleasures that were as refined and civilized as he himself aspired to be. The dandy shrank from anything not subject to calculation and control. "Floral Decorations" thus represents one respect in which Stevens modified aesthetic dandyism while absorbing it: characteristically, he is aesthete and dandy in a natural rather than artificial universe. This distinction seems to have eluded Alfred Kreymborg, who, agreeing with Munson and Untermeyer, called Stevens an "esthete, the hedonist par excellence of modern poetry," yet offered, as Stevens' only frank self-portrait, the poem "Nomad Exquisite" (written 1919).[33] Stevens sent this piece to Harriet Monroe on the back of a postcard, a circumstance which lends credence

33. *Our Singing Strength* (New York: Coward-McCann, 1929), pp. 500, 504.

to Kreymborg's sketch of his fellow poet tossing off perfect poems in railroad coaches bound for Florida.[34] But Stevens' nomad is not a tourist, passively regarding the southern landscape from the indoor side of a plate of glass. In him "come flinging" not images or impressions of fruits and flowers but the fruits and flowers themselves. Welling up inside him, the vital dew of Florida produces hymns as spontaneously as it produces palm trees and vines from the soil. To the extent that this nomad "sees" at all, he sees with the regardless animal vision of the young alligator.

The dandy praised artifice and perfection of surface partly, Baudelaire maintained, to distinguish himself from such specimens of *homo naturalis* as woman and the bourgeois.[35] Whistler, with his sure instinct for the statement which would most outrage the bourgeois, coined his bon mot to the effect that nature imitates art. (Oscar Wilde wished he had said that, and eventually he did.) Stevens, as his "Anecdote of the Jar" (1919) indicates, was sufficiently middle-class to appreciate what is sacrificed when art gains the upper hand. He also knew that the bourgeois is not as "natural" as Baudelaire let on; he is just as likely to take offense at a display of primitive vitality as at a display of artifice. Thus in "Disillusionment of Ten O'Clock" (1915) it is not the well-dressed dandy but "an old sailor, / Drunk and asleep in his boots," who represents the antithesis of the bourgeois "ghosts" who haunt their own houses in white nightgowns. Whereas the people who keep regular hours are unlikely to dream of baboons and periwinkles—natural if exotic items—the sailor dreams of catching tigers in "red weather." Whatever red weather may be (hot? stormy?), it would keep the dandy in his club. Nor would one find, in the wardrobe of any self-respecting son of Brummell, any of the parti-colored nightgowns offered as alternatives to white.

Closer in manner to the dandy than to the old sailor, but

34. *Our Singing Strength*, p. 501.
35. "Mon Coeur mis à nu," *Oeuvres complètes*, ed. F. F. Gautier and Y. G. Le Dantec, VI (1937), 272.

still possessed of a savagery the dandy would find distasteful, is Victoria Clementina of "Exposition of the Contents
of a Cab" (1919), whose cab ride through Central Park suggests a jungle queen's triumphal progress:

> Victoria Clementina, negress,
> Took seven white dogs
> To ride in a cab.
>
> Bells of the dogs chinked.
> Harness of the horses shuffled
> Like brazen shells.
>
> Oh-hé-hé! Fragrant puppets
> By the green lake-pallors,
> She too is flesh,
>
> And a breech-cloth might wear,
> Netted of topaz and ruby
> And savage blooms;
>
> Thridding the squawkiest jungle
> In a golden sedan,
> White dogs at bay.
>
> What breech-cloth might you wear—
> Except linen, embroidered
> By elderly women?
>
> > (OP 20–21)

As with "Peter Parasol," Stevens tried to withdraw this
poem from a group he had sent to *Poetry* because he felt
he had not yet learned to bring it off successfully (L 214).
It is hard to see where he thought he had failed, for "Exposition" succeeds nicely as an aesthetic prank; the verbal
extravagance of a line like "Thridding the squawkiest
jungle" parades before the reader nurtured on genteel
verse much as Victoria Clementina parades before the conventional folk by the lake. Further, by dwelling on the
breech-cloth Victoria Clementina would wear in another
setting, and contrasting its "topaz and ruby / And savage
blooms" with the embroidered linen worn by the per-
fumed onlookers, the poem hints at an erotic energy they
would find as intimidating as her panache.

Stevens exploits the erotic *épatant* more explicitly in

"The Ordinary Women" and "A High-Toned Old Christian Woman," first published together in the *Dial* in 1922. The women of the first poem, ghostlike as the bourgeoisie of "Disillusionment of Ten O'Clock," flit through the walls of a movie palace to seek in Hollywood fantasies ("guitars") the excitement lacking in their humdrum and sexually unfulfilled lives. Lighted by the "moonlight" of the silver screen, the spectral conclave remains hushed until the script calls for a love scene between boy and girl ("beta b and gamma g"). This elicits a "Ti-lill-o!" of titillation, whereupon the women become so enthralled in the celluloid illusion, with its rich costume and eloquent lovemaking, that the brick and mortar of the theater seem insubstantial by comparison.

The wickless halls return, however, as the last frame fades from the screen, leaving the women as impoverished spiritually as they had ever been. Their "heavenly script" is neither as heavenly nor as sustaining as that of the woman addressed in "A High-Toned Old Christian Woman." The poet attempts to ruffle the composure of this true believer by proposing a shocking version of Santayana's argument in *Interpretations of Poetry and Religion*— that poetry and religion are equally fictions of the human mind, reflecting the values of the human maker. If lewdness is human, why not project a heaven on this basis rather than the moral sentiment? This is the more conceivable inasmuch as the imagination is itself irreverent and protean: "fictive things / Wink as they will." "A High-Toned Old Christian Woman" is calculated to elicit from the woman—and those readers who share her outlook—the "wince" that concludes the poem.

When the Decadent writer took up the subject of erotic love at all, he tended to explore its more perverse manifestations; one thinks of Wilde's *Salomé* and Beardsley's *Venus and Tannhäuser*. Stevens, though he sometimes used erotic themes to shock, remained well within the burgher's conception of normal sexuality. This still left him room to range, from the bawdy "Lulu Gay" (1921, *OP* 26) to the near-sentimental "Two at Norfolk" (1931). On the one hand, he satirizes "caliper," the intellectual who can take the measure of every flower but not of his companion's passion ("Last Looks at the Lilacs," 1923); on the other hand, he wishes that Florida were less the harlot and more the sequestered inamorata ("O Florida, Venereal Soil," 1922). In his treatment of love as in his celebration of fine sensations, Stevens invoked the natural world as his norm: like a plant, love has its proper seasons for flowering, producing fruit, and finally resolving into dust. Consequently, in a poem like "Piano Practice at the Academy of the Holy Angels" (1919), he eschews the leering irony Laforgue had brought to the same subject in his "Complainte des pianos." Where Laforgue hears a precocious eroticism in the girls' finger exercises, Stevens merely reminds us that they will come seasonally to knowledge: "The time will come for these children, seated before their long black instruments, to strike the themes of love . . ." (*OP* 21).

In the natural scheme of things, ripeness is all. But ripeness was already becoming a memory for the poet of *Harmonium*, who was forty-four when the volume was published. This, together with his less than blissful experience of wedded life, may account for the note of resignation which is occasionally sounded in his treatments of love. In "Le Monocle de Mon Oncle" (1918), for example, it might well be Laforgue's worldly-wise Hamlet who lectures his mistress on the quirks of middle-aged romance, using an apple and gourds for props rather than Yorick's skull. To compare lovers with squashes is to imply that love follows the same deterministic course as other things in nature; a squash can choose neither to refrain from blooming nor to bloom indefinitely. The uncle, though he protests the "unconscionable treachery of fate" which operates through the sexual instinct to make a mockery of our pretensions to free will, yet remains philosophical about his lot. For him, "the firefly's quick, electric stroke / Ticks tediously the time of one more year." But the passion of the young pulses in harmony with a force as remote as Venus and as near as the planet beneath one's feet:

> In the high west there burns a furious star.
> It is for fiery boys that star was set
> And for sweet-smelling virgins close to them.
> The measure of the intensity of love
> Is measure, also, of the verve of earth.

In "Le Monocle," we view the world through the lens of someone who professes to be a "rose rabbi." Wistfully but without bitterness, he studies the course of love and other ephemeral "fluttering things." The more things change, he decides, the more they remain the same. The verve of earth is the perennial reality, the rest mere sentiment ("anecdotal bliss") and literature ("Memorabilia of the mystic spouts").But what if, to entertain a possibility that haunted Baudelaire and Laforgue, the verve of earth were itself beginning to flag? One thinks of Laforgue's "Couchant d'hiver" and especially the line "La Terre a fait son temps; ses reins n'en peuvent plus" on reading Stevens' "Anatomy of Monotony" (1931). Ordinarily, the poem suggests, the warmth of the sun and human companionship foster our illusion of well-being and distract us from the "barer sky" which perpetually confronts our maternal but moribund planet with an augury of its fate. Only at summer's end do we intuit the ultimate autumn which Baudelaire and Laforgue called "le gouffre" and against which they defended themselves by means of dandyism. "Anatomy of Monotony" finds the rose rabbi in a rare moment of spleen; reverting briefly to his earlier phase as "dark rabbi," he inscribes—so the poem's original title had it—his "Footnote To The Anatomy of Melancholy."[36]

Corresponding to the dandy's spleen, but proceeding

36. This title appears on a holograph draft of the poem. Stevens owned a copy of the Nonesuch *Anatomy of Melancholy* (London, 1925), which was sold at auction on 10 Mar. 1959 at Parke-Bernet Galleries.

from a somewhat different sense of the world, was the aesthete's ennui. Where the dandy saw too little, the aesthete occasionally saw too much. In "Banal Sojourn" (1919), one feels the "malady" which Stevens later characterized as "[t]he mildew of any late season, of any experience that has grown monotonous as, for instance, the experience of life" (L 464). Monotony claims even the rhythm of the piece, which consists of ponderous end-stopped "summer" lines bracketing an enjambed recollection of a fresher season. Here, as often in Stevens' seasonal mythology, summer is a state of excess, of cloying surfeit. One would rather have the sky "unfuzzed" by clouds and see the "Satan ear" of the black trees stripped of their wigs of foliage. By its very inertia, this swollen season invokes its opposite, a time when the moonlight descended swiftly through the clear atmosphere.

When monotony infects the imagination as well as the senses, the poet suffers the condition of "dumbness" which Stevens represents in "The Man Whose Pharynx Was Bad" (1921). Like the speaker of "Banal Sojourn," the poet of the ailing pharynx wishes that a change of weather would dispel his lassitude and indifference; then he might spout "new orations of the cold." Though he appears convinced that "time will not relent," his prognosis is favorable, for his cure is implicit in the terms of his complaint: if "summer" is here, can "winter" be far behind? In this sense, the poem illustrates Michel Benamou's contention that Laforguian boredom was temperamentally uncongenial to Stevens and mattered to him chiefly as something to be overcome.[37]

Pater's "Conclusion" likewise begins with a reminder that all things follow a natural cycle, "birth and gesture and death and the springing of violets from the grave." Rather than surrender to this rhythm, however, Pater at-

37. *Wallace Stevens and the Symbolist Imagination* (Princeton: Princeton University Press, 1972), p. 30.

tempts to stall it, to make of the moment a miniature eternity. His "desperate effort to see and touch," his compulsion to get "as many pulsations as possible into the given time" follow naturally from his protest against nature. Stevens, as his college marginalia and journal entries bear witness, was disposed to give life the nod over art. In *Harmonium*, he characteristically accedes to the passing of temporal things, even the most lovely, with the poise and equanimity that mark the last stanza of "Peter Quince at the Clavier" (1915):

> Beauty is momentary in the mind—
> The fitful tracing of a portal;
> But in the flesh it is immortal.
> The body dies; the body's beauty lives.
> So evenings die, in their green going,
> A wave, interminably flowing.
> So gardens die, their meek breath scenting
> The cowl of winter, done repenting.
> So maidens die, to the auroral
> Celebration of a maiden's choral.
> Susanna's music touched the bawdy strings
> Of those white elders; but, escaping,
> Left only death's ironic scraping.
> Now, in its immortality, it plays
> On the clear viol of her memory,
> And makes a constant sacrament of praise.

Susanna's is the beauty of living, perishable things. Though such beauty belongs to the world of process rather than the world of art or thought—a fact driven home by the insistent participles in the passage—it nevertheless escapes the "white elders" of decay and death. This it can do because it is memorable: it assumes new flesh whenever and wherever there is a Peter Quince to praise Susanna's beauty and so make it immortal. Paradoxically, of course, this memory is implanted in Peter Quince by a literary text, the Book of Daniel, and further promulgated by the artistry of Stevens' poem.

By planting himself in the seasonal cycle and awaiting its timely revelations, Stevens forestalled the morbid pursuit of novel sensation that marks some literature of the nineties. Oscar Wilde suggested the extreme to which this could go when he had Lord Henry Wotton propose to Dorian Gray that murder might be "simply a method of procuring extraordinary sensations."[38] Stevens flirts with Lord Henry's view in "Anecdotal Recovery" (*OP* 12–13), which appeared as the second poem of the "Lettres d'un Soldat" sequence (1918). When read in connection with its French epigraph, the poem implies that only those blinded by moral convention—one of the "habits" Pater advised the aesthete to shed—fail to recognize the "triumphant beauty" of the murderer's deed. Elsewhere, Stevens indulges in such grotesquerie as his subject allows, with the results to be seen in "The Worms at Heaven's Gate" and "The Emperor of Ice-Cream" (1922). Usually, however, his imagination attends the moment of natural change rather than searching out more exotic sensations.

Of all Stevens' poems, the one most frequently described as "Paterian" is "Sunday Morning" (1915). If the epithet were a suit, the poem might consider it a poor fit; but fit it does, after a fashion, and to review "Sunday Morning" here is to see at a glance how Stevens tailored aestheticism to his own sensibility. Some readers find the Paterian signature in the elegiac tone and gracefully cadenced, almost orotund style of a sentence like the following, here transcribed as prose:

> Although [Death] strews the leaves of sure obliteration on our paths, the path sick sorrow took, the many paths where triumph rang its brassy phrase, or love whispered a little out of tenderness, she makes the willow shiver in the sun for maidens who were wont to sit and gaze upon the grass, relinquished to their feet.

For others, "Sunday Morning" is thematically a Paterian poem, an opinion Stevens endorsed indirectly, when he called the poem "simply an expression of paganism" (*L*

---

38. "The Picture of Dorian Gray," *The Works of Oscar Wilde* (New York: Lamb, 1909), II: 386.

250). Pater singled out the element of paganism most germane to "Sunday Morning" when, in his essay on "Aesthetic Poetry," he observed,

> One characteristic of the pagan spirit the aesthetic poetry has, which is on its surface—the continual suggestion, pensive or passionate, of the shortness of life. This is contrasted with the bloom of the world, and gives new seduction to it—the sense of death and the desire of beauty: the desire of beauty quickened by the sense of death.[39]

Turning relentlessly upon the axis of its central theme, "Death is the mother of beauty," Stevens' poem is now pensive, now passionate, depending on whether it contemplates a lost belief or a present pleasure. The concluding stanza brings these into sharp juxtaposition:

> She hears, upon that water without sound,
> A voice that cries, "The tomb in Palestine
> Is not the porch of spirits lingering.
> It is the grave of Jesus, where he lay."
> We live in an old chaos of the sun,
> Or old dependency of day and night,
> Or island solitude, unsponsored, free,
> Of that wide water, inescapable.
> Deer walk upon our mountains, and the quail
> Whistle about us their spontaneous cries;
> Sweet berries ripen in the wilderness;
> And, in the isolation of the sky,
> At evening, casual flocks of pigeons make
> Ambiguous undulations as they sink,
> Downward to darkness, on extended wings.

Having journeyed in imagination to Palestine, the woman is persuaded by an oddly authoritative (but presumably not supernatural) voice that Jesus is dead and with him all hope of resurrection. Pursuing the implications of this disclosure, she concludes that we live on a physical and temporal island, at once free of divine despotism and shackled to a world of flux and death. Those pleasingly undulant

39. *Appreciations, with an Essay on Style* (London: Macmillan, 1889), p. 227.

pigeons' wings are not at all ambiguous in what they portend of the hereafter; the sky isolates us from transcendent glory as effectively as any mythological river.

Insofar as there is a cosmology behind the "new Cyrenaicism" of Pater's Marius or the "new hedonism" of Wilde's Dorian Gray, it is the same that informs the conclusion of "Sunday Morning": we live amid Democritus' atoms, in an uncreated "chaos of the sun." In such a universe, Pater taught, one should seek pleasure, not as an end in itself, but as a means to "fullness of life," a fullness which includes even "noble pain and sorrow."[40] Though the final lines of "Sunday Morning" stress the natural pleasures that render a purely naturalistic world tolerable, Stanza II had embraced a wider range of experience. "Divinity" is there equated syntactically with both pleasures and pains, grievings and elations; these in turn correspond to summer and winter, making the seasonal cycle the "measure" to which the woman must attune her soul.

The boys of Stanza V who bring plums and pears for the maidens to taste (their offering recalls Porphyro's to Madeline in Keats's "The Eve of St. Agnes") already dance to this measure. So do the men who chant their boisterous devotion to the sun in Stanza VII, where, as elsewhere in the poems of Harmonium, Stevens infuses Pater's pensive view of men that perish like dew with a quasi-religious reverence for natural process. Nature is not a god, despite the suggestions of pantheism Yvor Winters saw in this stanza.[41] But the sun appears to its worshipers "as a god might be." The sun resembles a god and in the larger economy of resemblance God may be an idealized likeness of the sun; paradise is likewise a resemblance abstracted from the windy lake, the trees, and the echoing hills. Stevens remains mindful of the distinction he tries to impress upon

40. *Marius the Epicurean: His Sensations and Ideas* (London: Macmillan, 1885), I: 163.

41. *In Defense of Reason* (New York: Swallow Press and William Morrow, 1947), pp. 432–33.

the high-toned old Christian woman—that poetry itself, rather than any of its creations, is the supreme fiction.

"Sunday Morning," inasmuch as it captures "the desire of beauty quickened by the sense of death," is what Pater called an "aesthetic" poem. Rather than choose between Pater's "pensive" and "passionate," Stevens incorporates both moods into the poem by means of diverse personae. The pensive attitude is struck by the woman who day-dreams over breakfast in a sunny chair, unable either to believe in imperishable bliss or to abandon herself to the balm and beauty of the earth. Beside her hesitation and minor, indoor dissipations, the boys' sexual offering of fruit and the men's orgiastic chant seem all the more passionate and unequivocal. They represent a piety both natural and naturalistic, one that Pater and the aesthetes could not have embraced in its pure form. The aesthete might, however, have shared the attitude of the poem's presiding consciousness, which is neither pensive, exactly, nor passionate. This consciousness, which might be identified as the poet's, is sympathetic to the woman's quandary yet remains slightly superior to it. Adelaide Kirby Morris might be thinking of "Sunday Morning" in particular when she says that Stevens, in his criticisms of religion, often assumes the "calm of a cataloguer of fossils or the scorn of a highly developed form for a vestigial one."[42] Maintaining his detachment, he assigns the pensive wish and the passionate act their roles in the drama of religious belief. Clearly the author of "Sunday Morning" wanted to appear more hard-headed than the pensive woman and more sophisticated than the passionate youths and men, even as he invested some of his most private feelings in them.

This self-protective strategy can be seen in other "aesthetic" poems in *Harmonium*. It is as though Stevens, hav-

---

42. *Wallace Stevens: Imagination and Faith* (Princeton: Princeton University Press, 1974), p. 47.

ing assumed the pose of aesthete, had suddenly caught sight of himself in a mirror; thereafter, his dismay and amusement became an integral part of the pose. The same might be said of his dandiacal poems, for the dandy is by definition someone who lives always as though reflected in a mirror; the dandy's vaunted wit sprang in the first place from an awareness of his own absurd pretensions.[43] Further compounding the aesthetic dandy's self-consciousness, in Stevens' case, was his burgherly sense of his own foppish creations.

Stevens' self-consciousness manifests itself in various ways. It appears in the overt self-mockery of "Depression before Spring" and, combined with mockery of another's pretense, in "Le Monocle de Mon Oncle." It appears in self-deprecating titles like "Jasmine's Beautiful Thoughts underneath the Willow" and "Discourse in a Cantina at Havana" (later, "Academic Discourse at Havana"). It shows in his choice of archaic or recherché words, such as "pardie," "besprent," "featly," "quotha," "arointing," "nuncle," "gat," "anon," "trumped," "writ," and "thridding." It prompts a turn of phrase which might be considered over-nice—

The melon-flower nor dew nor web of either
Is like to these—

or grandiloquent—"the unconscionable treachery of fate" (*CP* 72,17). Finally, in *Harmonium* as never again in Stevens' career, his self-consciousness sponsored a proliferation of comic personae.

While courting Elsie, Stevens had found it useful to hide his emotion behind the mask of Pierrot. Likewise, when he first ventured into print with the poems of *Harmonium*, he was no more ready for Yeats's enterprising nakedness than Yeats himself had been at that stage of his career. Though Pierrot never appears under his own name in *Har-*

43. Moers, p. 75.

monium, he is present in his avatars, characters bearing names like Bantam and Berserk, Carlos and Peter Quince, and of course Crispin.[44] Bantam and Berserk, from "Bantams in Pine-Woods" (1922) and "Anecdote of the Prince of Peacocks" (1923) respectively, represent but one side of the Pierrot consciousness—the subversive. To obtain the whole, with its seriousness as well as its irony, one must pair them with the heroes of imagination to whom they play anti-hero: Bantam with Chieftain Iffucan and Berserk with the Prince of Peacocks.

Carlos, the sole character in Stevens' play *Carlos among the Candles* (1917), is Pierrot complete. Carlos' elaborate candle-lighting experiment, though serious in its aesthetic implications, amounts to a burlesque of the Paterian consciousness. This self-proclaimed "modern" begins by lighting a single candle in a dark room. He then steps back to reflect that the candle and its aura of loneliness have created the self he is at that moment. "It is in the afternoon and in the evening," he muses, ". . . in effects, so drifting, that I know myself to be incalculable, since the causes of what I am are incalculable . . ." (*OP* 145). The use of spaced periods between Carlos' sentences suggests his moment-by-moment response to impressions. As he lights a second candle, the atmosphere of the room changes from lonely to companionable and effects a like change in Carlos: "The associations have drifted a little and changed, and I have followed in this change . . . If I see myself in other places in such a light, it is not as I saw myself before." The experiment continues until he has lighted six candles, a feat which moves him to exult, "In how short a time have I been solitary, then respectable—in a company so cold as to be stately, then elegant, then conscious of luxury, even magnificence; and now I come, gradually, to the beginning of splendor. Truly, I am a modern.

44. Robert Storey traces permutations of the Pierrot in Stevens' early poems and plays in *Pierrot: A Critical History of a Mask* (Princeton: Princeton University Press, 1978), pp. 167–92.

[*He dances around the room.*]

To have changed so often and so much . . . or to have been changed . . . to have been carried by the lighting of six candles through so many lives and to have been brought among so many people . . . This grows more wonderful."

That one's identity varies according to one's surroundings and sensations is a notion Stevens entertains elsewhere, in "Theory" (1917) and "Sea Surface Full of Clouds" (1924). Rather than identify too closely with Carlos, however, Stevens describes him in the stage directions as "an eccentric pedant of about forty" who dresses in black and is "over-nice in sounding his words" (*OP* 144). He takes a similar tack in "Peter Quince at the Clavier," whose title serves as an ironic stage direction. In this case, the image evoked—Shakespeare's rude mechanical pressing the delicate keyboard with his thick fingers—seems a gratuitous bit of self-deprecation, for the libretto which follows is both subtle and solemn. The title betrays Stevens' discomfort in the role of "serious poet" in the early poetry, where, to appropriate the words of the uncle of "Le Monocle," he usually affects to be either a "yeoman" or one of the "fops of fancy."

Broomstick of Stevens' play *Bowl, Cat and Broomstick* (1917) is one of the yeomen, though he subscribes to the highest standards in poetry. Believing that the poet must be himself in his day, Broomstick cannot share Bowl's enthusiasm for the stale poesies of Claire Dupray. "How little it would take to turn the poets into the only true comedians!" Broomstick exclaims upon reading her work (*PEM* 26). "There's no truer comedy than this hodge-podge of men and sunlight, women and moonlight, houses and clouds, and so on."

Taking this view as his point of departure in "The Comedian as the Letter C," Stevens recounts the adventures of Crispin, a poet who tries repeatedly to transcend his role as comedian but repeatedly fails. Leaving Bordeaux, where his poems had consisted of a hodge-podge of melancholy verses to autumn and yearly couplets to spring, he seeks to be himself in his day first in Yucatan, then Carolina. Crispin's transatlantic voyage is a crucial phase of his education, for it disabuses him of the notion, garnered chiefly from books, that "man is the intelligence of his soil." In the early version of "Comedian" entitled "From the Journal of Crispin," our hero learns that he cannot alter his mythology of the world without simultaneously and more significantly altering his mythology of self:

> It is not so much that one's mythology
> Is blotched by the sea. It was a boresome book,
> From which one trilled orations of the west,
> Based on the prints of Jupiter. . . .
> What counts is the mythology of self.
> That's blotched beyond unblotching.

It is one thing to see Jupiter "blotched" and to find only the dismembered remains of Triton in the waves; it is another and more unsettling experience to discover that "The sea / Severs not only lands but also selves." Yet Crispin, ever ready to serve grotesque apprenticeship to chance event, comes to preen himself on being a "starker, barer self / In a starker, barer world." In Yucatan he savors the savage, luxuriant, occasionally sublime reality of the land while poking fun at the sonneteers who take their cue from Petrarch. Crispin is not without his own backward lapses; as his ship steams toward Carolina, he briefly gives himself up to a romantic conception of the northern continent. What he actually finds is a seaport whose sights, sounds, and smells would serve admirably as the raw material for a realistic poem. Crispin promptly revises his unseaworthy thesis to read, "His soil is man's intelligence." Like Hawthorne in the Salem Custom House, however, he cannot make literary capital of the "Provocative paraphernalia" of commerce that surround him, endorse their value though he may. If (as he supposes) he is conditioned by his region to write in a certain way, he must nevertheless abandon hope of becoming a regional poet.

Crispin decides instead to found a colony of such poets and even projects an anthology of the Americas, to include contributions from Mississippi and Florida, California and Brazil. But an ironic truth soon dawns upon him: his soil, Bordeaux, is still very much his intelligence. He realizes that his utopian scheme is as romantic in its way as the poetry he had written before crossing the ocean. "From the Journal of Crispin" leaves our comedian at this impasse, unable either to advance or to retreat. He knows the world too well to masquerade as a romantic poet, himself too well to pose as a regional or realistic poet. He would seem, finally, to be the intelligence only of his own intelligence.

Though Stevens maintained that Crispin's story represents "the sort of life that millions of people live" (L 294), one is tempted to read it as a fable of his own career up to 1921. Certainly Crispin's journal records Stevens' progress in broad outline, if not in detail. "Bordeaux" was, by synecdoche, the France of his imagination and the country whence he had imported the dandyism of Barbey d'Aurevilly, Baudelaire, and Laforgue. Since this fictive France was nurtured in part by Pitts Sanborn's *Vie de Bordeaux* and the postcards which announced Sanborn's regular pilgrimages to that region, Stevens fittingly promised his friend the first chance at periodical publication of Crispin's adventures (L 229).[45] This side of the Atlantic, Carolina was a politic choice of American setting, considering that the Poetry Society of South Carolina sponsored the competition for which the poem was written.

The Carolinas were also part of a South Stevens had recently come to know more intimately and whose re-

---

45. Stevens' copy of *Vie de Bordeaux* (Philadelphia: Nicholas L. Brown, 1916) is inscribed by Sanborn and dated 30 Dec. 1916.

gional idiosyncrasies fascinated him. The rural South, especially, seemed to him to compensate for its material poverty with a luxuriance of vegetation and vernacular idiom. While writing "From the Journal of Crispin," Stevens was just getting to know Arthur Powell, an Atlanta attorney whom he retained to handle some of the Hartford's litigation in the South. Judge Powell's accents can be heard in the titles Stevens borrowed from him—"A High-Toned Old Christian Woman" and "Like Decorations in a Nigger Cemetery"—and also in the rich compendium of anecdote and personal reminiscence Powell published in 1943, under the title *I Can Go Home Again*. As Peter Brazeau has suggested, Powell's devotion to his region may well have prompted Stevens to relocate his "pine-spokesman" from Mississippi to Georgia when he revised "From the Journal of Crispin."[46]

Pursuing the likenesses between Stevens and his clown, one finds nothing in the poet's early career as dramatic and decisive as Crispin's sea crossing. Rather than being suddenly shredded by an elemental storm, Stevens' mythology of self apparently came out at the elbows gradually, like an old coat. That he found little between himself and the weather around 1921 is suggested by a letter Judge Powell wrote him years later, on reading Hi Simons' essay, "'The Comedian as the Letter C': Its Sense and Its Significance." "While I do not go as far as he does in looking upon 'The Comedian as the Letter C' as autobiographic," Powell said,

> still, of course, there is in it much of yourself and of the mental attitude of yourself toward yourself at a very formative period of your life—a period that was still in progress when first I met you.
>
> When one has cast off all his old clothes, even the nethermost, and has not gotten new ones, his nudity abashes him even in the presence of intimates; and, naturally, he seeks screenery of a sort; even if behind the screenery [*sic*] he is mak-

46. *Parts of a World: Wallace Stevens Remembered*, p. 101.

ing stitches upon new underwear and shirts. Of course, as for me, you did not need to get behind a bush to prevent my seeing very much of you in that phase of your life with which the peom [sic] deals—my literary eyes are too myoptic [sic] to see very far in that realm—and our business relations, our social relations, the good times we had in just working together and playing together, as "men of this world" were screen enough.[47]

It was probably tact as much as literary myopia that prevented Powell from studying too curiously the cut and condition of Stevens' old clothes. Intuitively, he understood that his friend required, perhaps then as never before, the disguise of the burgherly man of the world.

For Stevens as for Crispin, the old mythology of self was founded upon an old mythology of the world. By contrast with Crispin's classical mythology of Jupiter and Triton, however, Stevens' was inherently a mythology of disintegration. Literary decadence, Richard Le Gallienne complained in 1892, consists in "the euphuistic expression of isolated observations" and fails to relate those observations to any controlling center.[48] Arthur Symons, his fellow member of the Rhymers' Club, acknowledged even in his defense of the new literature that it was "really a new and beautiful and interesting disease."[49] When Stevens came to make a selection of his poems for *Harmonium*, he was appalled at their "miscellaneous" character. The earlier pieces seemed, he told Harriet Monroe, "like horrid cocoons from which later abortive insects have sprung," pastiche begetting pastiche (*L* 231).

Several reviewers echoed his self-criticism when *Harmonium* came to their attention. Among the more perceptive of these was John Gould Fletcher, who observed that in the course of the remarkable decade between 1913 and

47. Letter of 8 Apr. 1940.
48. Review of Churton Collins' *Illustrations of Tennyson*, reprinted in *Retrospective Reviews: A Literary Log* (London: John Lane, 1896), I: 24–25.
49. "The Decadent Movement in Literature," *Harper's*, Nov. 1893, p. 859.

1923 the most advanced American poets had become "prematurely disillusioned aesthetes, lacking in mental and moral orientation."[50] Stevens was one whose private reality had become "disintegrated against the banal, the ordinary, the commonplace, which is everyday reality," and this, Fletcher speculated, had led to the disintegration of personality represented obliquely in "The Comedian as the Letter C." "I make bold to say," Fletcher wrote in conclusion, "that Mr. Stevens is the most accomplished and not one of the least interesting of modern American poets. But for the future he must face a clear choice of evils: he must either expand his range to take in more of human experience, or give up writing altogether. 'Harmonium' is a sublimation which does not permit of a sequel."

Stevens in a sense embraced both of these alternatives (he would not have considered them "evils") even before *Harmonium* appeared, when he told Harriet Monroe that he wished to remain as obscure as possible until he had perfected "an authentic and fluent speech" for himself (*L* 231). He prefigured his own spell of obscurity in the two sections he added to "From the Journal of Crispin" to make it "The Comedian as the Letter C." These follow Crispin from his failure as a planter of colonies through his absorption in home and family to his anticlimactic realization that his fate is, after all, the fate of everyman. Lines like the following, which describe Crispin with his daughters, seem clairvoyant in retrospect:

> The chits came for his jigging, bluet-eyed,
> Hands without touch yet touching poignantly,
> Leaving no room upon his cloudy knee,
> Prophetic joint, for its diviner young.

Crispin's knee-joint was indeed prophetic. Many an editor who looked to Stevens for "diviner young" between 1924

---

50. "The Revival of Aestheticism," review of *The Pilgrimage of Festus*, by Conrad Aiken; *Cups of Illusion*, by Henry Bellaman; *Charlatan*, by Louis Grudin; *Less Lonely*, by Alfred Kreymborg; and *Harmonium*, by Wallace Stevens, *Freeman*, 19 Dec. 1923, pp. 355–56.

Wallace Stevens with daughter Holly, about 1925
(Courtesy of the Huntington Library)

and 1934 received this same excuse, though in a style less
Miltonic. He professed to be absorbed in his work, in en-
tertaining his new daughter or being entertained by the
radio. For once, even Ezra Pound had to take no for an
answer when he requested a poem of Stevens, using William Carlos Williams as intermediary.[51]

Yet Stevens' obscurity was not entirely unproductive.
He would later remember his silent decade as a time when
he began, as Fletcher had put it, to "expand his range."
Writing to Hi Simons in 1940, he remarked that Crispin's
pilgrimage illustrates what might be a paradigm of the inner life: one goes from romanticism to realism to fatalism
to "indifferentism" and possibly back to romanticism to
recommence the cycle (*L* 350). Then, in a postscript which
both confesses his identification with Crispin and suggests
their differences, Stevens added,

> About the time when I, personally, began to feel round for a
> new romanticism, I might naturally have been expected to
> start on a new cycle. Instead of doing so, I began to feel that I
> was on the edge: that I wanted to get to the center: that I was
> isolated, and that I wanted to share the common life. . . .
> People say that I live in a world of my own: that sort of thing.
> Instead of seeking therefore for a "relentless contact", I have
> been interested in what might be described as an attempt to
> achieve the normal, the central. . . . Of course, I don't agree
> with the people who say that I live in a world of my own; I
> think that I am perfectly normal, but I see that there is a cen-
> ter. For instance, a photograph of a lot of fat men and women
> in the woods, drinking beer and singing Hi-li Hi-lo convinces
> me that there is a normal that I ought to try to achieve.

If Stevens had no particular photograph in mind when
he dictated that last sentence, his memory could easily
have supplied one: a sepia-toned image of his Pennsylvania Dutch neighbors enjoying a holiday at Kuechler's

---

51. In a letter of 7 Sept. 1927, Stevens told Williams he had no poems
to send to Pound. Williams forwarded the letter to Pound, whence it
came to the Pound Collection at the Beinecke Library, Yale University. The
letter is reprinted in *Antaeus*, no. 36 (1980), pp. 146–47.

Roost. As an epitome of the normal, this image occupies a position somewhere on the continuum between "relentless contact" (here Stevens may be recalling the sometimes factitious localism of the *Broom* and *Contact* groups) and solipsism.[52] So defined, the normal is not unlike the "new romanticism" he would articulate in the thirties.

It is not very different, in fact, from the project that occupies his alter ego in the conclusion of "From the Journal of Crispin." Later canceled when the final sections of "The Comedian as the Letter C" were added, the passage reads,

> As Crispin in his attic shapes the book
> That will contain him, he requires this end:
> The book shall discourse of himself alone,
> Of what he was, and why, and of his place,
> And of its fitful pomp and parentage.
> Thereafter he may stalk in other spheres.

During his silent decade Stevens likewise labored in some attic of his mind to shape an authentic and fluent speech for himself. His experiment in aesthetic dandyism had taught him, as it taught Crispin, that

> Imagination soon exhausts itself
> In artifice too tenuous to sustain
> The vaporous moth upon its fickle wings.

Except when he was "a little off the normal," Stevens did not feel that he was truly "in the area of poetry" (L 287). But, as A. Walton Litz speculates, he may have stopped writing when he realized that his work had become all but detached from reality.[53] Only by applying himself to the near and the normal, even if this meant forgoing poetry for a time, could he recharge his exhausted imagination.

Such application might eventually produce its moments

---

52. Martha Strom discusses Stevens' relation to the localists in "Wallace Stevens' Revisions of Crispin's Journal: A Reaction against the 'Local,'" *American Literature* 54 (1982): 258–76.

53. *Introspective Voyager: The Poetic Development of Wallace Stevens* (New York: Oxford University Press, 1972), p. 151.

of fitful pomp and stalking in other spheres. This possibility, guardedly broached in the conclusion of "From the Journal of Crispin," is developed more fully in a poem Stevens wrote about the same time. "Anecdote of the Abnormal" (*OP* 23–24) begins by observing that, in nature, ordinary things sometimes assume an extraordinary aspect. There are regions, for example, where the grass has a "pale, Italianate sheen" not seen on ordinary grass. Corresponding to such privileged natural regions is the moral sphere Crispin longs to inhabit:

> Crispin-valet, Crispin-saint!
> The exhausted realist beholds
> His tattered manikin arise,
> Tuck in the straw,
> And stalk the skies.

Were Crispin ever to transcend his role as clown (or valet of French comedy), he would become, not the patron saint of shoemakers, but another *Harmonium* persona not considered thus far—Hoon of "Tea at the Palaz of Hoon" (1921). This regal figure, of all Stevens' early protagonists the one least qualified by irony, stalks the rarified aether of *la poésie pure*—an aesthetic program which also amounts to a mythology of self and world. Without a visit to Hoon in his palaz, one will not appreciate how Stevens' poems of the thirties, though they are not intimately autobiographical, might nevertheless be said to contain and discourse of himself alone.

· 4 ·

Pure Poet

In December 1936, Stevens received a letter from Stevens T. Mason, a Detroit lawyer who, like Judge Powell, occasionally handled surety claims for Stevens and knew him as poet as well as businessman. Mason was frankly perplexed. He reported that he and his wife had read the recently published *Owl's Clover* and had enjoyed it "as a piece of music or a lovely picture."[1] Only when he read Eda Lou Walton's review of the book in the *New York Times* did he glimpse what he took to be its "real meaning." He wondered if he were "hopelessly dumb" or if others had also required an explanation of the poem.

Readers who have shared Mason's confusion when confronted with *Owl's Clover*—and this category would exclude few who have taken it up since 1936—will be interested in Stevens' reply. "It is not possible," he began,

> to produce the music and imagery of poetry (at least, it is not possible for me), and at the same time to define the underlying idea with the clarity of a piece of chalk defining things on a blackboard. There are certain subjects, themselves musical and indefinite, of which this is not true. Unfortunately, however, those are not permissible subjects now-a-days: I don't mean to say permissible in the sense of permissible from the point of view of convention; I mean that we are just not interested in such subjects. Everything is overwhelmingly real now-a-days; and accordingly we are interested in reality.

Like a snapshot, this passage captures Stevens in a ges-

1. Letter of 8 Dec. 1936; reprinted, together with Stevens' reply of 10 Dec., in the *Wallace Stevens Journal* 4 (1980): 34–36.

ture at once characteristic and timely. Characteristically, he gives more weight to the music and imagery of his poems than to their ideas. Doubtless recalling his *Harmonium* period, he says there was a time when the poet with a predilection for music and image could choose matter congenial to his manner. For such a poet, the Depression brought a dislocation of sensibility. Unwilling to abandon his usual manner, he felt obliged—and not merely by an external pressure like literary convention—to address more "realistic" matter. The result was a book like *Owl's Clover*, in which, as Stevens went on to tell Mason, "one's real subject . . . is not the nominal subject but the poetic subject." The reader attuned to the nominal subject will see one thing in such a poem; the reader attuned to the poetic subject will see another. Both Mason and Walton had read the poem correctly, Stevens told his correspondent, for "a poem consists of all the constructions that can be placed upon it."

This was a stiff dose of poetic and critical theory for a short letter. Stevens admitted that he was particularly full of his subject, as he had lectured on it a few days previously at Harvard. Since he could not repeat the lecture for Mason's benefit, he recommended a book that would, he said, make a "complete poetic reader" of him—John Sparrow's *Sense and Poetry: Essays on the Place of Meaning in Contemporary Verse* (1934).[2] Though Stevens never cites Sparrow in his Harvard lecture, he apparently found much in *Sense and Poetry* to confirm, perhaps even to augment, his own argument.

Sparrow attempted in his collection of essays to define what he regarded as the emerging aesthetic of modern literature. As he saw it, writers of the day were no longer trying to imitate, criticize, or provide an escape from life; instead, the best of them sought to reproduce as fully as possible the "cultivated modern consciousness." Since the modern consciousness embraces more than discursive rea-

2. Published the same year in London by Constable and Company and in New Haven by the Yale University Press. In the following paragraphs, all direct quotations are from the "Introduction," pp. ix–xxiii.

son, its literature contains much that is illogical and even
unintelligible. In form, it is often as shapeless as consciousness itself. Of the influences which had done the most to
make literature what it was in 1934, Sparrow singled out
the psychologists' forays into the subconscious mind and
the experiments in poetic suggestion undertaken by Mallarmé and Rimbaud. The behaviorist school of criticism
further vindicated modern literary practice. Regarding all
"acts of the mind" (the phrase is one Stevens appropriated
some years later, in "Of Modern Poetry"), including poetic
composition, simply as physical reactions, the behaviorists
refused to adjudicate between "reasonable" and "unrea-
sonable" reactions. Sparrow aligned I. A. Richards with
the behaviorists, not in his critical assumptions, but in the
effect of his criticism. Citing Richards' distinction between
"reference" and "attitude" in poetry, he agreed with the
distinguished critic that attitude had gotten the upper
hand of late. Though Sparrow thought this a good thing
when properly managed, he deplored its consequences in
Joyce's *Finnegans Wake*.

Stevens, perhaps recalling Sparrow's assertion that in
modern literature "the irrational and the inartistic are alike
important elements," entitled his Harvard lecture "The Irrational Element in Poetry." Since he had lived through the
aesthetic revolution Sparrow described, he was able to
bring a personal perspective to it:

> When I was here at Harvard, a long time ago, it was a com-
> monplace to say that all the poetry had been written and all
> the paintings painted. It may be something of that sort that
> first interested us in the irrational. One of the great figures in
> the world since then has been Freud. While he is responsible
> for very little in poetry, as compared, for example, with his
> effect elsewhere, he has given the irrational a legitimacy that
> it never had before. More portentous influences have been
> Mallarmé and Rimbaud. (*OP* 218–29)

For the poet as for the psychologist and philosopher,
the irrational seemed a spacious new frontier. Like all frontiers, however, it has inflexible laws of its own, operating

in this case below the level of conscious control. Stevens both echoes the behaviorist view and entertains the possibility of a lapse in its rigor when he says, "If each of us is a biological mechanism, each poet is a poetic mechanism. To the extent that what he produces is mechanical: that is to say, beyond his power to change, it is irrational. Perhaps I do not mean wholly beyond his power to change, for he might, by an effort of the will, change it." Stevens goes on to say that the poet is impelled by irrational forces to choose a given subject and to adopt a given attitude toward it. Consequently,

> One is always writing about two things at the same time in poetry and it is this that produces the tension characteristic of poetry. One is the true subject and the other is the poetry of the subject. . . . In a poet who makes the true subject paramount and who merely embellishes it, the subject is constant and the development orderly. If the poetry of the subject is paramount, the true subject is not constant nor its development orderly. This is true in the case of Proust and Joyce, for example, in modern prose.

After thus restating Richards' distinction between reference and attitude in his own terms and concurring with Sparrow as to the formal consequences of a shift toward attitude, Stevens takes up the more fundamental question: why does one write poetry in the first place? He chooses to address this question in connection with the critical debate over *la poésie pure* which had only recently subsided in France.[3] At the center of the controversy was the Abbé Henri Brémond, to whose position Sparrow devotes the better part of a chapter in *Sense and Poetry*. The Abbé Brémond regarded poetry as a kind of prayer, which raises the soul to God by mysterious means having little to do

3. For an illuminating discussion of the French debate and Stevens' use of Croce in resolving some of the aesthetic issues it raised, see A. Walton Litz, "Wallace Stevens' Defense of Poetry: *La poésie pure*, the New Romantic, and the Pressure of Reality," in *Romantic and Modern*, ed. George Bornstein (Pittsburgh: University of Pittsburgh Press, 1977), pp. 111–32.

with the discursive content of the language. Though Stevens cannot accept the religious element in this notion, he uses it as a stalking horse to approach his own view of poetry, a view that might have seemed excessively mystical without Brémond's more extreme version. According to Stevens, one writes poetry not to find God but to find "the good which, in the Platonic sense, is synonymous with God."

Since even the Abbé Brémond had to admit that an absolutely pure poetry cannot be, Stevens is willing to settle for a few impurities in his secular ideal. While waiting for poetry to approach the condition of music, we will have to content ourselves with poems in which the nominal subject—a duck on a pond, for example, or the wind on a winter night—is subordinate to the poetry of the subject. Stevens has more to say about such poetry in his lecture, and especially about its role during an uncongenial period like the thirties. But without some sense of pure poetry as he practiced it prior to his lecture, one will miss both the polemical aim of "The Irrational Element in Poetry" and its personal significance for Stevens. The better to appreciate these dimensions of the lecture, we need to glance back at some of the poems he wrote during his *Harmonium* period, a time when, he later recalled, he "believed" in pure poetry (*L* 288).

Much as the French Parnassians had rebelled against the didactic and utilitarian poetry of their day, and the English Decadents against the high-minded seriousness of theirs, Stevens fled the genteel tradition that still held sway in Cambridge during his college years, notwithstanding the efforts of Santayana and other Harvard poets. The extreme attenuation of his 1908 and 1909 poems for Elsie, of "Carnet de Voyage" (1914), and even of *Harmonium* verses like "Tea," reflects his early horror of anything approaching solemn statement. When he did address more serious topics, as in "Sunday Morning," "Peter Quince at the Clavier," and "Le Monocle de Mon Oncle," he resorted to a sort of ventriloquism, using the aesthetic dandy, the clown, or another persona as his dummy. As an apprentice in the literary workshop of the late nineteenth century, Stevens had at his command three other tools of use to the pure poet—naturalism, impressionism, and symbolism. A fourth, imagism, was being forged even as he wrote the first poems of *Harmonium*.

One may not expect to find naturalism, a technique employed chiefly by writers of prose fiction, under the aegis of pure poetry. Since naturalism stresses reference over attitude, it would seem the very opposite of pure poetry; but in its effort to report the facts objectively, it equally eschews didacticism. When George Moore compiled his *Anthology of Pure Poetry* (1925), he defined pure poetry almost naturalistically as "something that the poet creates outside of his own personality," something that "contains no hint of subjectivity."[4] Though Stevens never assumed the full philosophical burden of literary Naturalism, with its materialistic determinism and its demotion of man, as Zola put it, from "l'homme métaphysique" to "l'homme physiologique,"[5] he did suggest in "The Snow Man" (1921) how the naturalistic outlook differs from the romantic. The romantic strategy had been to consummate at least temporary union with nature, the Emersonian Not-Me, by means of anthropomorphic fictions. Hence in the 1800 preface to *Lyrical Ballads* Wordsworth defined the poet as one who delights "to contemplate similar volitions and passions as manifested in the goings-on of the universe, and . . . to create them where he does not find them."[6] The speaker of "The Snow Man" is in this sense a romantic, for he entertains pathetic analogies—hears misery in the sound of the wind, for example—that are lost upon the

4. New York: Boni and Liveright, pp. 34–35.

5. "Le Roman expérimental," *Oeuvres complètes*, ed. Eugène Fasquelle, XXXVI (Paris: François Bernouard, 1928), 50.

6. *The Poetical Works of William Wordsworth*, ed. Ernest de Selincourt, 2nd ed., II (Oxford: Clarendon, 1952), 393.

snow man's "mind of winter." The snow man is incapable of pathos because he is all snow and no man. This limitation is of course his virtue: he is better qualified than the speaker of the poem to record objectively the scene before him, the "Nothing that is not there and the nothing that is."

What Wordsworth called "similar volitions and passions" in the"goings-on of the universe" are pointedly excluded from Stevens' "The Death of a Soldier" (1918). Like "The Snow Man," this poem likens a human experience to a season of the year. It does not, however, imply a sympathetic relation between the two. The soldier dies as the wind dies in autumn, his death affecting the course of the world as little as the terrestrial stillness of autumn affects the clouds in the sky; both world and clouds "go, nevertheless, / In their direction."[7] This brief elegy is one of the few poems Stevens wrote from the snow man's point of view, perhaps for the reason given in the last stanza of "The Snow Man": to behold nothing that is not there, the snow man must be "nothing himself." He is the sum of his impressions, identical, in this instance, with the nothing he does behold. His is the Lockean mind so detested by those laureates of the active soul, Coleridge and Emerson. On reading "The Snow Man," one begins to understand what Yeats, who numbered himself among the last Romantics, meant when he sadly conceded in 1931 that "the romantic movement, with its turbulent heroism, its self-assertion, is over, superseded by a new naturalism that leaves man helpless before the contents of his own mind."[8]

Akin to naturalism, inasmuch as it too left little room for heroic self-assertion and abandoned the poet to the con-

7. Earth-sky juxtapositions are common in the literature of World War I, as Paul Fussell points out in *The Great War and Modern Memory* (New York: Oxford University Press, 1975), pp. 51–63. Usually, however, the writer places the details of battle against a Ruskinian sunrise or sunset to achieve an ironic effect.

8. "Introduction" to J. M. Hone and M. M. Rossi, *Bishop Berkeley* (London: Faber, 1931), p. xxiii.

tents of his own mind, was the technique of impression-ism. Though often linked with symbolism and practiced on occasion by poets of the Symbolist school, impression-ism set itself a different objective. Whereas the Symbolist endeavored to construct a Jacob's ladder of suggestive and interrelated images leading to an ideal realm, the Impres-sionist tried to see life, not steadily or whole, but as accu-rately as possible in a given moment. Both strategies sought, Arthur Symons maintained, to convey the truth—symbolism the truth of the spiritual eye, impressionism the truth of the physical eye.[9] It was the latter that Symons tried to communicate in his impressionistic sketch "On the Beach," from the sequence entitled "At Dieppe":

> Night, a grey sky, a ghostly sea,
> The soft beginning of the rain;
> Black on the horizon, sails that wane
> Into the distance mistily.
>
> The tide is rising, I can hear
> The soft roar broadening far along;
> It cries and murmurs in my ear
> A sleepy old forgotten song.
>
> Softly the stealthy night descends,
> The black sails fade into the sky:
> Is not this, where the sea-line ends,
> The shore-line of infinity?
>
> I cannot think or dream; the grey
> Unending waste of sea and night,
> Dull, impotently infinite,
> Blots out the very hope of day.[10]

Beginning with elliptical notations of scene in the first stanza, the poem moves toward the feeble flight of meta-physical wit which concludes the third stanza. To pursue this flight beyond the sea-line would be to enter the realm of symbol. This adventure Symons declines, resigning himself to the impotent infinity of sea and mist that

9. "The Decadent Movement in Literature," p. 859.
10. *Poems by Arthur Symons* (New York: John Lane, 1921), I: 16.

stretches before the physical eye. Taking his cue from the scene, he progressively loses his capacity for integrity and self-definition, becoming at last, like Stevens' snow man, the nothing that is there.

"On the Beach" is the kind of poem Hugh Selwyn Mauberley might have written just prior to his final disintegration, which suggests that Pound's poem is as much an indictment of impressionism as it is of the "hedonistic" Paterian consciousness. Indeed, when Pater defined aesthetic criticism in his preface to *Studies in the History of the Renaissance* he simultaneously laid down the criteria of impressionistic criticism. What Pound found distasteful in aestheticism and impressionism—not to mention naturalism—was their passive attitude before the object, an attitude that could only produce, he thought, a mimetic art. "There are two opposed ways of thinking of a man," Pound wrote in 1914: "firstly, you may think of him as that toward which perception moves, as the toy of circumstance, as the plastic substance *receiving* impressions; secondly, you may think of him as directing a certain fluid force against circumstance, as *conceiving* instead of merely reflecting and observing."[11] Pound believed that these different views of perception would translate into different artistic objectives, with the receptive man seeking to "render" impressions and the conceptive man seeking to "present" an image.

Pound's opinion aside, literary impressionism was in generally good repute while Stevens was writing *Harmonium*, and boasted practitioners like Ford Madox Ford and Conrad Aiken. As with naturalism, however, it was a technique Stevens used only infrequently. *Carlos among the Candles* features an impressionistic experiment which has already been discussed, and another appears in *Bowl, Cat and Broomstick*, where Bowl reads Claire Dupray's "Le Bou-

11. "Vorticism," *Fortnightly Review*, 1 Sept. 1914, pp. 467–68; reprinted in *Gaudier-Brzeska: A Memoir* (New York: New Directions, 1960), pp. 81–94.

quet," a poem consisting of nothing more than the names of colors. "You read these rapidly," Bowl explains, "and so produce in the mind a visual impression like that produced by the actual sight of dahlias" (*PEM* 31). The experiment miscarries when Broomstick, hearing the word "white," is diverted from the dahlias to the vase, and so loses the picture altogether.

In one of his last lectures, Stevens would distinguish between "sensibility" and "imagination" in a way that recalls Pound's distinction between the receptive mind and the conceptive (*NA* 163–65). That he regarded the mere rendering of an object or scene as imaginative failure even in the early poetry is apparent in "Metaphors of a Magnifico" (1918). The title is ironic, for there is little of metaphor in the magnifico's perceptions. The poem recreates, instead, an impressionistic nightmare in which the meaning of a particular experience will not declare itself because it cannot be related to any other experience. The poem's humorously self-important persona does discriminate between an event as experienced and the same event as seen by a disinterested onlooker. To each of twenty men, there is one bridge and one village; hence their combined inventory of the scene would include twenty bridges and twenty villages. To the distant onlooker, the men appear to move as a single man across a single bridge into a single village. But the magnifico wants more than perceptual nicety; he wants the scene to declare its "meaning." Instead of metaphor, which would relate the present scene to a similar past experience, he gets tautology: twenty men crossing a bridge into a village are—here he pauses, awaiting a metaphor that never comes—twenty men crossing a bridge into a village. Since the magnifico cannot shape the scene by means of imagination, he must suffer his sensibility to be shaped by the scene. If there is any "poetry of the subject" in this poem, it resides not in the magnifico's purely referential statements but in Stevens' skillful manner of dramatizing their inadequacy.

Beginning where "Metaphors of a Magnifico" leaves off, "Of the Surface of Things" (1919) translates its nominal subject into the realm of pure poetry. The first stanza takes the speaker from a purely interior world to an outer world, where he describes the surface of things:

> In my room, the world is beyond my understanding;
> But when I walk I see that it consists of three or four hills and
>   a cloud.

This description does not allow him to approach any closer to "understanding" than the magnifico had come to "meaning." Understanding begins on a "balcony" between the inner and outer worlds, with a poetic simile:

> From my balcony, I survey the yellow air,
> Reading where I have written,
> "The spring is like a belle undressing."

The phrase "yellow air" suggests that the speaker has already begun to penetrate the surface of things. His momentum carries him to an "understanding" he can express only by means of the most extravagant metaphor:

> The gold tree is blue.
> The singer has pulled his cloak over his head.
> The moon is in the folds of the cloak.

The tree in its spring foliage is blue by virtue of the same imaginative liberty that permits yellow air. By reading the last stanza against the first, one can infer that the "cloak" is probably the cloud and the "singer" one of the hills. Compared with the spring-as-belle simile which sponsors these metaphors, they are connected more tenuously to their referents, hence are more expressive and original.

"Of the Surface of Things" allows the reader to watch Stevens as he proceeds from reference to attitude, from journalistic notation to pure poetry. In this respect it is unlike the many *Harmonium* poems that find him already ensconced on his "balcony." The reader determined to "understand" such a poem, in the sense of discovering its discursive meaning or the structure of its imagery, must recover the analogy, the "x resembles y," which first set the poem in motion. In Stevens' "The Paltry Nude Starts on a Spring Voyage"(1919), for example, the paltry nude is never identified in so many words as the spring sun; this must be inferred from her "archaic" status, from her noiseless traverse of the sea, from her cloud-touching height, from certain points of comparison with the "goldener nude" of summer. Another reader might infer a wave or the spring season generally, rather than the spring sun. This is because the subject of the poem's extended metaphor is all but tacit; the reader must interpret the predicate, "Venus."

Does it matter that, in a poem like "The Paltry Nude," one cannot specify more precisely the referent of the controlling image? Stevens did not think so, and told a correspondent in 1936 that there is a point at which intelligence destroys poetry (L 305). Like other poets of his generation, he had learned from the French Symbolists to cultivate mystery and suggestiveness as dimensions of meaning. Mallarmé, trying to distinguish the Symbolist strategy from the Parnassian, told an interviewer in 1891,

> The Parnassians take something in its entirety and simply exhibit it; in so doing, they fall short of mystery; they fail to give our minds that exquisite joy which consists of believing that we are creating something. To *name* an object is largely to destroy poetic enjoyment, which comes from gradual divination. The ideal is to *suggest* the object. It is the perfect use of this mystery which constitutes symbol. An object must be gradually evoked in order to show a state of soul; or else, choose an object and from it elicit a state of soul by means of a series of decodings.[12]

Following Mallarmé's prescription, "The Paltry Nude Starts on a Spring Voyage" invites the reader to divine the

12. "The Evolution of Literature," in *Mallarmé: Selected Prose Poems, Essays, and Letters*, trans. Bradford Cook (Baltimore: Johns Hopkins University Press, 1956), p. 21.

sun behind the nude and so take part in the creative process. The poem succeeds for the reader if he comes gradually to feel the "paltriness" or dilute quality of the early spring sunshine, especially when compared with the lustier "brine and bellowing" of the sea. Grander "states of soul" there may be, but this is at least the equal of those evoked in other poems where Stevens uses a symbol to invest a landscape with his feeling for it—"Infanta Marina" (1921), "The Bird with the Coppery, Keen Claws" (1921), and "The Public Square" (1923).

Of Mallarmé's alternative strategy, choosing an object and from it eliciting a state of soul by means of a series of "decodings," one finds an almost schematic example in Stevens' "Sea Surface Full of Clouds" (1924). In this case, the subject of the poem is known at the outset; all five sections describe atmospheric and tonal variations in the ocean and in the sky as reflected in the ocean's surface. The rhetorical strategy is also identical in each of the stanzas: the quality of light as it strikes the deck of an ocean liner is captured in an expressive image; the mood of the ocean is suggested; the nature of the perceiving consciousness is called into question; the perceiving consciousness identifies itself in French; and the reflections of the clouds moving upon the ocean surface are described. Despite their shared subject and approach, however, the five sections recreate different states of soul. The difference is readily seen when parallel phrases from any two sections are set beside each other and the key words emphasized— as they are here, for Sections I and V:

I	V
summer hued the deck	day / Came, *bowing* and *voluble* . . . / Good *clown*
rosy chocolate	Chinese chocolate
gilt umbrellas	*large* umbrellas
Paradisal green	*motley* green

perplexed machine	*obese* machine
like *limpid* water lay	perfected in *indolence*
evolved the moving blooms	Beheld the sovereign clouds as *jugglery*
Diffusing *balm* in that Pacific *calm*	the sea as *turquoise-turbaned Sambo*, neat / At tossing saucers

The first section of "Sea Surface" presents a scene of unspoiled innocence and serenity, while the last evokes the noisy, contrived high spirits of a carnival.

Reversing Carlos' procedure of deriving a self from the perceived world, each section then attempts to identify the self or state of soul which informs the perception:

I

Who, then, evolved the sea-blooms from the clouds
Diffusing balm in that Pacific calm?
C'était mon enfant, mon bijou, mon âme.

V

What pistache one, ingenious and droll,
Beheld the sovereign clouds as jugglery

And the sea as turquoise-turbaned Sambo, neat
At tossing saucers—cloudy-conjuring sea?
C'était mon esprit bâtard, l'ignominie.

The perceiving self implicit in the Eden of Section I is itself an unspoiled jewel; the self which perceives the circus of Section V is of dubious pedigree, a *bâtard* rather than an *enfant*.

Of course, this schematic reading of "Sea Surface" runs counter to the spirit in which it and most pure poetry was written. When a Yale undergraduate sent Stevens a copy of a thematic analysis of the poem he had written, Stevens protested,

> You appear to regard this, or some substitute for it, as giving the poem a validity that it would not possess as pure poetry.
> As a matter of fact, from my point of view, the quality called poetry is quite as precious as meaning. . . . If the purity

of a poem is a question not of the detachment of the poem but of the detachment that it produces in the reader, it is obvious that the repetition of a theme and the long-drawn-out rhythm that results from the repetition are merely mechanisms. But this again gets one into a lot of theory. (*L* 389–90)

Stevens did not want to encourage the excessive intellectualization he thought inimical to pure poetry by going further into "theory." But his comments indicate that he had well-defined aesthetic objectives. Like Mallarmé, he understood that poems are made of words, not ideas, and he tried to choose words which conduct the reader into that "absence in reality" (*CP* 176)—that interval, so to speak—between the ideas and things denoted literally. "Sea Surface" detaches one from a too-precise sense of its subject partly by means of its imagery. Pressed to define the phrase "Chinese chocolate" in Section V, few readers would hit upon the image Stevens intended: a large Chinese holding an incongruously small cup of chocolate (*L* 389). The extreme compression of the image gives it a purely suggestive quality that it shares with "porcelain chocolate," "obese machine," and other images in the poem. Similarly, the repetitious structure and rhythm of the poem mesmerize, even as they pretend to satisfy, one's demand for orderly development. Finally, just as one is ready to seize the key to a given section, a foreign language baffles and redirects the quest for meaning; it is to be found, not in translation, but in the sound of the words.

I have dwelt at some length on "Sea Surface Full of Clouds" because it illustrates what I take to be the theory informing better and subtler poems like "Thirteen Ways of Looking at a Blackbird" (1917), "Domination of Black" (1916), and "The Emperor of Ice-Cream" (1922). The first of these is, as Stevens remarked, a collection of "sensations" involving a blackbird or blackbirds (*L* 251). One might regard the poem's thirteen stanzas not so much as perspectives, as "ways of looking at" the blackbird, but as Mallarméan decodings calculated to elicit states of soul.

Each stanza has its peculiar state of soul—Stevens characterized the twelfth and thirteenth as, respectively, "the
compulsion . . . back of the things that we do" and "de-
spair" (*L* 340)—and the thirteen combine to produce another and more complex state, one in which fear mingles
with fascination, delight with foreboding.

From that ominous final stanza of "Thirteen Ways of
Looking at a Blackbird"—

> It was evening all afternoon.
> It was snowing
> And it was going to snow.
> The blackbird sat
> In the cedar-limbs—

two very different but equally "pure" *Harmonium* poems
take their departure: "Domination of Black" and "The Emperor of Ice-Cream." In the first of these, peacocks have
supplanted the more commonplace blackbirds and hemlocks have replaced the cedars. Moreover, the birds and
trees stand in a different relation to each other. The speaker
of "Domination of Black" associates the peacocks' tails
with other cheerful things—the flames turning in the fire-
place and colored leaves turning in the wind. Sensibly an-
tagonistic to these is the color of the hemlocks, the color of
night itself. On the merely mundane scale, this blackness
is not particularly frightening; but if the turning leaves
have their counterpart in the gathering planets, might not
the hemlocks have theirs as well, in a cosmic blackness?
Confronting such a threat, the speaker identifies with the
peacocks. These verses, or "turnings," with their brightly
revolving images and repetitive returns of phrase, "Like
the leaves themselves / Turning in the wind," are his cry of
protest.

"Domination of Black" is staged in the universe most
congenial to the Symbolist, a universe in which everything
is related to everything else in an intricate series of corre-
spondences. To pass through such a world, Baudelaire said

in his poem "Correspondances," is to pass through "forêts de symboles," none of them quite unfamiliar for all their mystery. Though Stevens' peacock is a bird of a different feather from the swan favored by Baudelaire and Mallarmé, it affords the same touch of exoticism. Like the Symbolists, Stevens "decoded" his symbol so as to divert the reader from his quest for discursive meaning. "I am sorry," he replied when asked to explain "Domination of Black," "that a poem of this sort has to contain any ideas at all, because its sole purpose is to fill the mind with the images & sounds that it contains. A mind that examines such a poem for its prose contents gets absolutely nothing from it" (L 251).

That Stevens could write a pure poem without recourse to Symbolist metaphysics or exoticism is brilliantly demonstrated in a piece like "The Emperor of Ice-Cream." Here, the impending night of "Thirteen Ways of Looking at a Blackbird" and "Domination of Black" has descended, quenching not only the woman's life but also any possibility of protest. Instead, the poem affixes its relentless beam upon the common, even repellent details of the woman's room and her corpse. In a voice that suggests the sideshow barker rather than the unctuous minister or funeral director, the speaker of the poem insists that the naturalistic "be" replace the religious or romantic "seem." He calls for a wake devoid of pomp and ceremony; the mourners (or are they celebrants?) are to wear their workaday clothes and one of them, the muscular cigar maker, will serve ice cream—a symbol not only of life's ephemeral pleasures but also, as Stevens told R. P. Blackmur, "of the materialism or realism proper to a refugee from the imagination."[13]

Not that "The Emperor of Ice-Cream" is an unimaginative poem. Though Stevens spoke of its "deliberately commonplace costume" when he chose it as his favorite in

13. Letter of 16 Nov. 1931; reprinted with an introduction by Holly Stevens in "Flux²," *Southern Review* 15 (1979): 773–74.

1933, he also said that it seemed to him to contain something of the "essential gaudiness" of poetry (*L* 263). These remarks appear contradictory until one remembers that Stevens, in keeping with a fundamental precept of pure poetry, typically inverted the usual hierarchy of subject and style. Since poetry is the true subject of a pure poem (*L* 297, *CP* 176), the ostensible subject is, relatively speaking, mere "costume." Such costume is not dispensable, however. "Poetry is like anything else," Stevens told Latimer; "it cannot be made suddenly to drop all its rags and stand out naked, fully disclosed" (*L* 303). Consequently, though the "essential gaudiness" of "The Emperor of Ice-Cream" lies in its expressive diction and oratorical flair, "The Emperor" does have clothes: the woman's wake. Because its costume is so prosaic—as compared, for example, with "Domination of Black"—the poem is a triumph of attitude over reference. Ostensibly an endorsement of "be," it testifies still more eloquently to the power of "seem." One is not surprised to learn that Stevens, when he tried to recall the inception of the poem years later, could remember the "state of mind" which gave rise to it but not the external occasion (*L* 264).

Consistent with his view of other pure poems, Stevens denied that the "point" or argument of "The Emperor of Ice-Cream" is equivalent to its meaning (*L* 500). In letters to both Blackmur and Leonard van Geyzel, he regretted the damage done to this poem by explanation. "Nothing has made me unhappier," he told Blackmur in 1931, "than the fact that I have in the past on one or two occasions explained."[14] Indeed he had, but rarely without some hand-wringing. Typical of these occasions is a letter he sent in 1928 to an editor who had included two of his poems in an anthology and sought elucidation of other *Harmonium* pieces. "It may or may not be like converting a piece of mysticism into a piece of logic," Stevens wrote by way of

14. "Flux²," p. 774.

preface to his comments. "But the feeling is much the same" (L 250). Like a repentant sinner who finds himself lapsing into old vices, he guiltily concluded the letter by protesting, "It is shocking to have to say this sort of thing. Please destroy these notes. I don't mind your saying what I have said here. But I don't want you to quote me. No more explanations."

Stevens disliked explaining because he feared that readers would lose interest in poems they could comprehend fully (L 294, 346). It was not a question of mystification. Rather, he understood that pure poetry succeeds when it detaches the reader from reason and reality and lifts him by the most tenuous of threads to another plane of experience. To explain is to make the reader overly conscious of those filaments and so to subvert their function. When that happens, something more valuable than understanding is lost, or so Stevens implied by a pair of rhetorical questions in "The Irrational Element in Poetry": "When we find in poetry that which gives us a momentary existence on an exquisite plane, is it necessary to ask the meaning of the poem? If the poem had a meaning and if its explanation destroyed the illusion, should we have gained or lost?" (OP 223).

We should obviously have lost, Stevens believed; and we would not be the only losers, for explanation redounds upon the explainer. "[T]here is a kind of secrecy between the poet and his poems," he told one correspondent, "which, once violated, affects the integrity of the poet" (L 361). On this occasion as on so many others, he denounced explanations in the course of explaining, an irony that must have left him feeling further compromised. Poetry was, after all, his piety; it was, to appropriate the words of Hemingway's Brett Ashley, what he had instead of God. Writing to Leonard van Geyzel about "The Emperor of Ice-Cream," Stevens did not hesitate to describe his personal investment in poetry as a form of belief. Conceding that others might benefit from analyzing the poem, he shied away from doing so himself. "You examine what you do as you go along," he said, "and you examine it afterwards, yet there is a point at which you are bound to stop. If you do not stop, you soon become like anyone else who no longer has anything in which to believe. If you don't believe in poetry, you cannot write it" (L 500).

Why, one wonders at this point, did Stevens not forswear explanations altogether if he thought them insidious to his poetry and his integrity as a poet? He may have found it difficult to withhold helpful information from correspondents like Ronald Lane Latimer and Hi Simons, who served him well as publisher and bibliographer-critic, respectively, and whom he could trust to receive his comments in the proper spirit. He may also have realized that his poems had begun to reach a larger audience, one unfamiliar with the conventions of pure poetry. This had not been a problem for the first readers of his poems, the people who edited and subscribed to magazines like *Trend*, *Rogue*, and *Others*. These immediately recognized him as a pure poet—indeed as one of the purest of the pure, a poet on the order of that rarified Rhymer, Richard Le Gallienne. Hence the whimsical tribute *Rogue* paid Stevens in the "Letters Not Yet Received" department of its first number:

> Dear Rogue:
> I never knew there was such a thing as poetry before, I just thought it was something we all were doing. However, Wallace Stevens has shown us. I am going to take up painting.
> > Undeniably,
> > Richard Sir Valliene[15]

Outside the *Trend-Rogue-Others* coterie, Stevens' poems fell into the hands of readers uninitiated in the aims and purposes of pure poetry or hostile to them. To these, his work seemed willfully obscure, mannered, and destitute of meaning. A legendary exchange between Stevens and Robert Frost suggests that the pure poet could not be sure

15. *Rogue*, 15 Mar. 1915, p. 3.

of a sympathetic hearing even from fellow poets. In one version of the story, Frost is supposed to have accused Stevens of lacking a subject; in another, he is said to have chided Stevens for writing "bric-a-brac."[16] In either version, Frost was simply repeating in friendly malice the charge many critics had laid at Stevens' door—that the clothes had no emperor, that his verse was merely "decorative." This epithet continued to pursue him like an old tin can tied to his ankle, and it was useless for him to protest, as he sometimes did, that one man's decoration is another's "essential gaudiness."

The conventions of pure poetry receded further from sight as the teens and twenties gave way to the thirties. "Everyone realizes," Stevens remarked to Latimer in 1936, "that now-a-days we are a good deal more exacting about the meaning of poetry than we used to be" (*L* 305). Stevens' "everyone" does not include readers who never knew a poetry in which meaning was not paramount, and those readers were understandably annoyed at what they took to be gratuitous obfuscations of meaning in his work, beginning with the arcane titles. During the *fin de siècle*, when formalistic titles were fashionable, Whistler could coax a knowing smile from anyone versed in contemporary art by a display of outrage at the hapless critic who quibbled with the literal accuracy of his caption for "Symphony in White No. III": *"Bon Dieu!* did this wise person expect white hair and chalked faces? And does he then, in his astounding consequence, believe that a symphony in F contains no other note, but shall be a continued repetition of F, F, F?"[17] By contrast, Stevens was almost apologetic when explaining the significance of the title of "The Comedian as the Letter C" in 1935. "When I wrote that poem," he said, "subject was not quite what it is today, and

16. Morse, p. 200; and Lawrance Thompson, *Robert Frost: The Years of Triumph* (New York: Rinehart, 1970), p. 666.

17. *The Gentle Art of Making Enemies* (1890; reprinted New York: Putnam, 1923), p. 45.

I suppose that I ought to confess that by the letter C I meant the sound of the letter C; what was in my mind was to play on that sound throughout the poem. While the sound of that letter has more or less variety, and includes, for instance, K and S, all its shades may be said to have a comic aspect. Consequently, the letter C is a comedian" (L 294).

Stevens felt, then, some obligation to explain his aesthetic objectives if not the meaning of a particular phrase or image. When a reader approached his poetry with improper expectations, he tried rather to modify than to gratify those expectations. He did not find it necessary, at first, to draft a literary manifesto preparing the way for his poems, since he worked within aesthetic programs—Naturalism, Impressionism, and especially Symbolism—that were well defined and widely disseminated by the turn of the century. He also benefited to some extent from the most widely publicized literary experiment of the early twentieth century, Imagism, even though his work did not appear in any of the Imagist anthologies.

Stevens seems, in fact, to have regarded Imagism as the most recent variety of pure poetry. When Latimer asked him in 1935 whether he accepted "the common opinion" that his verse was "essentially decorative," he replied, ". . . I was on the point of saying that I did not agree with the opinion that my verse is decorative, when I remembered that when HARMONIUM was in the making there was a time when I liked the idea of images and images alone, or images and the music of verse together. I then believed in *pure poetry*, as it was called" (L 288). Several weeks later, while explaining to Latimer why he had recently begun to introduce "impurities" into his poetry, Stevens used the terms "Imagism" and "pure poetry" interchangeably: "Imagism was a mild rebellion against didacticism. However, you will find that any continued reading of pure poetry is rather baffling" (L 302).

Though Stevens associated himself with Imagism

chiefly in its flight from the didactic, he shared other affinities with the movement as well. Like Pound, H. D., and Richard Aldington, he sought a Parnassian hardness and clarity of outline in his images. He preferred the active mind and "presentation" to impressionistic rendering of an object or scene. In sympathy with Pound's prescription for "absolute rhythm," he wrote free verse rigorously disciplined to his subject and intended effect.[18] He shared the Imagists' impatience with the realm of "permanent metaphor" invoked by some Symbolists. When Pound said that the image should present not just an object but "an intellectual and emotional complex," that the image should be an equation for a "state of consciousness," he was describing Stevens' practice as well as his own.

For all these similarities, however, Stevens wrote no more than a handful of poems which fit Pound's exacting criteria. Though Pound was willing to relax his rules to accommodate the "permanent part" of Dante's *Paradiso* and the deliberate rhythms of his own "The Return," he decreed that an Imagist poem should present its intellectual and emotional complex "in an instant of time" if it is to be a work of "the first intensity." Such a poem is what he called "a form of super-position": two things are named in rapid succession, preferably without the connective "like," so as to produce an instantaneous shock of recognition. This is the moment, Pound averred, "when a thing outward and objective transforms itself, or darts into a thing inward and subjective." Modesty did not prevent him from offering his "In a Station of the Metro" as a superlative example of the genre:

The apparition of these faces in the crowd:
Petals on a wet, black bough.[19]

18. This account of Pound's theory of Imagism is based on his essays "Vorticism," already cited, and "A Few Don'ts by an Imagiste," *Poetry* 1 (1913): 200–206.
19. As Hugh Witemeyer points out in *The Poetry of Ezra Pound: Forms and Renewal, 1908–1920* (Berkeley: University of California Press, 1969), p.

Among Stevens' earliest poems is one which suggests that he was sufficiently interested in Imagism to try his hand at the form. It is called "From a Junk" (1914):

A great fish plunges in the dark,
Its fins of rutted silver; sides,
Belabored with a foamy light;
And back, brilliant with scaly salt.
It glistens in the flapping wind,
Burns there and glistens wide and wide
Under the five-horned stars of night,
In wind and wave . . . It is the moon.[20]

By comparing this poem with "In a Station of the Metro," one can see why the Imagist aesthetic program sheds little light on Stevens' poetry. "From a Junk" lapses into riddle-like flatness because its author is not really interested in producing an instantaneous effect. He would prefer that the reader come at the moon by the process Mallarmé called "gradual divination," and not require the solution provided in the final sentence. Given a few more lines in which to develop his image, Stevens might have produced the lunar equivalent of "The Paltry Nude Starts on a Spring Voyage." But even in this shorter version, "From a Junk" contains much that Pound would have dismissed as mere description.

René Taupin, in a study of the influence of French Symbolism on American poetry to which Stevens contributed a comment, concludes that the Imagist image differs from the Symbolist symbol only in being more precise.[21] Yet this difference should not be underestimated. Stevens, who found the symbol more congenial to his form of pure poetry, reflected in two notebook entries upon the inadequacy of the image:

34, "apparition" is a word of suggestion rather than presentation, recalling "Apparuit" and other poems of Pound's pre-Imagist phase.
    20. *Trend* 8 (1914): 117.
    21. *L'Influence du symbolisme français sur la poésie américaine (de 1910 à 1920)* (Paris: Honoré Champion, 1929), p. 98.

Not all objects are equal. The vice of imagism was that it did not recognize this.

The bare image and the image as a symbol are the contrast: the image without meaning and the image as meaning. When the image is used to suggest something else, it is secondary. Poetry as an imaginative thing consists of more than lies on the surface. (*OP* 161)

These adages imply what Stevens says explicitly elsewhere, that he regarded Imagism as "a phase of realism" (*OP* 257). This was certainly one way to construe Pound's assertion that "the natural object is always the *adequate* symbol." At the same time, Stevens shares Pound's distaste for using the image in a "secondary" way, to suggest "something else" allegorically or allusively. He calls for an image that is meaningful, that delves beneath the surface of things, without having to be translated into other terms.

A poem which both illustrates and embodies Stevens' theory of the image is "Earthy Anecdote" (1918). This familiar story of the bucks that clatter across Oklahoma only to be repeatedly diverted by a "firecat" is still perplexing after decades of explication, and one can sympathize with the plight of Walter Pach, Stevens' friend and an organizer of the 1913 Armory Show, when he was faced with the task of illustrating the poem for the *Modern School*. On seeing Pach's illustration, which shows fin-like mountains rising above clouds, with the sun or moon in the upper right-hand corner, Stevens objected that he intended "actual animals, not original chaos" (*L* 209).

Pach might easily have managed the actual bucks befitting an "earthy" anecdote, but what was he to do with the firecat? Years later, he sent Stevens a postcard with a photograph of a rock formation which he said might serve as an image of this fabulous beast.[22] The firecat, Pach had every zoological reason to believe, is not actual in the same sense that the bucks are actual. It seems to represent some

22. Dated 19 Mar. 1923.

obstacle, whether mountain, rock formation, oil well, prairie fire, or even—since it appears every time the bucks are active—the sun. One might explain the poem in terms of its objective, spatial relationships, in which case one would arrive at some variation on the theme of Marcel Duchamp's painting "King and Queen Surrounded by Swift Nudes": "It is a theme of motion in a frame of static entities."[23] Or one might regard the poem as an emblem of one's own engagement with this kind of poem: like the bucks, one's clattering, discursive mind swerves left or right whenever it approaches the firecat, thus duplicating the pattern of bafflement and evasion in the anecdote. The poem continues to produce its intended effect—an effect that is also its subject—as long as the firecat remains a source of perplexity. Both poem and effect come to an end when the firecat closes his bright eyes and sleeps. Like so many poems written under the aegis of pure poetry, "Earthy Anecdote" has a self-reflexive quality that lends itself to semiotic and structuralist criticism.[24]

Stevens declined to explain "Earthy Anecdote" when the editor of the *Modern School* queried him about it, though he added, in a way to tease readers ever since, that there is "a good deal of theory" behind the poem (*L* 204). This presumably distinguished "Earthy Anecdote" from the bulk of American poetry of the time, which prompted him to complain that there was "practically no aesthetic theory back of it."[25] Mindful of Stevens' care in the ordonnance of his books, the reader is tempted to regard this poem, the first he encounters on opening *Harmonium*, as a sort of theoretical preface. It is an oblique preface, just as

23. Duchamp, quoted in MacLeod, p. 34. According to MacLeod, Duchamp's "King and Queen" was completed in 1912 and exhibited throughout the decade in Walter Arensberg's apartment, where Stevens may have seen it.

24. Terrance King notes the indebtedness of structuralist theory to French Symbolism in "The Semiotic Poetry of Wallace Stevens," *Semiotica* 23 (1978): 77–98; he distinguishes, however, between Symbolist "art-about-art" and what he takes to be Stevens' "art-about-signs."

25. Letter to Ferdinand Reyher, 13 May 1921 (Maryland).

the theory is oblique. As a propagandist for a theory of poetry, Stevens was no match for Pound or Amy Lowell. He did not appear publicly in the role of apologist for his kind of poetry until he delivered his Harvard lecture in 1936, and then he approached the lectern with some trepidation (*L* 313).

During the thirties, we shall see in the next chapter, he had every reason to be diffident, for he then occupied an embattled theoretical position. Even when he was writing the poems of *Harmonium*, however, his stance was apt to be as defensive as it was assertive. "Tea at the Palaz of Hoon" (1921), first published in tandem with "The Snow Man" in *Poetry*, is a case in point. At its simplest level, the poem is another of Stevens' anecdotes of the sun. Hoon, the *héro solaire*, has exchanged his noonday white for golds and purples on reaching the end of his daily promenade. Is he less himself—that is, is he more than himself—when swathed in regal colors? A critical onlooker has apparently implied as much, prompting Hoon to protest that his splendor is not masquerade but authentic self-expression. Like the snow man, he is identical with his world; unlike that passive man of winter, he is the onlie begetter of his universe:

> . . . I was the world in which I walked, and what I saw
> Or heard or felt came not but from myself;
> And there I found myself more truly and more strange.

Since, as Stevens puts it elsewhere, "All things in the sun are sun" (*CP* 104), these lines literally describe the sun's experience of the solar system. Figuratively, they suggest the creative life of both the romantic and the pure poet. Coleridge characterized the sensibility of the former when he said in his "Dejection: An Ode" that "we receive but what we give, / And in our life alone does Nature live. . . ." Similarly, the pure poet bathes his nominal subject in the imaginative effulgence which I. A. Richards called "attitude" and Stevens called the "poetry of the subject."

Especially to the naturalistic mind, such solipsism may seem well-nigh preposterous. Stevens has anticipated this objection not only in Hoon's initially defensive stance but also in the poem's title, which reduces our audience with Hoon from an affair of state to a routine domestic ceremony. However, as is often the case in Stevens' poetry, the irony is calculated rather to reinforce than to undercut a daring proposition. He could neither live with the sublime, as Harold Bloom has remarked, nor live without it and remain a poet.[26] Properly qualified, Hoon's self-assertion would eventually afford Stevens an escape from the aesthetic impasse to which he brought Crispin in "The Comedian as the Letter C." Hoon speaks for the self Crispin thought he had left in Bordeaux, the self that is the intelligence of its soil. Where Crispin sought to find himself through identification with a region, Hoon finds himself more truly and more "strange"—the adjective recalls those "strange creatures" Stevens found in his actor's trunk (SP 166) as well as the Romantic and Decadent cult of strangeness—by applying himself to what Stevens called "the idea of pure poetry: imagination, extended beyond local consciousness, . . . an idea to be held in common by South, West, North and East" (L 370).

Accordingly, until Stevens took up his genealogical study in the early forties and began to resume the connection with his native region that had been severed by the move to New York, he found Hoon's course more congenial than Crispin's. It was hardly the course of least resistance, though critics of the thirties sometimes characterized Hoon's palaz as an ivory tower. It was here, in the "loneliest air," that Stevens meditated the significance of pure poetry until it became the "new romantic" and finally the supreme fiction.

26. *Wallace Stevens: The Poems of Our Climate* (Ithaca: Cornell University Press, 1977), p. 140.

· 5 ·

Restatement of Romance

It seems, in retrospect, as though some historical demiurge invented the Great Depression and social unrest of the thirties specifically to test the pure poet's resolve. Not that his resolve would otherwise have gone untested by pressures extrinsic to his art. Even in the twenties, readers had begun to tire of pure poetry and to demand more in the way of didactic or at least thematic content; to this chorus leftist critics and New Critics lent their very different voices in the thirties. The economic slump merely compounded what was, after all, the most irksome of the pure poet's difficulties—the problem of making a living. In the best of times, he had not the market that was open to writers of prose and the more salable kinds of verse.

When Stevens likened the position of the poet in the thirties to that of "the mystic who wishes to contemplate God in the midst of evil" (*OP* 225), he was using an analogy which had long been applied to the lot of the artist in a commercial civilization. To Yeats it had seemed supremely ironic that the poet should have to labor under Adam's curse with the rest of mankind,

> and yet
> Be thought an idler by the noisy set
> Of bankers, schoolmasters, and clergymen
> The martyrs call the world.

To discriminate between poseur and serious artist generally exceeds the capacity of the "world," the *mundus* of the Christian martyrs and ascetics. Still less can the world discern, behind the artist's often casual style of life, the near-religious devotion to craft which Lafcadio Hearn remarked in Henri Murger's *Scènes de la vie de Bohème* (1849). "Under the levity of Henri Murger's picturesque Bohemianism," Hearn observed,

> there is a serious philosophy apparent which elevates the characters of his romance to heroism. They followed one principle faithfully—so faithfully that only the strong survived the ordeal—never to abandon the pursuit of an artistic vocation for any other occupation however lucrative—not even when she remained apparently deaf and blind to her worshippers. The conditions pictured by Murger have passed away in Paris as elsewhere: the old barriers to ambition have been greatly broken down. But I think the moral remains. So long as one can live and pursue his natural vocation in art, it is a duty with him never to abandon it if he believes that he has within him the elements of final success. Every time he labours at aught that is not art, he robs the divinity of what belongs to her.[1]

Hearn, Whistler, and other enthusiasts were drawn to the Latin Quarter much as the Puritans were drawn to the American wilderness, from a conviction that there they might worship their divinity in spirit and in truth. If the bohemian was somewhat irregular in the matter of gainful employment, this was because his goddess was a jealous goddess, requiring his undistracted devotion. Of course his devotion could not be entirely undistracted, for he had to earn his daily bread. Thence arose the artist's dilemma: either he risked his divinity's ire by rendering unto Mercury some of the things that were hers, or he neglected his vigils now and then to engage in profitable pastimes unrelated to his real work.

Stevens, who read Murger during a month of "bitter *far niente*" in 1905 (*SP* 154), chose the latter course, differing from his bohemian colleagues only in the calculation and perseverance with which he pursued it; he worked to se-

1. Quoted in Albert Parry and Harry T. Moore, *Garrets and Pretenders: A History of Bohemianism in America*, rev. ed. (New York: Dover, 1960), p. 164.

cure not a week or a month free from financial anxiety, but a lifetime. He devoted the period from 1901 to 1913 almost exclusively to profane pursuits so as to make oblation fit in 1923. After *Harmonium*, he dwelled apart from the sanctuary for another decade. Though Stevens occasionally had misgivings about this strategy, he did not hesitate to recommend it to less provident souls. When it appeared that Ronald Lane Latimer would have to give up the Alcestis Press, Stevens first tried to find a job for him at the Hartford.[2] Failing that, he urged Latimer to devote himself to business for a period of twenty-five years or so to earn the means to resume the printing of fine books (*L* 320). He also advised Victor Hammer, a printer who abhorred modern technology, to swallow his pride and connect himself after retirement with a commercial printing business.[3] "While I do not mean to compare my own situation with yours," he told Hammer, "nevertheless I find that having a job is one of the best things in the world that could happen to me. It introduces discipline and regularity into one's life. I am just as free as I want to be and of course I have nothing to worry about about money."[4]

In 1952, when Stevens wrote these words, he was already two years beyond the "mandatory" age of retirement at the Hartford, he obviously appreciated the discipline and regularity of a steady job even apart from its remuneration. He sometimes went so far as to suggest that his work was itself a kind of poetry. "Poetry and surety claims aren't as unlikely a combination as they may seem," he once remarked. "There is nothing perfunctory about them, for each case is different."[5] Nor was there anything perfunctory about Stevens' approach to insurance generally, to judge from his sole published essay on the subject. En-

2. Letter from Stevens to Latimer, 8 Sept. 1936 (Chicago).
3. Letter of 27 Sept. 1951 (copy at Huntington Library).
4. Letter of 7 Jan. 1952 (copy at Huntington Library).
5. Quoted by Lewis Nichols in "Talk with Mr. Stevens," *New York Times Book Review*, 3 Oct. 1954, p. 3.

titled "Insurance and Social Change," that essay might serve as prolegomenon to any future poetry of insurance.[6] He begins the piece by hypothesizing a perfectly insured future world. A citizen of this world can, by paying a token premium on his way to work each morning, insure himself against every misfortune, from disablement to finding a worm in his lunchtime apple. Stevens then uses this utopian yardstick to measure the distance insurance had come in Italy, Germany, Russia, and England. He concludes that, in countries which had experienced rapid social change, the government had absorbed or begun to absorb the function of insurer. Stevens proves himself the poet when he objects to such nationalization on aesthetic rather than fiscal or political grounds: "Under both systems, that is to say, under both Fascist and Communist systems, the finely-tailored agent, wearing a boutonniere, gives way to the letter carrier."

When Emerson urged the American scholar to enter the marketplace if only to learn its vocabulary, he anticipated one of the minor benefits Stevens derived from his job. Titles like "Agenda" and "Memorandum" (*OP* 41, 89); words like "ward," "pandect," "entailed," "femes," "in camera," "chits," "exchequering," and "fiscs" reflect his workaday immersion in the office routine, in law and finance. Casting about for a word to designate a philosophically legitimate range of thinking, Stevens turned naturally to the insurance term "permissible" (*L* 753). Commerce between his poetic and business vocabularies went beyond the matter of diction, as we shall see in the next chapter; the legal fictions he used and interpreted daily may well have informed his notion of the poetic supreme fiction.

Nevertheless, in evaluating Stevens' remarks concern-

6. *Hartford Agent* 29 (1937): 49–50; reprinted in the *Wallace Stevens Journal* 4 (1980): 37–39.

ing the intrinsic value of his business life and its contribution to his poetry, one must not forget that these were reflections—and to some extent rationalizations—after the
fact. He initially took up law because he could not make a
living at literature, and for years regarded the nine-to-five
routine as an onerous necessity. By dint of habit and long
association with his poetic ambitions, necessity became almost a virtue, the means scarcely distinguishable from the
end. Even then, however, a substantial jolt could revive
the distinction. When his daughter Holly decided to leave
college in 1942 and find work, Stevens wrote to dissuade
her from this course. He could understand why, in a time
of uncertainty, she might want to "find herself" in a job.
"But take my word for it," he advised, "that making your
living is a waste of time. None of the great things in life
have anything to do with making your living . . ."(L 426).
In words that recall his account of the poet's vocation in
"The Irrational Element in Poetry," he urged his daughter
to stay in college, where she could use her leisure to identify and devote herself to the good in her heart.

Especially after he began to assume a more public role
in the forties, Stevens labored to span the gap between his
business and literary lives, or at least to make the gap seem
less anomalous. But he was first and foremost a pure poet,
and, as such, appreciated his means of making a living
precisely because it was so remote from the "great things
in life." Not long before his death, he told an interviewer
that if he had lived an academic life—that is, a life devoted
professionally to the "great things"—he would have had
far less reason for writing poetry.[7] Ironically for a poet
whose work the academy has always found congenial, he
was wary of professorial meddling in poetic theory and
disapproved of writers who earned their livelihood by
teaching creative writing. In poetry as in almsgiving, he

7. Quoted in Lafferty, p. 131.

thought it better for the right hand not to know what the left was doing. He feared that if the two communicated too closely, the hand that wrote the poem would be sullied by the hand that accepted the paycheck. He applied the same principle to publishing his work. Except for the very early pieces he submitted to *Poetry*, he waited for poetry editors to approach him. Consequently, all but a handful of his poems appeared in little magazines rather than the glossier periodicals offering more handsome fees. Whenever he could do so gracefully, he returned payment for his poems or applied it toward a subscription to the magazine.

An episode which took place in 1946 suggests that his pecuniary disinterest amounted to a moral scruple. That October, R. P. Blackmur, Lionel Trilling, and Malcolm Cowley drafted a letter in which they asked certain writers to name the little magazines they deemed most worthy of financial assistance. Once these were identified, they planned to investigate means of obtaining support. In a reply addressed to Blackmur, Stevens protested that the scheme was not only unfeasible but possibly also insidious. He concluded his letter by saying,

> the objects in the attic of life never seemed dearer to me than now when I see the three of you approaching them with pots of gilding. I hope you won't think that I am not interested. Personally, I have a horror of the sort of thing that is done for money. That is about all there is nowadays. It has nothing whatever to do with what means anything to me nor, I believe, to you and to the other two men who signed your letter.[8]

Blackmur then clarified the group's intentions, prompting a more conciliatory and helpful response from Stevens. The poet had been confused, he said, by their use of the phrase "little magazines" to include organs affiliated with

---

8. Letter of 4 Nov. (Princeton). In 1951, Stevens advised Richard Wilbur to stop publishing in the *New Yorker*. "If you're a poet," he earnestly told Wilbur, "you must be prepared to be poor, if that's necessary. You must be like a monk. You must sacrifice yourself to your work" (quoted in Brazeau, p. 197).

colleges and universities, such as the *Kenyon Review* and the *Sewanee Review*. The literary magazine he considered most vital was free of academic association: the *Partisan Review*. Possibly, Stevens ventured, Blackmur and his associates might enlist support for contributors to serious magazines rather than the magazines themselves, thereby preventing the bulk of the money from going to the printer. But would this scheme—or any other involving a subsidy—be in the best interest of literature or even of the writer himself? Stevens had his doubts, and returned to the theme of his previous letter:

> If one believes that the great corrupting force in literary activity in this country is that its object is to make money, the successful writers of fiction seem to support one. In the last number of Alphabet & Image it is said that Crowell-Collier print 18,000,000 magazines (not pages, but magazines) a month. I have no doubt that this makes life easy for a great many talented writers, but it must also make them very unhappy when they look back on what they have done. As a writer faces the point of honor that concerns him as a writer, he must apparently choose between starvation and that form of publishing (or being published) in which it is possible to make money. His problem is how to support himself while engaged in the most honorable capacity. There is only one answer. He must support himself in some other way.[9]

Not to seem too dogmatic, Stevens allowed that the writer might make a comfortable living even from poetry and even without publishing in Crowell magazines—*Collier's* and the *Woman's Home Companion* being a couple of the more popular ones—but only if he happened to be a national institution like Robert Frost. Then he might parlay his reputation into a college appointment and augment his book royalties with fees from readings. If Stevens thought Frost had thereby deviated from the strictly honorable course, he tactfully avoided saying so in his letter to Blackmur. For himself and most serious writers, he saw the

9. Letter of 12 Nov. (Princeton).

choice in terms as absolute as those Lafcadio Hearn had seen in Murger: "For a writer who sticks stiffly to the point of honor the choice is between starvation and making a living in something else."

During the thirties, Stevens may have felt that he had literally earned the right to be a pure poet and could literally afford to continue in this role. With an income of over seventeen thousand dollars in the mid-thirties, he was more prosperous, comparatively speaking, than he would ever be again.[10] He bought a large colonial style home on Westerly Terrace in Hartford in 1932, when the economy struck bottom, and continued to enlarge his collection of press books and fine bindings. Not all of his expendable income went to conspicuous consumption, for he also sent checks regularly to his brother during the months preceding Garrett's death in 1937. In a man known for his financial caution, this largesse suggests a sense of confirmed well-being. Stevens benefited from the relative stability of the insurance business during the Depression, and his own firm prospered better than most (see L 263, 322). Once he was promoted to a vice-presidency in 1934, he had reason to believe that he would never need to compromise his poetry merely in order to make a living.

There was but one flaw in this otherwise perfect picture: he was not writing poetry and may have begun to wonder whether he would ever write it again. In "The Sun This March" (1930), his first poem to be published since "Red Loves Kit" a half-dozen years previously, his imagination warms to life just enough to remind him how stiff and dark it has become. Like Hoon, the "turning spirit" in Stevens' earlier self, the March sun finds itself in all it surveys. But now that cold and darkness have become Stevens' accustomed elements, he can no longer identify with this earlier self; he must appeal to it as "rabbi," as an external source of spiritual strength.

10. Brazeau records Stevens' salary between 1916 and 1948 in *Parts of a World*, p. 231n. For 1954, Stevens reported a gross annual income of $26,000—just $6,000 more than he had earned in 1936.

The sun proves true savant and rabbi of Stevens' soul in "The Brave Man" (1933), published with "A Fading of the Sun" in the *Harkness Hoot*. Though still external to the self, it exorcises his midnight devils: "Fears of my bed, / Fears of life and fears of death, / Run away." Might others derive courage from the same source? Stevens, as though reproaching himself for the solipsism of "A Brave Man," seeks to allay the anxieties of his fellow man in its companion piece. But "A Fading of the Sun" is little more than a homily on the value of inner resources. In it, Stevens exhorts others to do what he apparently cannot do himself— find within themselves the kind of satisfaction no longer available in the "book" of the external world. The first of Stevens' poems to allude to the social turmoil of the thirties, "A Fading of the Sun" suggests how far he was removed from the events that agitated other writers between 1923 and 1933: the Sacco and Vanzetti and Scottsboro trials, the Harlan County coal miners' strike, Trotsky's exile, and Hitler's inauguration of the Third Reich. He had sound aesthetic reasons for omitting these events from his poems, as we shall see; but he also moved in a cloud of material comfort which few cries of distress or challenge could penetrate. That began to change early in 1934, when he was approached by a young editor seeking contributions for a new poetry magazine he was about to launch.

Ronald Lane Latimer was rewarded with a windfall of eight poems, among them "The Idea of Order at Key West." Other editors shaking the same tree since 1924 had considered themselves fortunate if they received one or at most two poems. Latimer's unusual success might be attributed partly to timing; when Stevens was especially productive he tended to give all of his manuscript poems to the first editor who knocked at his door rather than parceling them out among several callers. But there was some imponderable quality in Latimer's letters, his sole means of contact with Stevens, that apparently struck a responsive chord in the poet. Perhaps it was simply Latimer's persistent interest in his work, an interest that was to have resulted in a critical study of Stevens' poetry (*L* 359). Certainly it was to Latimer's advantage that Stevens took him for a Harvard man and one who shared his social and political views.[11] In any case, Stevens later credited Latimer with starting him on his next volume, *Ideas of Order* (*L* 359).

Ideas was already in progress before Latimer contacted him, though Stevens did not know it. He regarded the eight poems he had published since the expanded edition of *Harmonium* (1931) as "things more or less improvised" and consigned these "reliquiae" to the attic after they appeared in print (*L* 271, 272). When Latimer proposed gathering these and his more recent work into a book to be published by the Alcestis Press, Stevens assembled a slender manuscript but found the collection "low and colorless" in tone (*L* 273). Usually, he allowed his poems to rise spontaneously into consciousness, then shaped and polished them. This time, given the incentive of Latimer's proposal, he set deliberately to work on pieces that would brighten the effect of the book. Hence what he told Latimer in his letter of January 8, 1935, is as much a tribute to Latimer's influence as it is a description of his method of composing the new poems: "One of the essential conditions to the writing of poetry is impetus. . . . Writing poetry is a conscious activity. While poems may very well occur, they had very much better be caused" (*L* 274).

As its title suggests, *Ideas of Order* embraces a plurality of orderings. Within the volume, the poems are arranged, as Stevens told Latimer, according to contrasts rather than any rigid scheme (*L* 279). Yet the various orderings can be divided into two main categories, depending on where they are sought—apart from the contemporary social situation, or within it. "How to Live. What to Do" (1935) best illustrates the first category. Stevens chose this as his favorite among the poems of *Ideas of Order* because, he said,

11. Stevens mentions in a letter of 11 Oct. 1935 (Chicago) that he had always thought of Latimer as a Harvard man; in a letter written the following spring, he assumes that Latimer shared his dismay at the "merely violent" phase of social change (*L* 309).

"It so definitely represents my way of thinking" (*L* 293). Possibly recalling his hikes with Elsie to the summit of Pulpit Rock near Reading, he portrays two people who climb a rocky prominence and so secure a place for themselves "away from the muck of the land / That they had left." Besides the man and his companion, the place is visited only by the wind, which, though cold, blows with a "heroic sound / Joyous and jubilant and sure."

This way of thinking met with little enthusiasm in the rest of the literary community, however. Writers at both ends of the political spectrum had grown intolerant of mountains and towers and every other lofty eminence that suggested escapism. On the right, certain of T. S. Eliot's camp-followers extended the master's suspicion of vague emotion to include, first poetry about nature or remote historical epochs, then all poetry not directly related to the problems of the day.[12] Writers on the left or sympathetic to it regarded the "escapist" writer as at best a victim of historical forces, at worst a covert fascist. Isidor Schneider, addressing the first of several Writers' Congresses which the Communist party organized during the thirties, insisted that poetry is by nature a social art and that the poet had been forced into his ivory tower by bourgeois individualism.[13] For Malcolm Cowley, it was an aesthetic creed that had driven the writer up his tower. Beginning in the late nineteenth century, according to Cowley, the "religion of art" movement compelled the writer continually to experiment in the direction of greater purity. Although the religion of art had produced such aesthetic monuments as *Madame Bovary*, *À la recherche du temps perdu*, and *Ulysses*, Cowley believed that "as a way of life it was completely bankrupt."[14] The growing roll of poet-suicides—Elinor Wylie in 1928, Vachel Lindsay in 1931, Hart Crane in 1932,

12. Graham Hough, *The Last Romantics* (London: Gerald Duckworth, 1949), p. 115.

13. "Proletarian Poetry," in *American Writers' Congress*, ed. Henry Hart (New York: International Publishers, 1935), pp. 114–20.

14. *Exile's Return*, p. 286.

Sara Teasdale in 1933—seemed to argue that literature was indeed on a fatal course.

Whatever their political persuasion, assailants of the ivory tower agreed that the pure poet had to descend to the street and rejoin the human community. Pure poetry had been, after all, a brief aberration in the long history of literature. Now it was time to resume the more humane and less perilous road that writers had traveled for centuries. Stevens, having recently recovered from a paralysis of the imagination, was not unsympathetic to this view. A dozen adages he wrote during the thirties indicate that he appreciated the role which reality—or, more precisely, a sense of reality—plays in the creative process. He understood, too, that one's sense of reality changes from one era to the next, and that the writer must accommodate this change in his work. During the Depression, people might and did seek escape in popular fiction like Margaret Mitchell's *Gone with the Wind* (1936). But, disillusioned by nearly everything else, the serious-minded tolerated less illusion in ostensibly serious art.

Stevens did not have to read the generally tepid reviews which greeted the second edition of *Harmonium* in 1931 to discern the change of climate. In "Sad Strains of a Gay Waltz" (1935), he bids adieu to the pure poet of his first book and thereby to a literary epoch. There was a time, he recalls, when Hoon had "found all form and order in solitude." Now those structures have vanished, and Hoon surveys a world beset by mobs of men who have been liberated from the oppression of the old social and economic institutions but who now lack direction and meaning in their lives. Who will provide articulate forms for these inarticulate masses? Not Hoon, who still hankers for the solitude of his palaz. Not the artist who works within prescribed aesthetic forms, for these, like the waltz, had come to seem "so much motionless sound." The final lines of "Sad Strains" prophesy a musical messiah who will be properly irreverent toward the prevailing mode. In his forms and through them, the troubled masses of humanity will acquire the dynamism and shadowed lucidity of a stream of flowing water.

That Stevens himself aspired to the role of "harmonious skeptic" is suggested by the poem he placed first in the Alcestis *Ideas of Order.* Realizing that "Sailing after Lunch" (1935) might seem as cryptic in its way as the "Earthy Anecdote" which had prefaced *Harmonium,* he paraphrased it for Latimer as follows:

> While it should make its own point, and while I am against explanations, the thing is an abridgment of at least a temporary theory of poetry. When people speak of the romantic, they do so in what the French commonly call a *pejorative* sense. But poetry is essentially romantic, only the romantic of poetry must be something constantly new and, therefore, just the opposite of what is spoken of as the romantic. Without this new romantic, one gets nowhere; with it, the most casual things take on transcendence, and the poet rushes brightly, and so on. What one is always doing is keeping the romantic pure: eliminating from it what people speak of as the romantic. (L 277)

If "Sailing after Lunch" is a prospectus for a new romantic poetry, it is also a confession that Stevens had not yet sloughed off the old, pejorative romanticism. He dreams of rushing brightly through the summer air, but still sails round in waltz-like circles. Far from being a harmonious skeptic, he is admittedly "A most inappropriate man / In a most unpropitious place." How was he to get under way, to advance toward a more skeptical music? Though Stevens feared being influenced by other poets and ordinarily refused to review their work or write prefaces to their books, he made two exceptions in the mid-thirties. The preface to William Carlos Williams' *Collected Poems 1921–1931* (1934, *OP* 254–57) and the review of Marianne Moore's *Selected Poems* (1935, *OP* 247–54) afforded him the opportunity to think out loud about the new romanticism.

"There are so many things to say about him," Stevens

announces at the outset of the Williams preface. "The first is that he is a romantic poet. This will horrify him." Indeed it did, though it was not the word "romantic" that offended Williams, or even the "sentimental" that appears further on. Rather, it was the epithet "anti-poetic." [15] Williams had placed the word "antipoetry" in the mouths of hostile critics in the first prose section of *Spring and All* (1923), and may have assumed that Stevens, like his imaginary critics, was accusing him of writing poetry à la mode, with fashionably unmusical lines on ignoble subjects.

Stevens in fact takes pains to preclude these connotations of the word, as he does the negative overtones of "sentimental." What fascinated him in Williams' work was neither quality in isolation but rather their potency when combined; "one might run through these pages," he says of Williams' *Collected Poems*, "and point out how often the essential poetry is the result of the conjunction of the unreal and the real, the sentimental and the anti-poetic, the constant interaction of two opposites. This seems to define Williams and his poetry." He describes Williams' kind of romantic poet memorably as "one who still dwells in an ivory tower, but who insists that life would be intolerable except for the fact that one has, from the top, such an exceptional view of the public dump and the advertising signs of Snider's Catsup, Ivory Soap and Chevrolet Cars; he is the hermit who dwells alone with the sun and moon, but insists on taking a rotten newspaper."

The words "sentimental" and "anti-poetic" are not the most politic Stevens might have chosen, and they may betray his private estimation of Williams' work. He felt that Williams represented "a somewhat exhausted phase of the romantic" (*L* 279), a phase that was neither skeptical nor musical enough. By contrast, Marianne Moore seemed to be breaking up older forms in order to pursue something

15. For Williams' reaction to the preface, see his *I Wanted to Write a Poem*, ed. Edith Heal (Boston: Beacon, 1958), p. 52.

genuinely new, a "fresh romantic" (L 279). Consequently, he approached her *Selected Poems* with more enthusiasm and tact. He devotes the first part of his review to examining Moore's skillfully modulated music—a music too subtle for an earlier time, perhaps, but just right for the present. Her imagery combines the romantic with the skeptical in a pleasing blend: her moon vines are trained on fishing twine, her imaginary gardens have real toads in them. This is the new romanticism at its best, and Stevens cannot resist pointing out that this same quality of "cross-fertilization" or "hybridization" distinguishes the best work of a notorious anti-romantic, T. S. Eliot. Eliot and Irving Babbitt cannot disparage the romantic, Stevens maintains, without disparaging poetry itself.

In the Moore review and "Sailing after Lunch," which Stevens called "expressions of the same thing" (L 282), he envisions a poetry romantic in the non-pejorative sense and even locates that poetry in specific phrases and images. Of all the poems in *Ideas of Order*, "The Idea of Order at Key West" best illustrates the principle of "cross-fertilization" or "hybridization"—qua principle. But its eloquent periods, its imagery of singer and sea and wind belong rather to the world of the Symbolists than the Depression. In "Mozart, 1935" (1935), Stevens comes closer to translating principle into practice: for the singer of "The Idea of Order," he substitutes a pianist; for the sea, an angry crowd. Much as the singer at Key West incorporates the sea into her song and so orders it, the pianist is exhorted to "Play the present, its hoo-hoo-hoo, / Its shoo-shoo-shoo, its ric-a-nic, / Its envious cachinnation." However, he will demonstrate his concern for the present not in his choice of music, which will still be Mozart, but in his interpretation of the score. He will somehow infuse the unclouded concerto with his awareness of various kinds of "clouds": the winter weather, the angry cries, the body in rags. Nor will he leave his ivory tower. Assuming a stance appropriate to his music and in keeping with the lofty pronoun "Thou," he will brave the hostility of the crowd, assured that this is ultimately the means "By which sorrow is released, / Dismissed, absolved / In a starry placating."

"Mozart, 1935" was among the last poems Stevens wrote for *Ideas of Order*, and it typifies his contrary impulses in that volume. On the one hand he wanted, as he put it in "Sailing after Lunch," "To expunge all people and be a pupil / Of the gorgeous wheel"—to escape the disturbances of the thirties and in a transcendent solar isolation devote himself to pure poetry. On the other hand, he wanted to incorporate his new sense of reality—or his sense of a new reality—in his poems. One kind of reader will see in "Mozart, 1935" a moment of equipoise or studied ambivalence; another will see mere confusion. It was one of the latter who reviewed *Ideas of Order* for the *New Masses* magazine.

Neither Stanley Burnshaw's famous review nor Stevens' response to it can be fairly assessed without an understanding of their context; a quarter of a century after the affair, Burnshaw appealed to literary historians to do him that justice.[16] As a young Marxist critic, Burnshaw subscribed to an ideology whose literary adherents were legion in the mid-thirties. Though many poets still published in "aesthetic" magazines like *Poetry* and the *Hound and Horn*, the preëminence of journals like the *New Republic*, the *Nation*, the *Partisan Review*, and the *New Masses* fostered the notion that most writers had "gone left." While no precise dates can be assigned to the leftist episode in American literature, the years 1917 and 1939 serve as convenient boundaries and 1935 as the high-water mark. Before 1917, particularly in the tolerant ambience of Greenwich Village, revolution mingled easily with aestheticism—often, indeed, in the same writer. But the Draft Law of 1917 polarized the Village into two factions: those rebelling chiefly against puritanism and those in revolt

16. "Wallace Stevens and the Statue," *Sewanee Review* 69 (1961): 355–56.

against the capitalist system.[17] The latter group, faced with the prospect of fleeing the country or going to Leavenworth, had a hard time of it. News of the October Revolution in Russia brightened their horizons, however, and they found an American Communist party eager to enlist their talents in the postwar decade. Largely ignored by the public at large, the party gained prestige among writers with each progressive cause it championed.

With the crash of 1929, the literary left felt at once vindicated and infused with a new sense of purpose. Next to a vigorous Soviet Russia, the West appeared morally as well as economically bankrupt.[18] Hence the communist ideal, especially as implemented in Russia, held considerable appeal for American writers. Fifty-two of them, including Sherwood Anderson, Dos Passos, and Edmund Wilson, endorsed the Communist platform in the presidential election of 1932. Many more came over to the left a few months later, when Hitler seized power in Germany. Few of these writers actually joined the party, most preferring to serve the cause as fellow travelers. They found a congenial forum for their views in the *New Republic*, an index of liberal thought since 1914. More doctrinaire—and usually less gifted—converts turned to the *New Masses*, which had first appeared in 1926. Under editors like Michael Gold and Granville Hicks, the *New Masses* tolerated none of the bohemian high jinks of the old *Masses*, published between 1910 and 1917. After 1934, in fact, the *New Masses* no longer pretended to be a cultural journal. It became, in party secretary Earl Browder's words, "a *political* weekly with strong cultural interests."[19] Though not run by the Communist party, it toed the party line.

Prior to 1935, Gold and Hicks had used the editorial columns of the *New Masses* to badger the politically uncom-

17. Cowley, *Exile's Return*, p. 77.
18. Daniel Aaron, *Writers on the Left: Episodes in American Literary Communism* (New York: Harcourt, 1961), p. 148. The rest of this chapter is indebted to Aaron's invaluable study at many points.
19. "Communism and Literature," in *American Writers' Congress*, p. 70.

mitted or "middle-ground" writer into declaring for communism or fascism. The middle ground was in their view nothing less than "incipient fascism." In April 1935, however, the *New Masses* printed an essay whose line of reasoning and moderate tone anticipated the "popular front" strategy that the Communist International adopted a few months later. "'Middle-Ground' Writers" opens with the obligatory crisis rhetoric: "At this moment in our history, when fascization gains ground with every hour, the duty of the Marxist critic becomes deepened in seriousness and responsibility."[20] Self-important declarations of this sort had typically prepared the way for yet more blood-letting in the middle ground. But not this time, for, continues the essay, the left "can afford to drive away no one who can be turned into a friend of the revolutionary movement."

The essay goes on to paint a sympathetic portrait of the "confused" middle-ground writer who, in an effort to salvage fragments of order from the wreckage of capitalism, "begins to magnify into supreme importance such so-called 'principles' as heroism in battle, love of country, noble episodes in history, unnamed self-sacrificing martyrs, etc." The wavering writer must be made to see that there is no middle ground between communism and fascism, and that only communism is compatible with creativity. Nevertheless, the Marxist critic who brandishes hammer and sickle is apt to frighten the waverer into the enemy camp before he can persuade him of his friendly intentions. Hence the leftist critic should exercise his "politico-aesthetic leadership" by "critically analyzing rather than excoriating the dangerous philosophic chaos of incipient fascism, the so-called middle ground."

The author of "'Middle-Ground' Writers" was Stanley Burnshaw, an intelligent and articulate newcomer to the pages of the *New Masses*. A few months later, he had an opportunity to apply the principles of popular front criti-

20. *New Masses*, 30 Apr. 1935, p. 19.

cism to Haniel Long's *Pittsburgh Memoranda* and Stevens' *Ideas of Order*. The review, entitled "Turmoil in the Middle Ground," is for the most part conciliatory, even diffident, in tone.[21] A poet and translator himself, Burnshaw appreciated the damage done to Stevens' poems by paraphrase, and candidly admits that he is often unsure of their meaning. He does say of Stevens' poetry, "It is the kind of verse that people concerned with the murderous world collapse can hardly swallow today except in tiny doses." But this was his retrospective judgment of *Harmonium*, and he understood as well as anyone the convention governing that volume: "It was tacitly assumed that one read him for pure poetic sensation; if he had 'a message' it was carefully buried and would take no end of labor to exhume." As for *Ideas of Order*, Burnshaw says that its poems gave the lie to the leftist cliché that middle-ground writers had all "tramped off to some escapist limbo." Indeed, these poems confronted social agitation at some peril to psychic poise; they were "the record of a man who, having lost his footing, now scrambles to stand up and keep his balance." If Stevens and Long had done little to subvert capitalism, they could nevertheless be considered "potential allies as well as potential enemies."

When the review came to Stevens' attention, probably through Latimer, who had sent a copy of *Ideas of Order* to the *New Masses*, he was at first irritated and defensive. He characterized the whole left as "a mob of wailers" and the *New Masses* as "just one more wailing place" (*L* 287). But equanimity soon returned, and a few weeks later he could think it "extraordinarily stimulating" to have been exposed to the leftist point of view (*L* 296). Certainly the review stimulated his imagination as no other external incident of the thirties had done. Within a few weeks of the Burnshaw review, he wrote to Latimer, "I have just finished a poem

21. *New Masses*, 1 Oct. 1935, pp. 41–42; the review is reprinted in Burnshaw's "Wallace Stevens and the Statue," pp. 363–66.

that might be of some interest. You will remember that Mr. Burnshaw applied the point of view of the practical Communist to IDEAS OF ORDER; in MR. BURNSHAW AND THE STATUE I have tried to reverse the process: that is to say, apply the point of view of a poet to Communism" (*L* 289). Stevens eventually sent the poem to Alfred Kreymborg, who, drifting to larboard since his days with *Others*, had become editor of the *New Caravan*.

A single poem could not, of course, exhaust the poetic possibilities in communism. During the winter of 1936, Stevens applied his imagination to communism in two more poems, "A Duck for Dinner" and "Sombre Figuration." These three, together with "The Old Woman and the Statue" and "The Greenest Continent," would compose the volume entitled *Owl's Clover* (1936). By his own admission, Stevens was out of his element in writing about Marxism even from a poetic point of view (*L* 292). Nevertheless, with an instinct for the more vulnerable aspects of communism, he concentrated his attention first on its concept of history, then went on to consider its cult of the proletarian and glorification of reason.

In "Mr. Burnshaw and the Statue" (*OP* 46–52), Mr. Burnshaw contemplates a group of marble horses that represent contemporary civilization. He naturally ridicules these relics of capitalism, since according to the Marxist dialectic contemporary civilization must make way for a future millennium: "Everything is dead / Except the future. Always everything / That is is dead except what ought to be." In his review of *Ideas of Order*, Burnshaw had regretted the "insolence" of a line in "The Comedian as the Letter C": "For realists, what is is what should be." This bald assertion savored of Pope's "Whatever is is right," though Burnshaw wondered—and with good reason—whether the line was not tinged with self-mockery. In "Mr. Burnshaw," Stevens turns the tables on his critic by having him express a Marxist precept in the same rhetorical form but without the redeeming irony. Not that Stevens had any quarrel with the precept insofar as it states a law of inevitable change. Shortly after finishing the poem he told Latimer, "The only possible order of life is one in which all order is incessantly changing. Marxism may or may not destroy the existing sentiment of the marvellous; if it does, it will create another" (L 291–92).

Surely the Marxist millennium partook of the marvellous. Not himself a reader of the *New Masses*, Stevens probably did not know that Burnshaw had faulted the "deliberately regressive framework of totalitarianism" in his earlier essay for denying writers "the common literary hope of a vague golden future age." The Mr. Burnshaw of the poem errs, however, when he tries to capture that vague future age in a monument whose inscription reads, *"The Mass / Appoints These Marbles Of Itself To Be / Itself."* If the millennium is to be achieved through change and destruction, there is no reason to suppose that change and destruction will cease once the millennium arrives. Accordingly, another voice, one having the same arbitrary authority as the voice in Stanza VIII of "Sunday Morning," responds to Mr. Burnshaw by offering an equally valid though far less comforting vision of the future. In the alternate vision, all the "dead things"—including sculptor and statue—are deposited in an enormous trash can at the world's end. But this apocalypse of ruin has its hopeful side, too, for it is a prelude to rebirth; indeed, the light which illuminates this wreckage is already suffused with the rosy hue of new life.

The choral interludes which punctuate this dialogue on the future seem at first to offer stylistic relief without advancing the argument of the poem. However, they do suggest that change has different ethical consequences depending on how it is received. Whereas the commune that erects a monument to itself is unlikely to surpass its monument, the society that is willing to evolve at random and more slowly toward its ideal will not only enjoy greater serenity but may also achieve a higher type. Hence the question which concludes Section VI is also a challenge:

> Shall you,
> Then, fear a drastic community evolved
> From the whirling, slowly and by trial; or fear
> Men gathering for a mighty flight of men,
> An abysmal migration into a possible blue?

Following this question, the maidens of the chorus are invited to dance and sing in a manner that recalls the men chanting in orgy on a summer morn in "Sunday Morning." But the tone is different: the men sing in the elegiac mode, knowing well the heavenly fellowship of men that perish, while the maidens are to sing rhapsodically of the future, "like damsels captured by the sky, / Seized by that possible blue."

If "Mr. Burnshaw and the Statue" is, in one sense, the "justification of leftism" Stevens called it (L 295), it is also and more obviously a critique of leftism. The poem applauds the Marxist insistence on change, revolution, and the future of man; but it denies that civilization must develop along predetermined, Hegelian lines. The Marxist dialectic, as Karl Popper would argue in a book published a decade later, is founded on the historicist delusion that one can abstract quasi-scientific laws from history and use them to predict the future.[22] As historical goal, Stevens' "drastic community" partakes of the same delusion as the Marxist millennium; but it does not entail the further delusion that this goal will be achieved by logical, predictable means.

"A Duck for Dinner" (OP 60–66), written several months after "Mr. Burnshaw," examines the communist cult of the proletarian and its aesthetic implications. As in "Mr. Burnshaw," there are two voices. The poet is skeptical, inclined to deride the Marxist future as a displaced

22. *The Open Society and Its Enemies* (London: Routledge, 1945).

Christian heaven, merely a "diverting of the dream / Of heaven from heaven to the future." The Bulgar who speaks for the proletariat insists, to the contrary, that his Sunday strolls have nothing to do with worship or angels. The workers, he contends, do "rise a bit" with each duck they consume. Moreover, they have begun to create from Swedish hands, English noses, and Italian eyes a collective self that will eventually command a hearing.

Though derided by the skeptic as a "calico idea," the Bulgar's composite European worker had potent appeal for Communists and fellow travelers of the thirties. By calling itself the Soviet Union, Russia implied that it could accommodate people of all nations and ethnic groups. National chauvinism, Earl Browder scarcely needed to remind the first Writers' Congress, "is the characteristic of reaction, of fascism; those who will build the new world, who will help humanity find the way out of chaos and destruction, will be internationalists."[23]

The fascists were not only nationalists, but notorious hero-worshipers; even the United States had its reactionary demagogues in Huey Long and Father Coughlin, to name just two. In that era of widespread confusion, it was inevitable that the left—including the literary left—should also have had its heroes. "This is an age," Malcolm Cowley told the first Writers' Congress in 1935, "when Messiahs are being invoked not only by unemployed preachers and engineers and by shopkeepers who have lost their shops, but also by bewildered novelists and by poets no longer able to write poetry."[24] Marx and Lenin, Cowley stressed, were not Messiahs but "scientists of action." John Reed, though he was the inspiration for John Reed Clubs throughout the country, represented a primitive phase of the class struggle. To idolize a living Communist leader, like Stalin, would savor of fascism. Hence the idealized

23. "Communism and Literature," p. 70.
24. "What the Revolutionary Movement Can Do for a Writer," in *American Writers' Congress*, p. 59.

type of the proletarian worker was made to bear the burden of leftist hero-worship. So entrenched was the symbol of the worker by the time of the first Writers' Congress that Kenneth Burke nearly brought the roof about his ears when he proposed replacing "the worker" with "the people" as a myth whose appeal was less exclusive.[25] His audience protested that, while the Nazi "folk" might be mythical, the worker was as real as a wrench.

The worker-hero was, in fact, both real and mythical. The party made so much of the distinction between proletarian and petit bourgeois that the bona fide worker acquired for many writers a romantic glamor. Writers on the staff of the *Daily Worker* affected workman's shirts, while other intellectuals styled themselves "brain workers."[26] As prophesied in the pages of the *New Masses* and parodied by Robert Sage in *transition,* the communist author of the future would be one who worked in a factory all day, then sat down at night before a bare table to write "page after page of virile lyric literature—the real stuff."[27]

In addition to being the ideal artist, the worker was expected to be the ideal connoisseur of art. Malcolm Cowley anticipated that the proletariat would not only welcome art but would be "immeasurably more eager" and "quicker to grasp essentials" than those bourgeois philistines who had supported art from impure motives.[28] What is more, the art form of the millennium would break down the barrier between artist and audience. In a 1922 *Liberator* essay, Michael Gold imagined a millennial May Day festival featuring a thousand mechanical orchestras, with "color-organs" to project patterns onto the sky. Gold's rhapsody reaches its climax as a great cantata wells up from the assembly:

25. "Revolutionary Symbolism in America," in *American Writers' Congress,* pp. 87–94; for the ensuing debate, see pp. 166–71.
26. Aaron, p. 46.
27. "Mr. Gold's Spring Model," *transition,* no. 15 (1929), pp. 184–88.
28. *Exile's Return,* p. 302.

"not a man, woman, child or dog is outside the communion of this night; the world is wonderful; it is the drama
of the proletarian revolution; it is the proletarian art."[29]

By the mid-thirties, it seemed less certain that great art
would come from the working class or from committed
leftists as a group. Communist art bore less resemblance
to Gold's May Day festival than it did to the "Concerto for
Airplane and [Pianoforte]" played by Basilewsky in Stevens' "A Duck for Dinner." Somehow, communism had
failed to produce inspired music, and this raised the more
fundamental question as to whether any communist work
of art—indeed, whether any party social program—could
escape the fate of Basilewsky's abortive concerto:

> . . . In an age of concentric mobs would any sphere
> Escape all deformation, much less this,
> This source and patriarch of other spheres,
> This base of every future, vibrant spring,
> The volcano Apostrophe, the sea Behold?

To the extent that social regimentation deforms the imagination, the "base of every future," it deforms all products
of the imagination. This was still Stevens' opinion a dozen
years later, when he wrote to a friend, "I cannot help feeling that communism, in spite of its organization, in spite
of its revolutionary program and detonations, is the bunk:
something specious, the refuge of failure" (L 621–22). Living "in clusters," he went on to say, makes for few "living
individuals." The poet of "A Duck for Dinner" speaks Stevens' mind when he concludes, "As the man the state, not
as the state the man."

To counter the effects of social regimentation and assure
future progress would require, Stevens hypothesized, a
leader of superhuman capacity (L 371–72). Therefore, after
dismissing Basilewsky and the Marxist "architect" or theo-

---

29. "Prize-Fights vs. Color Organs," *Liberator*, Mar. 1922, p. 27.

retician, he projects a hero of increasingly mythic—and decreasingly human—stature:

> . . . What man of folk-lore shall rebuild the world,
> What lesser man shall measure sun and moon,
> What super-animal dictate our fates?

Section II of the poem features a "buckskin" who bears some resemblance to Stevens' fellow Pennsylvanian, Daniel Boone. Is he the man of folk-lore who will rebuild the world? Apparently not, though he serves well enough as a foil to the Bulgar's urban proletariat. Unlike the buckskin, who carries souvenirs from the Old World to sustain him in the New, today's hero must imagine the future and so create it (*L* 372).

The sculptor of the marble horses—surprisingly, considering how he is treated in "Mr. Burnshaw and the Statue"—is such a hero. Through the medium of his sculpture, which here represents "something pure and something lofty" according to Stevens (*L* 372), he has "touched another race, / Above our race, yet of ourselves transformed." The sculptor is consequently hailed as an authentic patron of the future. In discarding the worker ideal for the man of imagination, Stevens seems merely to exchange one future-obsessed hero for another. But just as the "drastic community" of "Mr. Burnshaw and the Statue" will evolve more slowly and more at random than the Marxist millennium, so the man of imagination will proceed by fits of visionary insight rather than calculation.

How these tactics vary appears more clearly in the last poem of Stevens' Marxist trilogy, "Sombre Figuration" (*OP* 66–71). Communists prided themselves on their "scientific" approach to history and social progress, and celebrated the machine as "the external expression of the rational ideal."[30] They continually distinguished themselves

---

30. Kenneth Burke, "The Relation between Literature and Science," in *The Writer in a Changing World* [papers and proceedings of the second

from the fascists in this respect. The fascists were propo-
nents of "cultural Neanderthalism"[31] who had burned
books upon seizing power in Germany, who refused to
debate the issues with anti-fascists, who wanted to return
to a handicraft and agrarian economy. Neither art nor science could thrive under fascism for, Stanley Burnshaw
asserted in "'Middle-Ground' Writers," fascism "is compelled to pull the intellect backward by a noose of anti-
reason that strangles creative science and art. It must install a so-called 'reasoning by blood' as its 'intellectual'
rationalization of a chauvinist racialism and the cult
of war."

Yet if many writers of the twenties and thirties saw communism as the guarantor of culture and reasoned discourse, others thought its Marxist logic inhumanly reduc-
tive. They were inclined to share Stevens' opinion,
expressed in "Esthétique du Mal" (1944), that "The cause /
Creates a logic not to be distinguished / From lunacy" (Section XIV). In "A Duck for Dinner," Stevens characterizes
the proletariat as "theoretical people" who, even on Sunday strolls, "keep to the paths of the skeleton architect / Of
the park." In "Sombre Figuration," he suggests that Marxism perpetuates the rationalistic "age of the solid" which
had begun in the seventeenth century. "We have grown
weary of the man that thinks," says Stevens, for "He thinks
and it is not true." The logician must be supplanted by the
"man below," or "subman," who

> Imagines and it is true, as if he thought
> By imagining, anti-logician, quick
> With a logic of transforming certitudes.

The subman, Frank Doggett has pointed out, stands for

Writers' Congress, 1937], ed. Henry Hart (New York: Equinox Coopera-
tive Press, 1937), p. 160.

31. Moishe Nadir, "The Writer in a Minority Language," in *American
Writers' Congress*, p. 157.

the imagination in its involuntary aspect; as such, he is the source of the irrational element in poetry.[32] He is also a kind of racial subconscious whose memory of the past enables him to intuit the future, since "memory's lord is the lord of prophecy." Even in the twenties, Stevens indicates in an elaborately symbolic passage, men experienced the social turmoil to come as a sense of foreboding.

What, then, lies beyond the thirties? Here the subman beholds the statue, in this poem an emblem of normal, workaday reality, and his prophetic vision evaporates. As the "night" of the imagination recedes and the subman grows mute, the poet wonders if perhaps he had not wanted all along

> merely to be
> For the gaudium of being, Jocundus instead
> Of the black-blooded scholar, the man of the cloud, to be
> The medium man among other medium men. . . .

Nothing prepares the reader for this conclusion, and he may well find fault with the machinery of Jocundus' lowering. Yet the device would become a familiar one in Stevens' later work: no sooner is the subman or superman announced than *l'homme moyen sensuel* makes his entrance. One sees the pattern of "Sombre Figuration" duplicated a year later in Stevens' Harvard lecture; after speaking movingly of the seductions of the unknown, he concludes with an allusion to Eliot's sensualist: "For the poet, the irrational is elemental; but neither poetry nor life is commonly at its dynamic utmost. We know Sweeney as he is and, for the most part, prefer him that way and without too much effulgence and, no doubt, always shall" (*OP* 229).

Jocundus and Sweeney are two avatars of "medium man," the figure who, liberated from both the politico's logic and the poet's imagination, enjoys a world without design or doctrine. Medium man represented the side of

32. *Wallace Stevens: The Making of the Poem* (Baltimore: Johns Hopkins University Press, 1980), p. 11.

Stevens that was notoriously fond of good food and drink and those subtler pleasures named in the epigraph to "Evening without Angels" (1934): "air and light, the joy of having a body, the voluptuousness of looking."[33] Together with "major man," a version of the "super-animal" first projected in "A Duck for Dinner," he would dominate Stevens' mythology of self in the decade following *Owl's Clover*. Though otherwise very different, these personae share an "irrational" character that may be due partly to an excess—or what Stevens thought to be an excess—of the rational in Marxism.

Indirectly, then, Stanley Burnshaw may have helped to shape Stevens' poetry from *The Man with the Blue Guitar and Other Poems* (1937) through *Transport to Summer* (1947). As the three more political poems of *Owl's Clover* indicate, however, he failed to lure the poet from the middle ground into the leftist camp. If anything, Stevens' political views became more "confused," ideologically speaking, after the review. He labeled the leftist program variously a "magnificent cause" and a "grubby faith" (*L* 287, *NA* 143). Fascism he called "a form of disillusionment with about everything else," yet described himself in an unguarded moment as "pro-Mussolini" (*L* 289; cf. *L* 295).[34]

As a private citizen, Stevens occupied a position to the right of center. He subscribed to an "up-to-date capitalism" and favored social reform over social revolution (*L* 292, 309). He professed to be "headed left" yet regretted the

33. Stevens took his epigraph from Mario Manlio Rossi's "Essay on the Character of Swift," trans. J. M. Hone, *Life and Letters* 8 (1932): 356, and transcribed it in *Sur Plusieurs Beaux Sujects*, Cahier I, pp. 7–8. I am grateful to George S. Lensing for identifying the source of the notebook entry.

34. One would like to know how many of Stevens' compatriots shared this view of Mussolini in 1935. According to a survey conducted by the American Institute of Public Opinion in the fall of 1938, Americans preferred the Italian dictator to Stalin and Hitler and did not want Roosevelt to criticize him for his warlike attitude; see *Public Opinion 1935–1946*, ed. Hadley Cantril (Princeton: Princeton University Press, 1951), p. 163.

drift of American policy toward the very near left of the Democratic party (L 286, 767). Though he hoped to see the workers' lot improved, he looked askance at the growing power of the labor unions (L 351). As a public man of letters, however, he was more sympathetic to the left, especially when compared with literary peers like Yeats, Pound, and Eliot. In a note which appeared about the same time as Burnshaw's review, he did his best to find qualities he could praise in the poetry of Martha Champion, editor of a magazine founded to indoctrinate children in the mysteries of the class struggle.[35] Magazines like the *New Republic*, the *Nation*, and the *Partisan Review* frequently asked him for poems during the thirties. His curiously ambivalent elegy for the Spanish Loyalists, "The Men That Are Falling," was designated by the *Nation* its prize poem of 1936. The *Partisan Review*, shortly after it turned anti-Stalinist, published his "Life on a Battleship" (1939, OP 77–81), a poetic critique of totalitarianism.

When Kenneth Rexroth complained to Malcolm Cowley in 1938 that "real"—that is to say, non-literary—people were fed up with "funny ideas about what Marx should of thought about Wallace Stevens," he was expressing the battle fatigue of many literary combatants as the decade drew to a close.[36] What Marx thought about Stevens and Stevens thought about Marx mattered even less after the Nazi-Soviet Pact of August 1939. For leftist writers who had accepted Trotsky's exile in 1929, who had somehow rationalized the mass treason trials of 1936–38, who had borne with the party's philistinism, factionalism, and interminable meetings, this was the final disillusionment. Thereafter, the literary community was less polarized along political lines, and writers could meet once again on the common ground of their craft.

35. Stevens' note appeared in *Trial Balances*, ed. Ann Winslow (New York: Macmillan, 1935), pp. 155–57; reprinted in *OP* 264–66.
36. Quoted in Aaron, p. 341n.

Ultimately, it was craft rather than ideology that preoccupied Stevens as he worked on *Owl's Clover*. His comments on the volume as a whole and especially on "The Old Woman and the Statue" and "The Greenest Continent" indicate that he had clearly defined aesthetic objectives, however "confused" his politics may have seemed. Rather than continue to play Mozart to the masses, as he had done in *Ideas of Order*, he wanted, he told Latimer, "to make poetry out of commonplaces: the day's news" (*L* 311n). This was apparently his aim even before the Burnshaw review, when he sat down to write "The Old Woman and the Statue" (*OP* 43–46). Recalling his state of mind at the time of its composition, he later said,

> the subject that I had in mind was the effect of the depression on the interest in art. I wanted a confronting of the world as it had been imagined in art and as it was then in fact. If I dropped into a gallery I found that I had no interest in what I saw. The air was charged with anxieties and tensions. . . . I wanted to deal with exactly such a subject and I chose that as a bit of reality, actuality, the contemporaneous. But I wanted the result to be poetry so far as I was able to write poetry. (*OP* 219)

The old woman of the poem represents not only the Depression era but also a depression of spirit; to her, the art of a happier time seems impertinent and scarcely credible. The marble horses seem to race with the wind until she approaches, whereupon they collapse into a heap and take on the dark coloring of her mind. Only after she has passed do they gallop again, as glorious as ever. As Stevens' comment on the poem suggests, the old woman personified an aspect of himself during the thirties: he found little satisfaction in the art of the galleries and perhaps, by extension, in the pure poetry of *Harmonium*. In *Owl's Clover*, he tried to fashion a poetry that would stand up to the old woman's scrutiny.

"The Old Woman and the Statue" succeeds as a poem

because its subject, the confrontation between art and the Depression, lends itself to Stevens' dual objective. Moreover, the woman is a sufficiently generalized symbol of the Depression as not to raise specific social and political questions. Stevens faced a severer test of his new aesthetic when he undertook "Mr. Burnshaw and the Statue." In this poem, he told Latimer, he wanted on the one hand to make contact with "normal ideas," on the other hand to bring out "the poetry of the thing" (*L* 289). This time, the subject lent itself to ideas but not to "poetry," which then became almost exclusively a function of style. Stevens sensed the disparity between the poem's matter and its "largely gaseous" manner even before he finished it, and confessed to Latimer, "the poem is a source of a good deal of trouble to me at the moment, because, having purposely used a good many stock figures (what is now called *Victorian ideology*) it seems most un-Burnshawesque" (*L* 289).

More Burnshawesque and therefore more appropriate to a poem dealing with Marxism would have been the "accurate, impersonal, lucid, compelling" style, stripped of "romantic rhetoric," which Edmund Wilson identified as the communist contribution to literature.[37] In choosing a more elevated style, Stevens may have proceeded on the assumption that only thus could he raise the day's news to the status of poetry. Because he could not bring himself to write plainly of the commonplace, like William Carlos Williams, he began to chafe under the constraint of his subject matter. While composing "The Greenest Continent" (*OP* 52–60) early in 1936, he sent Latimer a progress report in which he wondered aloud, "Is poetry that is to have a contemporary significance merely to be a collection of contemporary images, or is it actually to deal with the commonplace of the day? I think the latter, but the result seems rather boring" (*L* 308).

The subject of "The Greenest Continent," as Stevens de-

37. "The Literary Class War: II," *New Republic*, 11 May 1932, p. 348.

scribed it in the same letter to Latimer, is the white man in Africa (*L* 307–8). He equated this subject with "[w]hat one reads in the papers," which suggests that the poem may have been inspired by Mussolini's invasion of Ethiopia and Stevens' exchange with Latimer on this event the previous fall (*L* 289–90, 295). In the poem, the military invasion has become a theological and aesthetic invasion, as European angels try to inflict their gods and art upon African bushmen. The angels win the battle but lose the war, since the statue, here a symbol for all northern ideas of order, proves meaningless in the jungle. But profound as the differences are between European and African, they are not irreconcilable. In the final section of the poem, Stevens envisions the sort of divinity they might share: Ananke—the fateful, impassive, changeless presence who ordains the shape of all lesser gods and artifacts.

Stevens later remarked that Ananke was "an importation from Italy" (*L* 370)—specifically from the Italian philosopher Mario Rossi, with whom he had corresponded in 1934.[38] Rossi had used the word in the classical sense of fate or necessity, as does Stevens in Stanza XII of "Like Decorations in a Nigger Cemetery" (1935). In "The Greenest Continent," however, "Ananke" stands for "essential imagination" (*L* 370). In effect, it symbolizes pure poetry, an entity alike indifferent to regional differences and the day's news. Ananke's heaven is the "spirit's episcopate" evoked in Section III. There, in that realm "Beyond thought's regulation," each man enjoys a Hoon-like solitude; there he listens as the voices of human confusion resolve into the music of the spheres and contemplates a central, solar dome that betokens, not the future, as it does

38. Rossi's "Essay on the Character of Swift" (cited above) prompted Stevens to write to Rossi early in 1934. Though Rossi's letter of reply, dated 17 or 18 Apr. 1934, has apparently been lost, Stevens excerpted part of it in *Sur Plusieurs Beaux Sujects*, Cahier I, p. 8. In 1940, he sent the letter to Hi Simons (see *L* 347), who made a "true copy" now in the Hi Simons Papers at the University of Chicago Library.

for the proletariat of "A Duck for Dinner," but the beautiful, the good, and the true:

> There each man,
> Through long cloud-cloister-porches, walked alone,
> Noble within perfecting solitude,
> Like a solitude of the sun, in which the mind
> Acquired transparence and beheld itself
> And beheld the source from which transparence came;
> And there he heard the voices that were once
> The confusion of men's voices, intricate
> Made extricate by meanings, meanings made
> Into a music never touched to sound.
> There, too, he saw, since he must see, the domes
> Of azure round an upper dome, brightest
> Because it rose above them all, stippled
> By waverings of stars, the joy of day
> And its immaculate fire, the middle dome,
> The temple of the altar where each man
> Beheld the truth and knew it to be true.

Here, for perhaps the only time in *Owl's Clover*, subject and style are perfectly wedded. But that subject is not the day's news. Located at the center of *Owl's Clover*, this lyrical passage challenges the book's ostensible purpose, the making of poetry from commonplaces, and reasserts the purpose Stevens had always found more congenial, the making of pure poetry. Though he went on to write "A Duck for Dinner" and "Sombre Figuration" in the mode of "Mr. Burnshaw and the Statue," he complained as he neared the end of *Owl's Clover* that its style, particularly its blank verse, involved him in a "constant struggle with clichés, both of word and thought."[39] A month after the book was published, he could sympathize with the judgment of the reviewer to whom he wrote, "What I tried to do in OWL'S CLOVER was to dip aspects of the contemporaneous in the poetic. You seem to think that I have produced a lot of Easter eggs, and perhaps I have. We shall both have to wait to see what happens next . . ." (*L* 314).

39. Letter to Latimer, 23 Mar. 1936 (Chicago).

What happened next was "The Man with the Blue Guitar" (1937), a sequence whose thirty-three short sections differ markedly from *Owl's Clover* both in style and in handling of subject. Terse, sometimes fragmentary sentences replace the more grandiloquent periods of the earlier poem. Words and phrases are repeated over and over, as though Stevens were trying to wring a tune from a handful of notes. This style lends itself to representing a world devoid of imagination, as in the following passages:

> There are no shadows in our sun,
>
> Day is desire and night is sleep.
> There are no shadows anywhere.
>
> The earth, for us, is flat and bare.
> There are no shadows.
> (Section V)

> The earth is not earth but a stone,
> Not the mother that held men as they fell
>
> But stone, but like a stone, no: not
> The mother, but an oppressor, but like
>
> An oppressor that grudges them their death,
> As it grudges the living that they live.
> (Section XVI)

In proportion as the style of "The Man with the Blue Guitar" has become more astringent, the subject matter has become less contemporaneous, thus narrowing the gap between manner and matter which had troubled *Owl's Clover*. The day's news is still there, in allusions to political demagoguery (Section X), to war and schemes for material progress (XVI), to unrealized utopian and millennial dreams (XXVI, XXXIII), to conflict between employer and employee (XXXI). But these topical references are sufficiently generalized that, in context, they serve as metaphors or instances of the imagination's struggle with reality.

Like *Owl's Clover*, "The Man with the Blue Guitar" is often contentious in tone; but the contention is of a different sort. Yeats might have been describing the difference when he said that we make rhetoric out of the quarrel with others, poetry of the quarrel with ourselves. The first half-dozen sections of "The Man with the Blue Guitar" represent the quarrel with others, as society makes demands upon the poet which he cannot satisfy without ceasing to be a poet. In Section XV, the guitarist compares his efforts with Picasso's avowedly social art and wonders whether his tune is not merely a snatch from a popular song, something remembered rather than created. For the most part, however, he does not apologize for subordinating rhetoric to poetry as he quarrels with himself over his relation to his own poems, to a more heroic self, and to reality.

We have already touched on the first of these, the poet's relation to his "jocular procreations" (Section XXXII), in Chapter Three; we will take up the second, his relation to "man number one" (III), in connection with the "major man" of the forties. The poet's argument with reality is the same that took place behind the scenes of *Owl's Clover* as Stevens labored to make poetry of the commonplace. In "The Man with the Blue Guitar," this dispute takes the center of the stage. Both poetry and the commonplace, imagination and reality, have their moments of uncontested triumph. Corresponding to the unalloyed realism of Sections V and XVI, quoted above, is the pure imagination of Section XIII, a "blue sleek with a hundred chins, / The amorist Adjective aflame." More often, however, imagination and reality are held in tension or equilibrium, whether that of the lion in the lute confronting the lion locked in stone (Section XIX), the undertaker's duet with God (XXIII), or the comedian spinning the world upon his nose (XXV).

This struggle cannot be resolved, nor should it be. Section XXII comes closest to stating the theme of "The Man with the Blue Guitar," and its poetic strategy, when it simply gives each contender its due. Coming to this poem from *Owl's Clover* one feels that its opening proposition—

Poetry is the subject of the poem,
From this the poem issues and

To this returns—

was for Stevens a hard-won victory and not merely an aesthetic cliché. Explaining these lines to Hi Simons, Stevens wrote, "Poetry is the spirit, as the poem is the body. Crudely stated, poetry is the imagination. But here poetry is used as the poetic, without the slightest pejorative innuendo. I have in mind pure poetry. The purpose of writing poetry is to attain pure poetry" (L 363–64).

In its transit from poetry to poetry—that is, from imagination to pure poetry—the individual poem is fleshed out with the phenomena of reality. From the standpoint of poetry, this incarnation is ephemeral and impure, an "absence in reality." But this view bruises body to pleasure soul. As the poem sees it, this "absence" is its reality, the very stuff of its existence. Speaking therefore as advocate for the poem, the poet goes on to ask,

Is it
An absence for the poem, which acquires

Its true appearances there, sun's green,
Cloud's red, earth feeling, sky that thinks?

From these it takes. Perhaps it gives,
In the universal intercourse.

This give and take or "intercourse" between imagination and reality recalls the "cross-fertilization" or "hybridization" Stevens admired in the work of Williams and Moore. In this "new romantic"—again, "without the slightest pejorative innuendo"—body contributes as much to spirit as spirit to body. The two may in fact be indistinguishable, if reality can pass for an absence in reality. Consequently, Stevens proceeded to tell Simons in his note on the poem, "There is nothing that exists exclusively by reason of the imagination, or that does not exist in some form in reality. Thus, reality = the imagination, and the imagination = reality."[40]

One could not mistake one of these terms for the other in *Owl's Clover*, where the commonplace is "dipped" in poetry without being quickened by it. If that book seems in retrospect to have been an aberration in Stevens' career, wrong as a divagation to Moscow, it nevertheless taught him how much of the day's news, and what kind, he could successfully admit into his poems. He learned that a poem, like mankind, cannot bear very much reality—at least it cannot bear much reality into the realm of pure poetry. Once the volatile essence of a poem has evaporated, its realistic residue is apt to seem pitifully inert. Stevens might have been recalling the lesson of *Owl's Clover* years later, when he told a correspondent, "Nothing in the world is deader than yesterday's political (or realistic) poetry" (*L* 760).

Furthermore, after *Owl's Clover* Stevens could never again be so unconsciously, so innocently the pure poet he had been in *Harmonium*. He had entered the thirties believing that his integrity as a writer—an integrity he carefully preserved, to the extent of refusing remuneration for his poems—guaranteed the integrity of his work, and that the integrity of the work would command instant conviction. Once he understood that the ivory tower was vulnerable and that poetry is quickly blunted in its defense, he took up the weapon of prose. Shortly after completing *Owl's Clover*, apparently, he prepared a dust-jacket statement for the Knopf trade edition of *Ideas of Order* (1936), in which he warns the reader that the volume "is essentially a book

40. Helen Vendler correctly observes that in "The Man with the Blue Guitar" the mind confronts the world without any "sacred parental presences" of the kind which appear in *Owl's Clover*; see *On Extended Wings: Wallace Stevens' Longer Poems* (Cambridge, Mass.: Harvard University Press, 1969), p. 120. Her phrase nicely anticipates, however, what the "poetry" of Section XXII would become in Stevens' final phase.

of pure poetry," concerned only indirectly with social and political ideas of order. "I believe," he goes on to say, "that, in any society, the poet should be the exponent of the imagination of that society. . . . The more realistic life may be, the more it needs the stimulus of the imagination."

Later that same year, he told his audience at Harvard that people most need to regroup their spiritual forces in poetry when they are preoccupied with daily events and uncertain about the future (*OP* 225). At Princeton five years later, he spoke of poetry as "a violence from within that protects us from a violence without" (*NA* 36). What he had to say about "resistance" and "escapism" in these lectures he pursued almost belligerently at Yale in 1948; then, alluding to the era that had ended with the crash of 1929, he asserted,

> There was a time when the ivory tower was merely a place of seclusion, like a cottage on a hill-top or a cabin by the sea. Today, it is a kind of lock-up of which our intellectual constables are the appointed wardens. Is it not time that someone questioned this degradation, not for the purpose of restoring the isolation of the tower but in order to establish the integrity of its builder? Our rowdy gun-men may not appreciate what comes from that tower. Others do. Was there ever any poetry more wholly the poetry of the ivory tower than the poetry of Mallarmé? Was there ever any music more wholly the music of the ivory tower than the music of Debussy? . . . The ivory tower was offensive if the man who lived in it wrote, there, of himself for himself. It was not offensive if he used it because he could do nothing without concentration, as no one can, and because, there, he could most effectively struggle to get at his subject, even if his subject happened to be the community and other people, and nothing else. (*NA* 121–23)

The ivory tower poet had little to fear from intelligent criticism of the kind Stanley Burnshaw practiced; but the social unrest that preceded and followed World War II afforded less responsible critics, the "rowdy gun-men," an opportunity to assault work they barely understood. Unless the pure poet explained his objectives and demonstrated their humane value to a larger audience, the gun-men would find plenty of hands ready to take up brickbats. Accordingly Stevens, overcoming a deep-seated aversion to public speaking, took to the podium (the soapbox was not his style) to promote what he called "a confidence in the spiritual role of the poet" (L 340). Poetry remained the ultimate subject of his poems and lectures in the decade following *Owl's Clover*. But often between the issue and the return this austere subject assumed the costume of two figures who first strode the stage in that book: medium man and major man.

Supreme Fiction and Medium Man

Towers have figured in the landscape of war ever since that first military engineer realized how they might be used to espy the enemy, signal his approach, and bombard him with discomfiting objects. To the general rule that towers and wars flourish together, the ivory tower would seem to be an exception. Not in Stevens' case, however. During World War II, he suggested how poetry, even the purest sort, might serve the soldier and the soldier poetry. Furthermore, if the social critics of the thirties provided him with the incentive to mount his defense of the ivory tower, the war provided him with the opportunity, when it prevented the American expatriate Henry Church from returning to France in 1939, after a visit to his native land.

Though Church was descended from a founder of the American firm of Church and Dwight, manufacturers of bicarbonate of soda, and sat on its board of directors, he had spent most of his adult life in Europe, wandering from one resort to another before settling in Ville d'Avray, near Paris. There, together with Jean Paulhan, editor of *La Nou velle Revue Française* and *éminence grise* of French letters, he founded the little magazine *Mesures*. Church dabbled in verse and puppet plays, but served the cause of modern literature and art chiefly as a patron. He first contacted Stevens in March 1939, when he wrote requesting permission to have several *Harmonium* poems translated for a special American number of *Mesures*. Till then, only "Peter Quince at the Clavier" had been translated and published in France, so Stevens must have been pleased at this recognition from one of the capitals of his imagination. He was apparently also intrigued to find that the editor of *Mesures*, a magazine to which he had subscribed for five years, was a fellow countryman, and one with ties to Hartford (*L* 338). Possibly for these reasons he dropped his usual reserve and spoke early in his correspondence with Church of the purpose closest to his heart:

> I am, in the long run, interested in pure poetry. No doubt from the Marxian point of view this sort of thing is incredible, but pure poetry is rather older and tougher than Marx and will remain so. My own way out toward the future involves a confidence in the spiritual role of the poet, who will somehow have to assist the painter, etc. (any artist, to tell the truth) in restoring to the imagination what it is losing at such a catastrophic pace, and in supporting what it has gained. (*L* 340)

This passage captures Stevens as he stood in 1939, glancing over his shoulder at his recent encounter with the left and looking forward with a sense of mission to the project that would engage him for the rest of his career. He had reason to believe that Church, even more than Latimer, would sympathize with this ambition. He tended to idealize the editor of *Mesures* as a man who successfully straddled the worlds of business and art, and once told Church that he had lived the life he would have chosen for himself (*L* 401). In Church's desultory letters, written in a potpourri of English, French, and German and only slightly more legible when typed, Stevens discerned an "intricate" personality (*L* 401). Church himself had no illusions about his effectiveness as a businessman—he once complained that the other directors of Church and Dwight twisted him around their little finger[1]—and his letters will strike most readers as self-indulgent rather than scintillating or profound. But he was not an uncreative man, especially if, as Stevens once asserted, money is a kind of poetry (*OP* 165).

The value of money, as of poetry, appears in the specific

---

1. Letter to Stevens, 24 Apr. 1945.

transaction. How was Church to use his wealth most creatively? This question confronted him anew in 1939, when he found himself unable to return to Ville d'Avray after a summer vacation in the United States. By the following April he had fixed upon two projects, which he submitted to Stevens for comment. Since the Paris *Mesures* was imperiled by the war, he wanted in the first place to start an American version of the magazine in Princeton, where he and his wife had taken up residence. He also wanted to set up a foundation to award scholarships to promising artists and writers. Stevens, speaking first as a disinterested party, turned over some of the legal and financial issues entailed in Church's projects. Then, as though chafing at the limitations of both schemes and hankering for something of grander scope, he proposed that Church found a chair of poetry at Harvard "for the study of the history of poetic thought and of the theory of poetry" (*L* 358).

Stevens' suggestion piqued Church's interest. That fall, he executed a will providing for the Henry and Barbara Church Foundation. Though set up to award scholarships, the Foundation could also be empowered to fund a chair of poetry if the idea proved feasible. Church had first to settle on a location for the chair. Stevens had suggested his alma mater, but Allen Tate and Lawrance Thompson of Princeton argued that their institution would be a better choice, as Harvard already had the Charles Eliot Norton Chair.[2] More crucial was the choice of first incumbent. With a man like Jean Paulhan, Stevens believed, the chair might transcend its academic setting; with a less expansive spirit it would probably come to nothing (*L* 358, 378). Whether Paulhan was ever invited is not clear; in any case, he remained in Paris, where he eventually joined the French Resistance and founded an underground literary review. While mulling over the choice of location and incumbent, Church decided to explore the scope and pur-

2. Letter from Church to Stevens, 29 June 1940.

pose of the chair indirectly, through a series of four lectures to be given at Princeton in the spring of 1941. These were to be delivered under the aegis of *Mesures*, whose publication in America now seemed out of the question. Not without some difficulty, Church persuaded Stevens to deliver one of the lectures.

Stevens' lecture, "The Noble Rider and the Sound of Words," is at once his most ambitious and most satisfactory attempt to define the nature of poetry and the spiritual role of the poet. He opens his lecture with an experiment in reading, choosing for his text Plato's description of the soul as a charioteer drawn across the heavens by a pair of winged horses, one of noble, the other of ignoble breed. As one reads this passage, Stevens suggests, one's emotional response traces a course analogous to that of the mismatched team, beginning in exultation and ending in disappointment. Assuming that Plato's first readers were able to sustain enthusiasm for this trope, one must confront the question Stevens poses at the outset of his lecture: what has happened to the imagination since Plato's day?

Plato's parable is the first of five "episodes" which Stevens uses to sketch the history of imaginative representation. The others, all featuring horse-mounted figures, include Verrocchio's formidable statue of Bartolommeo Colleoni; Cervantes' romance of Don Quixote; Clark Mills's homely statue of Andrew Jackson in Lafayette Square, Washington; and a reproduction of a painting called "Wooden Horses," which depicts, with a realism almost grotesque, four people riding on a merry-go-round. As one proceeds chronologically from Plato's metaphor to "Wooden Horses," Stevens observes, one finds less and less of the quality he calls "nobility." The word is a peculiar one in this context, and recalls T. S. Eliot's rejection of any "semi-ethical criterion" like "sublimity" in judging literary merit.[3] Stevens apparently wanted to retain the ethical con-

3. "Tradition and the Individual Talent," in *Selected Essays* (New York: Harcourt, Brace, 1950), p. 8. In a letter to Elsie of 26 May 1909, Stevens had associated nobility with Matthew Arnold's famous definition of po-

notations of "nobility," for he defines it not only as the "symbol or alter ego" of imagination but also as "our spiritual height and depth" (*NA* 7, 33–34). The term is not inappropriate when applied to human figures, and it does permit Stevens to exploit the noble-ignoble contrast in Plato's image: nobility is the immortal essence of poetry, that which enables it to soar until the ignoble element drags it down to earth. The ignoble element is, in a word, reality.

The palpable decline in nobility from Plato's chariot to "Wooden Horses" suggests that imagination has had to give ground before reality. Especially since the crash of 1929, Stevens contends, reality has exerted progressively more pressure upon the human spirit. The war then being fought in Europe was but one part of a "war-like whole" whose other parts included the assault on authority, anti-intellectualism, loss of religious faith, violations of privacy, lack of pride in one's work, and even—here Stevens airs one of his pet peeves—the affront of an income tax. The modern sensibility is inevitably shaped by this pressure and can no longer yield itself to works of art in which the noble or imaginative element predominates; hence the history of poetry, like that of the other arts, is a "cemetery of nobilities."

What should the poet do about this state of affairs? Pander to the modern taste for realism? Try to stem the tide by creating images of exaggerated nobility? Stevens denies, in the first place, that the poet has any social or moral obligation whatsoever; such an obligation would be merely another pressure of the ignoble sort. But he is responsible to the imagination, which, Stevens says, is inseparable from society. Indirectly, then, the poet performs a spiritual function in society, though few people—admittedly an elite—will knowingly benefit from his victories. He helps us to live our lives by creating "supreme fictions," poems or poetic images that strike a perfectly satisfactory balance

---

etry, observing that "what counts in poetry, is the 'noble elucidation of a difficult world,' the noble 'criticism of Life.'"

between the reality and imagination of the day. Such fictions "magnify us in our own eyes," unlike "Wooden Horses" or Mills's statue of Andrew Jackson, but magnify us credibly, unlike Plato's charioteer or Verrocchio's statue of Bartolommeo Colleoni.

Whether people can surrender themselves to a given fiction depends, in the last analysis, on the style in which it is couched. In poetry, style is music as well as image, the sound of words as well as the noble rider. Stevens turns to this aspect of his topic in a passage that echoes his poem "Of Modern Poetry," published the year before he delivered his lecture:

> The deepening need for words to express our thoughts and feelings which, we are sure, are all the truth that we shall ever experience, having no illusions, makes us listen to words when we hear them, loving them and feeling them, makes us search the sound of them, for a finality, a perfection, an unalterable vibration, which it is only within the power of the acutest poet to give them. . . . A poet's words are of things that do not exist without the words. Thus, the image of the charioteer and of the winged horses, which has been held to be precious for all of time that matters, was created by words of things that never existed without the words. A description of Verrocchio's statue could be the integration of an illusion equal to the statue itself. (*NA* 32–33)

To the "acutest poet" we turn for acutest speech—speech that persuades us to accept as "all the truth that we shall ever experience" things that "do not exist without the words." Lacking other illusions (those once afforded by religion, for example), we might still suspend our disbelief in the illusions of poetry.

In the closing paragraph of "The Noble Rider and the Sound of Words," Stevens compares nobility, that quality which distinguishes noble from ignoble riders, to a wave in water. Just as a wave is a force and not the water of which it is composed, so nobility is a force not to be confused with its manifestations. Thus "nobility" inherited the place in his vocabulary previously occupied by "pure poetry," "imagination," "the romantic," "Ananke," and simply "poetry." A year later, he retrieved from his early poem "A High-Toned Old Christian Woman" another phrase for the same thing: the "supreme fiction." This was apparently the singular—and singularly supreme—version of the "supreme fictions" of which he speaks in "The Noble Rider." But the phrase differs in genealogy and connotation from literary-historical terms like "pure poetry" and "the romantic," from a mythological term like "Ananke," and from a quasi-ethical term like "nobility."

Stevens' supreme fiction might be characterized most simply as a form of willful illusion. "The final belief," he contends in an adage, "is to believe in a fiction, which you know to be a fiction, there being nothing else. The exquisite truth is to know that it is a fiction and that you believe in it willingly" (*OP* 163). In this respect, the supreme fiction belongs to a tradition of literary illusions that includes some of Poe's poems, Huysmans' *À Rebours*, Villiers de l'Isle-Adam's *Axël*, Tennyson's "The Lady of Shalott," and Mallarmé's prose poem "Le Nénuphar blanc." In these and other nineteenth-century works, an exquisite illusion is deliberately contrived and sustained in the face of a sordid or humdrum reality.

Stevens would also have been at least remotely conscious of the legal and philosophical history behind the word "fiction." As a lawyer, he was working daily with patently false concepts which nevertheless served the ends of justice; indeed, the eminent legal philosopher Pierre de Tourtoulon once remarked that the lawyer who finds it difficult to grasp fictions may as well renounce his practice.[4] During Stevens' career as a lawyer, legal fictions came under the scrutiny of Lon L. Fuller, Morris R. Cohen, and other American philosophers. Like their colleagues in Germany, these men had been inspired by Hans Vaihinger's

4. *Philosophy in the Development of Law*, trans. Martha McC. Read, Modern Legal Philosophy Series, XIII (New York: Macmillan, 1922), p. 391.

Die Philosophie des Als Ob (1911), a monumental study which became available in English in 1924 under the title *The Philosophy of 'As If.'*[5] Vaihinger recommended that fictions be regarded as scaffolding, to be removed once the intellectual edifice—be it legal, mathematical, scientific, religious, philosophical, or aesthetic—is complete. He warned against the error, one to which he thought the religious believer especially prone, of turning the fiction ("as if") into hypothesis ("if") and finally dogma ("because").

Between Stevens' supreme fiction and Vaihinger's more systematic theory there are striking affinities, as several readers have noted.[6] Yet there is no evidence that Stevens ever read the German philosopher or even heard of him; in fact, he spoke in 1948 of a "science of illusions" as though no one had yet attempted such a study (*NA* 139). He had, however, read Nietzsche, to whom, as one of the precursors of fictionalism, Vaihinger devotes many pages. We shall see in the next chapter how Stevens absorbed and modified Nietzsche's notion of the hero while disclaiming any direct influence. If he also derived his supreme fiction from a passage in Nietzsche, it was apparently not the one Henry Church once quoted as a possible gloss on "Notes toward a Supreme Fiction."[7] Translated, the aphorism from *Beyond Good and Evil* reads,

> Why might not the world *which concerns us*—be a fiction? And to anyone who suggested: "But to a fiction belongs an originator [*Urheber*]?"—might it not be bluntly replied: *Why*? May not this "belong" also belong to the fiction?[8]

5. Trans. C. K. Ogden (London: Routledge and Kegan Paul, 1924).

6. See, for example, Henry Campbell, "Some Facts about the Theory of Fictions," *University of Mississippi Studies in English* 1 (1960): 51–65; Frank Doggett, *Stevens' Poetry of Thought* (Baltimore: Johns Hopkins University Press, 1966), pp. 98–119; and Frank Kermode, *The Sense of an Ending* (New York: Oxford University Press, 1967), pp. 35–64.

7. Letter to Stevens, 19 Apr. 1943.

8. *The Complete Works of Friedrich Nietzsche*, ed. Oscar Levy, XII (London: Foulis, 1909), 50. The Levy edition (18 vols., 1909–13) introduced English and American readers, including Stevens, to Nietzsche; hence I

Stevens thought this passage only tangentially related to "Notes"; but in his reply to Church he suggested a more pertinent source or analogue of his supreme fiction:

> The *Fiktion* of Aphorism 34 is the commonplace idea that the world exists only in the mind. So considered it is an unreal thing, in which logic does not have a place. Since an *Urheber* is a projection of logic, it is easy to dispose of him by disposing of logic. . . . This is quite a different fiction from that of the NOTES, even though it is present in the NOTES. We are confronted by a choice of ideas: the idea of God and the idea of man. The purpose of the NOTES is to suggest the possibility of a third idea: the idea of a fictive being, or state, or thing as the object of belief by way of making up for that element in humanism which is its chief defect.[9]

The fiction of Nietzsche's aphorism is present in the first poem of "Notes" as the "invented world" man creates for himself; but the supreme fiction of the poem is, as Stevens tells Church, a religious surrogate rather than an epistemological concept, a thing one might believe in rather than simply perceive or know. As such, it belongs to the history of religious thought, whatever its literary, legal, and philosophical antecedents. Specifically, it belongs to a phase of Stevens' religious development, whose progress we might briefly review here.

Stevens was raised a Presbyterian and later remembered that his mother, who was devoutly religious, always read a chapter of the Bible to her children before sending them to bed each night (*SP* 254). This traditional faith appears to have sustained him at least through his secondary schooling. In a speech he delivered as a senior at the Reading Boys' High School, he affirmed his belief in the teeth of that bugbear of the nineteenth century, the "higher criticism": "Think you that Jesus of Nazareth would not have convinced the Jews that He was the Son of God, as He has

---

use it here and in Chapter Seven despite its occasionally unreliable translations.

9. Letter of 21 Apr.

convinced us, if the chance had offered? Christianity would be a myth if it had not had the chance to produce conviction of its nobility, its godliness. . . ."[10] If this passage strains to illustrate the orator's main theme, the importance of opportunity, it nevertheless suggests that Jesus was the first of Stevens' noble riders.[11]

At Harvard, Stevens both lost his faith and found it anew, in the form it would take during most of his adult life. The College had, at the turn of the century, a reputation for being "atheistical,"[12] which meant simply that its windows were open to the winds of every doctrine. The prevailing easterlies had for over half a century been unsettling to religious orthodoxy, for they carried new theories, invested with all the authority of science, respecting the origins of man and the universe. From Germany came a still more radical, though necessarily speculative, account of the genesis of God. Speaking to English and American readers through George Eliot's translation, Ludwig Feuerbach argued in *The Essence of Christianity* (1841, translation 1854) that

> [r]eligion, at least the Christian, is the relation of man to himself, or more correctly to his own nature (*i.e.*, his subjective nature); but a relation to it, viewed as a nature apart from his own. The divine being is nothing else than the human being, or, rather, the human nature purified, freed from the limits of the individual man, made objective—*i.e.*, contemplated and revered as another, a distinct being. All the attributes of the divine nature are, therefore, attributes of the human nature.[13]

The militant American atheist Colonel Robert Green Ingersoll reduced Feuerbach's cautious prose to vivid aphorism when he preached on the text, "An honest God is the

10. "Greatest Need of the Age," p. 5, col. 2.
11. In her fine study of Stevens' transvaluation of traditional Christian beliefs and forms, Adelaide Kirby Morris argues that Stevens' heroes of the thirties and forties continue to recall, even as they depart from, the Jesus of the gospels; see *Wallace Stevens: Imagination and Faith*, pp. 121–35.
12. Hapgood, *The Changing Years*, p. 54.
13. Reprinted New York: Harper, 1957, p. 14.

noblest work of man."[14] This was a new way to roast an old chestnut, but no longer, in 1874, an original thesis.

Assailed from without by an array of scientific evidence and from within by the suspicion that his faith might be mere anthropomorphism, the thoughtful young man born in the late nineteenth century was reduced to the state of mind Stevens confided to his journal in 1906; alluding to the sacred groves of the Romans, he fretted,

> I wish that groves still *were* sacred—or, at least, that something was: that there was still something free from doubt, that day unto day still uttered speech, and night unto night still showed wisdom. I grow tired of the want of faith—the instinct of faith. Self-consciousness convinces me of something, but whether it be something Past, Present or Future I do not know. . . . It would be much *nicer* to have things definite— both human and divine. One wants to be decent and to know the reason why. (*SP* 158–59)[15]

To have things definite: this much no longer seemed possible. One could be sure only that one still wanted to believe, that one possessed the instinct of faith. Did this preclude the practice of religion? Not necessarily. Barbara Charlesworth notes that Pater's Marius, though he cannot assent fully to the truths of Christianity, still proceeds *as if* they were true.[16] Thus he qualifies as a "pragmatic" martyr, one whose mode of faith William James articulated in *The Will to Believe* (1897), published just months before Stevens entered Harvard.[17]

James addresses his book, as he had addressed the lectures which make it up, to those whose capacity for faith has been paralyzed by the notion that they cannot believe

14. *The Gods and Other Lectures* (Peoria, Ill.: n.p., 1874), p. 7.

15. Morris points out that the first sentence of this passage echoes Psalm 19:2—"Day unto day uttereth speech, and night unto night sheweth knowledge" (p. 40).

16. *Dark Passages*, p. 50.

17. *The Will to Believe and Other Essays in Popular Philosophy* (New York: Longmans). I draw chiefly upon the title essay, pp. 1–31, in the summary which follows.

anything for which scientific evidence is lacking. Such persons have every right, he argues, to adopt an attitude of belief toward the postulates of religion. Since these postulates have not been demonstrated intellectually, they must be regarded as hypotheses rather than dogma. But one is not obliged to remain skeptical, for skepticism is itself based on the hypothesis that there is no truth. The skeptical attitude is in fact less defensible than the dogmatic, for, besides being *practically* indistinguishable from dogmatic atheism, it interferes with further testing of religious hypotheses. In his anxiety to avoid error, the skeptic may absent himself from the laboratory altogether and so lose the opportunity for discovering truth.

For James, that hypothesis is best which works best. In a given situation, he concedes, both skeptical and religious hypotheses may "work"; but one will produce better results than the other. By way of illustration, he offers the example of a mountain climber who finds himself in a position from which he can escape only by leaping across a chasm. Never having confronted such a challenge before, he cannot be intellectually certain that he will leap the chasm successfully. If he doubts his ability, he will probably fail; if he believes, he stands a better chance of succeeding. Although his hypothesis is verified in either case, he will have less time to savor his intellectual victory if he chooses to doubt. James concedes that we are disposed by temperament and training to regard some religious hypotheses as "live" and others as "dead." One may not be able to believe in a particular kind of God or accept the articles of a particular creed. But one is better advised, James believed, to take the risk of "precursive" or "voluntarily adopted" faith rather than remain immobilized by doubt.

In effect, *The Will to Believe* reconstructed the religious universe on the *dubito* much as Descartes had rebuilt the physical universe on the *cogito*. James's message was received enthusiastically, and it passed quickly into intellectual and popular culture. When a professor of philosophy at Columbia University tried to envision the religion of the future for readers of the *New Republic* in 1924, he predicted that it would retain some of the old dogmas, but transformed into hypotheses and so rendered intellectually respectable. "The most fantastic theory of the supernatural," he averred, "if held as a hypothesis, is honorable, and belief in it is honest and to be respected."[18]

Stevens, though he never took a course from James at Harvard and may not have read *The Will to Believe*, was at least familiar with the gist of the book. Writing to a Harvard classmate in 1943 concerning *Notes toward a Supreme Fiction*, he invoked James to help explain the attitude behind his poem:

> Underlying it is the idea that, in the various predicaments of belief, it might be possible to yield, or to try to yield, ourselves to a declared fiction.
> This is the same thing as saying that it might be possible for us to believe in something that we know to be untrue. Of course, we do that every day, but we don't make the most of the fact that we do it out of the need to believe, what in your day, and mine, in Cambridge was called the will to believe.
> (*L* 443)

A fiction is not, of course, a hypothesis; as defined by Stevens, the fiction is known to be untrue, whereas a hypothesis is simply unverified. Yet Stevens' attitude—what might be called his religious disposition—is the one James advocated. It explains not only his willingness to pass beyond skepticism in speculative "notes" but also some of the apparent contradictions between his religious beliefs and practice. Though he ceased after college to regard the Presbyterian God as a "live" hypothesis, he denied that he was an atheist (*L* 735). He might call the institutional church "largely a relic," declare that he hated the look of a Bible, and protest that he was not in the least religious (*L* 140, 102, 96). But he continued, his letters indicate, to at-

18. William Pepperell Montague, "The Promethean Challenge to Religion," *New Republic*, 6 Aug. 1924, p. 294.

tend church services, to read the Bible, and to weigh various religious hypotheses. "I ought to say," he told one correspondent in 1940, "that it is a habit of mind with me to be thinking of some substitute for religion. I don't necessarily mean some substitute for the church, because no one believes in the church as an institution more than I do. My trouble, and the trouble of a great many people, is the loss of belief in the sort of God in Whom we were all brought up to believe" (*L* 348). Near the end of his life, we shall see, Stevens affirmed his belief in the church as an institution, though probably not in his childhood God, by accepting instruction and baptism in the Roman Catholic faith.

In several *Harmonium* poems, Stevens delights in poking fun at religious orthodoxy. "A High-Toned Old Christian Woman," for example, finds him inviting the woman to regard an article of dogma as hypothesis and then to consider what sort of religion might be built on a contrary and equally plausible hypothesis. The poem supports Daniel Fuchs's thesis, that Stevens' wit is directed mainly at fictions which have failed him.[19] Its title indicates, however, that the woman's self-righteous manner is as much the object of satire as her beliefs. That the author of "A High-Toned Old Christian Woman" was not altogether the village atheist he seems to be is suggested by another *Harmonium* piece, "Palace of the Babies" (1921). The first four stanzas of this poem represent a "disbeliever" who walks in the moonlight outside a "palace," probably a church, inhabited by believers. The reader is invited to share the skeptic's low esteem for the faithful: they are "babies," immature if innocent, and nourished on the dreams which come in sleep. If this is faith, then Stevens was justified in asserting that "[l]oss of faith is growth" (*OP* 172). But is the skeptic any less dogmatic, in his way? The last two

19. *The Comic Spirit of Wallace Stevens* (Durham: Duke University Press, 1963), p. 30.

stanzas of the poem imply that skepticism may also be a form of willful ignorance:

> Night nursed not him in whose dark mind
> The clambering wings of birds of black revolved,
> Making harsh torment of the solitude.

> The walker in the moonlight walked alone,
> And in his heart his disbelief lay cold.
> His broad-brimmed hat came close upon his eyes.

Like the rationalists in the sixth of "Six Significant Landscapes" (1916), the disbeliever trims his thinking to the cut of his hat; he will not expose his eyes to illusory "moonlight." Besides restricting his vision, his mental haberdashery leaves him isolated and, ironically, benighted. In place of the agreeable angels' wings which animate the dreams of the believers, he has only the "harsh torment" of crows' wings.

Between dogmatic belief and dogmatic disbelief, James had cleared the ground for precursive faith, a willingness to believe. It was this position that Stevens occupied until about 1940, when he adopted the more active posture of voluntary or willed belief. That year he published "Asides on the Oboe," which begins with an ultimatum:

> The prologues are over. It is a question, now,
> Of final belief. So, say that final belief
> Must be in a fiction. It is time to choose.

It is the voluntary aspect of Stevens' proposed belief, together with its fictive object, that has scandalized some of his readers, beginning with the college student who told him it is impossible to believe in something known to be untrue (L 430). Stevens was thus taking a significant step beyond James, who had defended the right to believe in something not known to be false. Stevens was apparently combining James's will to believe with an object of belief conceived in non-Jamesian terms. That object may have come from James's colleague and former student, George

Santayana, whose *Interpretations of Poetry and Religion* (1900) appeared during Stevens' last year at Harvard.[20]

According to Santayana, poetry and religion are both human fabrications, designed to express and at least partly to satisfy man's longing for the ideal. Identical in essence, they differ only in their relation to practical affairs. Religion is poetry in which we believe, usually without knowing it to be poetry, hence it affects our behavior. We continue to believe in a given religious myth as long as it satisfies our sense of poetic propriety. Thus the Christian system, a kind of epic poem and allegory of human experience, succeeded paganism, Neo-Platonism, and Judaism when their appeal began to wane. Today, Christianity is in decline because certain of its doctrines—that of eternal punishment, for example—have become distasteful or meaningless; they are incredible because they violate our sense of poetic propriety.

Up to this point, Santayana was developing a corollary of Feuerbach's thesis, that man had created God in his ideal image and likeness. Like Feuerbach, he takes some pleasure in unmasking religion, which has traditionally preferred to disguise its poetry under the more eulogistic terms "revelation" and "prophecy." But Santayana does not recommend that we exorcise our gods, as Freud would later advise in *The Future of an Illusion* (1927). On the contrary, he attacks those who try to make religion scientifically respectable by reducing the element of poetic mythology. A residual mythology is still mythology, but with less of that which endears it to the imagination; one cannot love abstract concepts or logical categories. Rather than seek to abolish the imagination, positive science should recognize it as an ally. Whereas mysticism attempts to sub-

20. New York: Scribners, 1900. For Santayana's reaction to *The Will to Believe*, see his "William James," in *Character and Opinion in the United States* (New York: Scribners, 1920), pp. 64–96, passim; for James's reaction to Santayana's *Poetry and Religion*, see Ralph Barton Perry, *The Thought and Character of William James* (Boston: Little, Brown, 1935), II: 319–20.

vert the understanding and reason, imagination builds upon them, enabling them to reach the sphere toward which they tend.

Santayana is pessimistic regarding the immediate future of religion, for he can see no new mythology rising from the ruins of Christianity. This he considers a great loss, as much to poetry as to religion. Apart from religion, poetry is speech for its own sake; in the hands of the Symbolists it had become a kind of stained glass window, devised rather to be seen for itself than to admit light. Though "pure," such poetry can become frivolous and demoralizing. Santayana contends that the highest poetry is identical with religion; as such, it permits us to glimpse the ideal—not so as to persuade us that the ideal is reality, but to give direction and meaning to our daily lives. The supreme poet, then, would be a prophet and not merely a euphuist. Santayana implies that if religion has a future it lies in the deliberate creation of a satisfactory myth or poem, known by at least some of its believers (those, certainly, who have read *Poetry and Religion*) to be a human fiction.

Stevens was editor of the *Harvard Advocate* when it published an unsigned review of *Poetry and Religion*.[21] Whether he wrote the review or even read the book may never be known; but he repeatedly echoes Santayana's thesis in his lectures and letters. In "The Figure of the Youth as Virile Poet" (1943), for example, he speaks of the idea of God as the "supreme poetic idea" and our notions of heaven and hell as "merely poetry not so called, even if poetry that involves us vitally" (*NA* 51). In "Two or Three Ideas" (1951), he maintains that we create our gods out of a need for the perfection they represent. The gods satisfy this need to the extent that they exhibit the sort of stylistic "propriety" and "felicity" one finds in a good poem. Much as Santayana had dismissed mere euphuism, Stevens re-

21. Quoted in Morse, pp. 54–55.

jects "eccentric and dissociated" poetry (*OP* 207, 211). In neither of these lectures does Stevens allude to Santayana; but his late poem "To an Old Philosopher in Rome" (1952) indicates that he was familiar with Santayana's philosophic enterprise—his aspiration toward an ideal realm which informed his vision of the real world. When Stevens characterizes the old philosopher as "a citizen of heaven though still of Rome" he recalls Santayana's assertion, in *Poetry and Religion*, that religion serves "to make us citizens, by anticipation, in the world we crave."[22]

Stevens was inevitably reminded of his former mentor when, in October 1940, he drafted a memorandum defining the scope of the Henry Church Chair of Poetry and the character of its ideal first incumbent. He balked only at what he took to be an excess of "the religious and the philosophic" in Santayana (*L* 378).[23] This was a curious reservation, especially in light of the task he assigned the chair's incumbent in the same memorandum:

> The major poetic idea in the world is and always has been the idea of God. One of the visible movements of the modern imagination is the movement away from the idea of God. The poetry that created the idea of God will either adapt it to our different intelligence, or create a substitute for it, or make it unnecessary. . . . The knowledge of poetry is a part of philosophy, and a part of science; the import of poetry is the import of the spirit. The figures of the essential poets should be spiritual figures. (*L* 378)

If Santayana's religious and philosophical interests disqualified him from lecturing on a major poetic idea to take the place of God in the modern imagination, who, then, was qualified? Stevens would have protested that he himself lacked the proper credentials, even if he had been free to accept the position. Nevertheless, a year and a half after

22. Page vi.
23. In a holograph draft of the memorandum, Stevens says not that he considered the religious and philosophic side of Santayana "too dominant" (*L* 378), but that it "would call for conversion."

drafting his memorandum he began work on "Notes to-ward a Supreme Fiction" (1942), a sequence whose thirty poems range widely over past and possible mythologies of self in search of one that might stand in the place of God. To consider "Notes" carefully is also to consider the themes which preoccupy Stevens in the two volumes that belong to this phase of his career, *Parts of a World* (1942) and *Transport to Summer* (1947).

"Notes toward a Supreme Fiction" is fittingly dedicated to the sponsor of the proposed Henry Church Chair of Poetry, inasmuch as it grew out of Stevens' effort to define the chair's purpose and scope. But if Church was the im-petus to "Notes" in the way that Latimer had been the impetus to *Ideas of Order*, he was not its source. That from which the poem issues and to which it returns is, as ever, poetry; and it is poetry, personified as Interior Paramour, that Stevens addresses in the invocation: "And for what, except for you, do I feel love?" From this intimate chamber, where even the "extremest book of the wisest man" is an impertinence, it might seem a far journey to the classroom where the poet lectures on the first of his three proposi-tions. Yet he speaks with an authority that proceeds from his privileged relationship with his subject.

Paradoxically, this professor advocates ignorance. "You must become an ignorant man again," he tells his student in the first poem of "It Must Be Abstract," "And see the sun again with an ignorant eye. . . ." Many of Stevens' poems roughly contemporary with "Notes" recur to igno-rance as though it were a state of pastoral innocence prior to rationalistic or imaginative sophistication. In "The Sense of the Sleight-of-Hand-Man" (1939), for example, he spec-ulates that only the ignorant man may be able to "mate his life with life / That is the sensual, pearly spouse." Thus wedded, the ignorant man enjoys a sensuous rapport with reality that Stevens sometimes calls "belief" to distinguish it from mere knowledge. "Of Bright & Blue Birds & the Gala Sun" (1940) celebrates this *gaya scienza*, "A gaiety that is being, not merely knowing, / The will to be and to be total in belief." In Stevens' seasonal mythology, summer is preëminently the time of ignorance and belief—hence the "Credences of Summer" he professes in another long poem that shares with "Notes" the pages of *Transport to Summer*.

Together with the special kind of "poverty" invoked later in "Notes," ignorance and belief define the experience of the figure Stevens called "medium man" in the final poem of *Owl's Clover*. What sort of poetry would the ephebe write were he to become a medium man? Probably none at all, for Jocundus of "Sombre Figuration" is "indifferent to the poet's hum" (*OP* 71). In trying to represent medium man's experience poetically, Stevens was trying to represent the ineffable—ineffable not because it transcended speech, but because it lay too deep for words. Supposing, however, that medium man could produce poetry commensurate with his vision, that poetry might be the kind described by Baudelaire in a passage Stevens transcribed into his commonplace book in 1950: "la grande poésie est bête: elle croit."[24] How far this poetry of belief might travel in the direction of the beastlike is suggested by a letter Stevens wrote to the young Cuban editor José Rodríguez Feo in 1945. After observing that "perhaps the only really happy man, or the only man with any wide range of possible happiness, is the ignorant man," he proceeded to compare the ignorant man with Rodríguez Feo's mule, Pompilio: "The elaboration of the most commonplace ideas as, for example, the idea of God, has been terribly destructive of such ideas. But the ignorant man has no ideas. His trouble is that he still feels. Pompilio does not even feel. Pompilio is the blank realist who sees only what there is to see without feeling, without imagination, but with large eyes that require no spectacles" (*L* 512).

Under Stevens' tutelage, the ephebe runs little risk of

24. *Sur Plusieurs Beaux Sujects*, Cahier II, p. 18.

the metamorphosis suffered by Bottom in *Midsummer Night's Dream*. The ignorant man, as Stevens' letter indicates, is not a "blank realist," without feeling for what he sees. Furthermore, the injunction to become an ignorant man again points, like Jesus' "You must become a child again," to a means rather than an end. Glossing this part of "Notes," Stevens remarked, "One of the approaches to fiction is by way of its opposite: reality, the truth, the thing observed, the purity of the eye" (*L* 444). By whatever name, this "opposite" serves as a kind of true north from which to measure imaginative declination. Like true north, it cannot be experienced directly. When the ephebe penetrates to the "quick" of the sun we have invented in myth and metaphor, he will see not the thing itself, the "something that never could be named," but his idea or mental image of the thing. If the ephebe cannot escape his own mind and know the sun as sun, however, he can still know it in its "first idea," that primitive distortion of the sun which Stevens calls a "falseness close to kin" in Section VI.

When Stevens calls the sun "gold flourisher" at the end of Section I, he presumably strikes close to its first idea. He also violates the spirit if not the letter of his prohibition against naming the sun, thus betraying in himself the "motive for metaphor" whose cogency he records in a 1943 poem (*CP* 288). This prepares us for the cyclic progress described in Section II, from metaphor to first idea and from first idea back to metaphor. To contemplate the first idea of anything is "not to have," a condition of salutary poverty that may, if prolonged, become the "destitution" evoked in Section IX of "Esthétique du Mal" (1944). Desiring the exhilaration of change, as one desires spring after winter, one then contrives those metaphoric "ravishments" that satisfy until another sort of tedium, the "ennui of apartments," sets in.[25] The mind comes full circle when

25. I construe "apartments" less literally than Harold Bloom, who regards this passage as a rather intrusive expression of Stevens' "distaste at

it returns from exhausted metaphor, "what is not," to the first idea.

The following section describes this same cycle in less invidious terms. Where Section II emphasizes the ennui one feels at either extreme, Section III stresses their "immaculate" or "candid" character. The last three tercets illustrate the thesis of the first four: to call the moon Diana, let us say, would conduce to more of the "stale moonlight" dismissed at the end of Section II; to call it an Arabian is to establish a startling relation between things ordinarily "strange" to one another. We exercise our poetic license to the full when, going beyond this visual relationship, we invent an incantation for the normally silent moon; its "hoobla-hoobla-hoobla-how" then rimes with the dove's "hoobla-hoo" and the ocean's "hoo." Our "saying" thus enables us to share the refreshment of the man on the dump of a 1938 poem, whose radical imagination launches the moon into the spring night, above the accumulated trash of moon-metaphors (CP 201–3).

Section III suggests how poetry, otherwise so alien to medium man's experience, can nevertheless approximate it. Words, as Stevens says in "Variations on a Summer Day," XIV, "Are the eye grown larger, more intense." Words can, of course, imprison; with only a little exaggeration, Stevens maintains in "Description without Place," III, that the world today is what Calvin, Queen Anne of England, Pablo Neruda, Nietzsche, and Lenin described it to be. But used by someone who knows how to restore their candor, words can also liberate. Barbara Church's phrase "blue and white Munich," casually dropped in a letter, had this effect upon Stevens in 1948, dramatically revising his somber image of the German city (L 605). He recalled the phrase a few months later in his lecture "Imagination as Value" (NA 140) and also reflected on its emotional impact in a letter

---

being surrounded by apartment-dwellers" (p. 179). Compare the "romantic tenements / Of rose and ice" in "Man and Bottle" (1940).

to Rodríguez Feo: "It is like changing records on a gramophone to speak of the red and the almost artificial green of mango skins and then speak of blue and white Munich. But unless we do these things to reality, the damned thing closes in [on] us, walls us up and buries us alive" (L 599).

Section VII rounds out the first group of poems in "It Must Be Abstract" and sets the stage for the second. The ignorance or candor of Sections I–VI is largely a willed state, as suggested by locutions like "You must become an ignorant man," "The sun / Must bear no name," and "We say: At night an Arabian." In Section VII, medium man's experience is not "achieved"; it simply "happens." Unlike the anxious confrontation between the ephebe and brute reality represented in Section V, this is a time when mind embraces world "As a man and woman meet and love forthwith." Like the "latest freed man" of a poem first published together with "The Man on the Dump," one is then almost preternaturally awake, and the "academies" or established structurings of the world seem to lose their solidity. It is, too, a time without myth. The professor of Section I had cautioned his ephebe not to suppose a Creator of the first idea, since a transcendent "inventing mind" would be itself an invention. In Section IV, he had asserted that the world was already in place, "Venerable and articulate and complete," before humanity arrived to colonize heaven with its gods. Is it tragic that the sky should reciprocate only the faintest echoes of the "sweeping meanings" we project onto it? For most of us, as for the woman in "Sunday Morning," this is undeniably "hard . . . in spite of blazoned days"; but not for medium man, who maintains that "It feels good as it is without the giant, / A thinker of the first idea."

One who is content to enjoy the world without ascribing its "Swiss perfection" to an immortal watchmaker will probably also be satisfied with the man in the old coat and sagging pantaloons of Section X. This Chaplinesque figure stands for the mass of humanity; as such, he balks the dreams of those who, like the rabbi and chieftain, long to surpass the human condition. As in Section I, Stevens exhorts the ephebe to adhere closely to this first idea, to propound it plainly. Such discipline is, however, preliminary to the ephebe's ultimate task, which is to render the "final elegance" of this inelegant creature. The "commonal" has its heroic as well as its pathetic dimension, and once the outsetting bard has graduated from the school of ignorance he will undertake the task outlined in "The Noble Rider and the Sound of Words": he will magnify us in our own eyes by fashioning credible fictions of nobility.

Sections VIII through X represent these noble fictions collectively under the epithet "major man," a phrase that suggests our supreme idea of man in much the same way that "gold flourisher" suggests our supreme idea of the sun.[26] Major man is otherwise to remain nameless, unlike the merely humanistic figure named MacCullough in Section VIII. Were MacCullough to read about God (the anthropomorphic "pensive giant") in the book of nature, his experience might parallel ours as we begin to read Plato's parable of the chariot drawn by two horses, before the trope fails us. He might intuit, in the sound of the ocean surf, the nobility of a being "leaner" or more abstract than himself. Since the ocean-text is description ("phrase," "deepened speech") as well as place ("wave"), one can speak legitimately of its rhetorical mode. According to Section IX, that mode should be neither "reason's click-clack" nor "romantic intoning" but reason and revery subsumed in "accurate song."

Section IX epitomizes Stevens' difficulty in projecting a supreme fiction. The mind cannot abide an abstract "idea of man" any more than it can remain content with a "first

26. I reserve the title "major man" for the ideal hero evoked in "Abstract," VIII–X, departing in this respect from Frank Doggett, who includes the man in sagging pantaloons, the planter on the blue island, and even MacCullough among the "major men" of "Notes"; see *Stevens' Poetry of Thought*, pp. 101, 108, and *Wallace Stevens: The Making of the Poem*, pp. 100–101.

idea" of reality; it moves impulsively toward mythology and metaphor. Nor is this a degenerative movement, if the fiction is to be an object of belief. Merely rational systems, Santayana had pointed out, leave nothing for the imagination and feelings to dwell upon. Stevens had recognized as much before he began writing "Notes," when he observed that it is easier to believe in something created by imagination than to believe in the imagination itself (*L* 370). That fiction, he noted years later, might well take the form of "an agreed-on super-man" (*L* 789). Thus humanized, the supreme fiction dwells in the same aura of affection that surrounds the Interior Paramour in the invocation to the poem: "The hot of him is purest in the heart." What Stevens demands in the line immediately preceding this one—"Dismiss him from your images"—is consequently neither possible nor desirable, for to strip the supreme fiction entirely of its human imagery, to make it truly abstract, is effectively to dislodge it from the heart.

Wary none the less of over-specifying the supreme fiction, Stevens retreats from the something created by imagination to imagination itself. He alludes to major man just once more in "Notes," and then obliquely, in Section IX of "It Must Give Pleasure." The two parts which follow "It Must Be Abstract" differ from it in another respect. Unifying the ten poems of "Abstract" is an obvious formal convention, the Master Poet instructing an imaginary disciple in the intricacies of his craft. Though the Master departs from this frame to apostrophize his muse in Section IX, he otherwise adheres to it, opening and closing "Abstract" with sentences addressed to the ephebe. The twenty poems ranged under the headings "It Must Change" and "It Must Give Pleasure" are formally more eclectic, consisting of anecdotes, skits, meditations, and apostrophes to the muse and various other figures. Satire, which is used sparingly in "Abstract" (in Sections V and VIII, for example) becomes more prominent in "Change" and "Pleasure."

It is a satirical piece, Section III, that affords the easiest

transition from "Abstract" to "Change." Were major man
to be given a name and represented in a definite image, he
would suffer the fate of General Du Puy, a "noble rider" in
the mold of Clark Mills's statue of General Jackson. Fixed
in bronze, the General cannot change to meet our changing requirements for nobility. To another generation, this
"strongly-heightened effigy" might have served as an appealing image of heroism; but now the doctors and lawyers
who pass the statue on their Sunday promenades find it
absurd rather than uplifting. The General has become at
best an object of antiquarian interest, at worst the sort of
"rubbish" the man on the dump must surmount.

The ceaseless activity of Section I differs little, in terms
of its effect upon the reader, from the General's rigid inac-
tivity. Another statue, the parcel-gilded seraph, is the appropriate genius of this scene, whose elements remain ge-
nerically the same even though one generation of violets,
doves, girls, bees, and hyacinths succeeds another. Such
repetition provokes, not the pleasure accruing to genuine
change, but disgust. Surrounded by evidence of Eros, one
nevertheless feels that the "obvious acid" of Thanatos dic-
tates this constant inconstancy.

Death may, of course, be the mother of beauty. Remove
even this potential for change and one has the scene of
Section II, utterly static but for the "red-blue dazzle" of the
flag. The President of the Immortals sees to it that there is
no change of death in this American paradise. In lines that
recall the mock-heroic apotheosis of Belinda's famous lock
of hair, he resurrects the bee whose blunt booming concluded Section I. As the questions of the next-to-last tercet
imply, however, this "spring" is not an awakening but another form of sleep.

Representing the same kind of stasis and repetition as
General Du Puy, the parcel-gilded seraph, and the immor-
talized bee is the "bird / Of stone" in Section VI, whose
plaintive "Bethou me" (he sounds more like a catbird than
a sparrow, as Stevens recognized—L 435, 438) contends

with the harsher cries of the wren, jay, and robin. By contrast with the silent raindrops, represented as clappers lacking bells to strike against, the chorus in the glade constitutes a gong "heavenly" in the pejorative sense: living in the repetitious world of Section I, the birds aspire to the changeless eternity of Section II. The sparrow in particular would remake the world and its animating spirit in his own image, like Eve in "Abstract," IV, or Shelley in his "Ode to the West Wind." Lest we feel overly superior to this tireless chorister, the final lines of the poem remind us that his song, which Stevens later characterized as "the spirit's own seduction" (L 438), is not so different from our own "seducing hymn[s]." Whether tuneless or tuneful, all the hymns will end, having seduced only their singers.

Sections I–III and VI proceed by satire's indirection. In Section IV, located strategically between the anecdotes of General Du Puy and the planter on the blue island, we find their direction out. The poem locates the origin of change in the fruitful embrace of opposites, including the embrace of the imagined and the real. From this coupling will issue neither blunt booming nor heavenly gong, but the "particulars of rapture." Section VII of "Change," like the corresponding section of "Abstract," begins by stressing the raptures of the real enjoyed by the ignorant man. This time, however, his bliss is said to be accessible in the text of reality written, paradoxically, by the "scholar," the man of imagination. Compelled as surely as the ignorant man by Eros, the scholar attends less to certainty than to its fluctuations, less to perception than to its changes of degree.

The scholar has several avatars in "It Must Change," any one of whom might serve as exemplar for the ephebe who was cowed by reality in "Abstract," V. There is the Shelleyan Ozymandias of Section VIII, who makes amends for the Shelleyan sparrow by clothing reality, Nanzia Nunzio, in the fictions which proceed from his thought and feeling for her. There is also the "vagabond in metaphor" of Section X, whose imagination turns the park into a Theatre of Trope. Like Stevens on one of his visits to the pond in Elizabeth Park, he sits beside the lake and witnesses the changes wrought by Shelley's west wind: swans become seraphs and saints, the blank surface is relieved by "iris frettings." Time will record these "amours" of imagination and reality, and in that sense they will end, like the sparrow's "Bethou me"—but not before they have accomplished a transformation of self commensurate with their transformation of the world.

Time has already recorded the amours of the planter in Section V, a poem that might serve as elegy for any hero of the imagination. A native of the melon-colored land of reality, a land never far from his thoughts, the planter went on to cultivate a blue island of imagination. Though his "plantation" has fallen into a state of disrepair—the house has collapsed and the fruit trees have run wild—his fictions have a vitality that outlives their maker. Like the mansion and landscape in "A Postcard from the Volcano" (1936), the planter's island still testifies to the labor and affection of its former occupant, still manifests what he felt at what he saw. What would a man of his vision most regret leaving at death—the red land from which he had emigrated, or those unsubdued islands to the south, laden with fictive fruit more exotic than his own oranges and limes? Neither, as it turns out. This amorist reserves his final sigh for one of the particulars of rapture, the banjo's twang. By a happy coincidence, it appears that this poem was to Stevens what the banjo's twang was to the planter (L 435).

I suspect that the "great banana tree, / Which pierces clouds and bends on half the world" is Stevens' impression of the tropical sun, described previously in the poem as "the greenest sun." In this extreme south of the imagination, the melon of reality might seem inexplicably common, like the "gibberish of the vulgate" invoked in Section IX. In the red land, conversely, those southern bananas might seem equally unintelligible, a "poet's gibberish."

Like the planter of Section V, the poet of Section IX mediates between these extremes; standing at the frontiers of sensibility, he strives to translate the vulgate of experience into his own tongue without losing its "peculiar potency." That potency inheres in a combination—what Stevens had called a "cross-fertilization" when defining his "new romantic" in the thirties (OP 252)—of the real and the imaginary and lends poignancy to the most anomalous poem, the "luminous flittering / Or the concentration of a cloudy day [.]" Stevens might have been paraphrasing Section IX when he told a correspondent in 1945 that "a poem must have a peculiarity, as if it was the momentarily complete idiom of that which prompts it, even if that which prompts it is the vaguest emotion" (L 500). Section IX thus restates in more schematic terms the lesson the ephebe learns at the end of "It Must Be Abstract": the way to the final elegance lies through the commonal, plainly propounded.

The ten poems of "It Must Give Pleasure" seem, on the one hand, even more eclectic and less rigorously subordinated to the thesis stated in their title than those in "It Must Change." On the other hand, there is greater continuity from poem to poem, especially as one nears the end of the sequence; the Canon Aspirin anecdote occupies two consecutive sections, while the next three sections pursue a line of thought having to do with an angel. Several of the situations and personae in "Pleasure" are familiar: the marriage of the great captain and Bawda in IV echoes the relationship of Ozymandias and Nanzia Nunzio and other "amours" in "Abstract" and "Change"; Section IX includes an encore by the wren and robin of "Change," IV. However, the reader must not respond automatically to themes and motifs he has encountered previously in "Notes," for "It Must Give Pleasure" invites him to reconsider his attitude toward such things as self-projection, repetition, and naming.

One seeking a ready transition from "It Must Change" to "It Must Give Pleasure" will find it in Section III, which

represents Jehovah as we might know him today if religious revelation had ended with the Old Testament. This
once majestic and potent figure has become a great stone
face, planted in the imagination as implacably as a statue
in a garden. The adjectives that pervade the first five tercets of the poem allow no latitude of emotional response,
being all of a kind: "lasting," "unending," "weathered,"
"worn," "spent," "tedious," "faded," "dull," "used." Not
until the adamant visage has possessed us completely does
Stevens remind us that its domination is purely hypothetical. Jesus released us from the old regime by his death and
the harrowing of a hell more imaginative than theological.
Whether or not Jesus really rose from the dead—Stevens'
"Or so they said" commits him to the "saying" or myth
but not to historical fact—the gospel story illustrates one
quality of the supreme fiction: it gives pleasure through
change. Manifesting their pleasure, Jesus' disciples ca-
rouse (the word and its context recall the "chant in orgy"
of "Sunday Morning" and the "jovial hullabaloo" of "A
High-Toned Old Christian Woman") and children scatter
flowers whose variety and freshness contrast with the stale
adjectives of the old dispensation.

Section III is concerned more with the effects of change
than its cause, which is presumably a fertile embrace of
opposites in the manner of "Change," IV. One can be sure
that Stevens' Orphic Jesus would not come to life for the
anonymous persona of Section VII, who tries to precipitate
change by fiat. This builder of capitols recalls the "skeleton
architects" of *Owl's Clover* and anticipates Konstantinov,
the "logical lunatic" of "Esthétique du Mal," XIV. In "The
Blue Buildings in the Summer Air" (1938), Stevens associates another communist ideologue, Lenin, with his religious counterpart, Cotton Mather, in the attempt to inflict
alien rational structures on "summer" reality rather than
seeking, as this section puts it, "To discover an order as
of / A season, to discover summer and know it." Though
Stevens' wry "It is a brave affair" establishes his distance

from his persona, this imposer of orders has something in common with the poet who wrote *Ideas of Order* in the early thirties. That Stevens can still be heard in the voice which insists on "discovery" as compulsively as the builder of capitols insists on "imposition": "It is possible, possible, possible. It must / Be possible."

By his own account, Stevens felt less compelled to dispose his world according to ideas of order after the mid-thirties. "You know," he wrote to Latimer several months after *Ideas* was published, "the truth is that I had hardly interested myself in [order] (perhaps as another version of pastoral) when I came across some such phrase as this: 'man's passionate disorder', and I have since been very much interested in disorder" (*L* 300).[27] That interest is announced in the title of *Parts of a World*, many of whose poems seek rather to subvert the tyranny of old orders than to suggest new ones. Some of the more intriguing poems in the volume explore the relation between language and that tyrant of tyrants, "the truth." "Where was it one first heard of the truth?" asks the man on the dump in a poem already alluded to. The answer to his question, "The the," exhibits this unprepossessing word in two roles—first in its usual, subordinate role as syntactic particle; then in the unusual role it has usurped from a noun like "truth." The speaker of "On the Road Home," first published with "The Man on the Dump," pursues one implication of his linguistic statement, "Words are not forms of a single word," when he goes on to say, "In the sum of the parts, there are only the parts. / The world must be measured by eye. . . ."

Among the characters in "It Must Give Pleasure," the

<hr />

27. Stevens encountered the phrase "the passionate disorder in the hearts of men" in "Doughty as an Influence To-Day," review of *Charles M. Doughty: A Study of His Prose and Verse*, by Anne Treneer; and *Selected Passages from "The Dawn in Britain*," ed. Barker Fairley, *Times Literary Supplement*, 9 Nov. 1935, p. 716. He transcribed several paragraphs from the review into *Sur Plusieurs Beaux Sujects*, Cahier I, pp. 12, 13–14.

blue woman in Section II and Canon Aspirin's sister in Section V come closest to measuring the world by eye. Stevens' comment on the blue woman indicates that she is his impression of the weather—doubtless the sky in particular—on a cool, clear morning in April (*L* 444); hence her color does not signal, as it often does in Stevens, the impulse to alter reality. On the contrary, the blue woman tactfully permits things to change according to laws of their own, without transforming them metaphorically or insisting upon the metaphors latent in a name like "argentines" or a phrase like "frothy clouds." Even when she looks forward to August heat and the coral berries of the dogwood, phenomena recalled from summers past, she demands that memory give the strictest account of these things.[28] To the blue woman's coldly delineating eye the Canon's sister adds the dimension of feeling. She regards reality as her daughters and affectionately dresses it in the pastels of an idea close to the first idea. Its "pauvred color" befits its "poverty," that condition of "not to have" so dear to the ignorant man ("Abstract," II). From the Canon's point of view, his sister's ecstasy is "sensible" in both of the usual senses of the word: it denotes the sensuous character of her experience and her good judgment in defying dreams.[29]

The canon's name, as Stevens cryptically remarked, is supposed to suggest the kind of person he is (*L* 427). He is the kind who applauds his sister's disposition in his "canonical" capacity—that is, as one committed to an ordinary, daytime reality, the life "According to canon" evoked

28. The corals of the dogwood seem at first to be a present (that is, an April) reality; but the blue woman is probably looking at an ornamental flowering dogwood, whose flowers are either white or, less frequently, a pink she would not mistake for coral. Besides being the right color, the late summer fruit of the flowering dogwood resembles the beads on a coral necklace.

29. For a dissenting view of the Canon's sister as a rigid ascetic in the mold of the high-toned old Christian woman, see Morris, pp. 51, 56.

in "From the Journal of Crispin." [30] The final tercets of Section V hint at the "aspiring" side of the man suggested by his surname; where his sister had resisted the least rhetorical flourish, he indulges in a fugue of praise. Section VI develops this side of him more fully. While his sister seeks, for the sake of her "children," a sleep unmuddled by dreams, the Canon probes the margins of experience in his dreams. His Miltonic flight takes him first to an extreme sense of fact, then, after a visit en route to his "nieces," to an extreme of imagination—in effect, from the "not to have" of "Abstract," II, to having "what is not." Must one choose between these kinds of nothingness? The Canon shrewdly chooses both, along with the intermediate gradations of being. He thus anticipates the speaker of "Someone Puts a Pineapple Together" (1947, *NA* 83–87), who declines to choose between the "angel" or first idea of the fruit and any of twelve highly imaginative ways of looking at it. Instead, he allows these aspects to collect, like the planes of a Cézanne painting, into an image of the whole—what the Canon embraces as the "amassing harmony" of his experience.

Harold Bloom regards Canon Aspirin as the type of the High Romantic poet and therefore as the sort of precursor whom Stevens, anxious about such an influence, would go on to satirize as the builder of capitols in Section VII.[31] Must we assume, however, that the pronoun "he" in Section VII refers to the Canon? Such an identification runs counter to everything we have learned about the man in the preceding two poems. In fact, I doubt that the Canon, who has chosen both the "angel" of reality and its imaginative transformations, would approve of either of the

30. *Wallace Stevens: A Celebration*, p. 43. Stevens first published "The Man on the Dump," "The Latest Freed Man," "On the Road Home," and nine other poems in the *Southern Review* (Autumn 1938) under the collective title "Canonica."

31. *Wallace Stevens: The Poems of Our Climate*, p. 210.

courses proposed in Section VII. The speaker who dismisses the builder of capitols tries rather desperately, I have suggested, to conjure the angel of reality. His compulsion, too, is the object of satire in other poems of the period, like "Landscape with Boat" and "Mrs. Alfred Uruguay" (both 1940). This poses a problem, for the voice of Section VII blends imperceptibly with that of the final three sections of "Notes," and the voice of these sections is, as Helen Vendler has observed, Stevens' own or as close to Stevens' as poetic convention permits.[32] In defense of this speaker, it should be said that he manifests two virtues which might redeem him in the eyes of someone as sophisticated as the Canon. First, he acknowledges that the first idea will not conform to his preconception of it; glimpsed in the sort of "irrational moment" described in Section I, it will seem a beast rather than an angel, "disgorged" rather than born or created. Second, he realizes by the end of the poem that he must solicit the angel with "proper sound," not peremptory command.

Between Sections VII and VIII, Stevens (to name him flatly) apparently strikes the proper chord, for the angel, his image of what was "Not to be realized" in "Abstract," VI, becomes minutely realized as it plunges from its luminous cloud into the violet abyss.[33] In its "majesty," a quality akin to the "nobility" of the hero, the angel comes to represent not only the first idea of reality but also the first idea of man. As a fiction potentially supreme, it prompts what would have to be the central question in a poem written avowedly to "create something as valid as the idea of God has been" (L 435): "What am I to believe?" Upon asking a similar question, the man on the dump comes to believe in himself, "as superior as the ear / To a crow's voice[.]" In this poem, Stevens likewise professes belief in the self as

32. On Extended Wings, p. 197.
33. The "violent abyss" of Transport to Summer and the Collected Poems is a misprint for "violet abyss," as Holly Stevens notes in PEM 403.

inventor of angels. That self is at once his poverty and his glory. The gist of "Notes toward a Supreme Fiction" is contained in a line which embraces both conditions, the impoverishment of medium man and the rich existence of Jehovah: "I have not but I am and as I am, I am." This is not Coleridge's notion of the creative imagination as a "repetition in the finite mind of the eternal act of creation in the infinite I AM," but the reverse: it is the infinite I am seen to be a repetition of the finite I am. The imagination is superior to what it imagines even as the ear is superior to what it hears.

In the pride of his rediscovered powers, Stevens enjoys an "expressible bliss" that combines the "accessible bliss" of medium man ("Change," VII) with a sense of creative mastery. Like medium man, he can live without the "solacing majesty" of angels—not because he is indifferent to it, but because he knows he is never really without it. The "golden hand" that supplies his spiritual needs is his own. Coming hard upon the heels of these affirmative lines, the final tercet of Section VIII strikes some readers as an oddly disillusioned coda to the poem. Does Stevens cancel the value of fictions, including a fiction like his angel, when he calls them "escapades of death"? The phrase has a distinctly pejorative sense in the case of the Cinderella who tries to escape an unpleasant reality by converting the "as if" of poetry into religious dogma; such a person is happy as long as he can obscure from himself the mechanism by which he projects his own bountiful hand into "external regions." The phrase has a more neutral sense for the believer who neither dissociates himself from his fictions nor pretends they will last forever. His is the different kind of exaltation Stevens describes in a 1951 lecture, where he says, "Modern reality is a reality of decreation, in which our revelations are not the revelations of belief, but the precious portents of our own powers. The greatest truth we could hope to discover, in whatever field we discovered

it, is that man's truth is the final resolution of everything"
(*NA* 175).

It is assuredly not a disillusioned or even a daunted Stevens who continues to revel in his angelic portent in Section IX: "I can / Do all that angels can." At first, he seems
to enjoy the repetitious song of the wren and the robin less
than he enjoys angels. With the concessive "at least" of
line 8, however, his angelic perspective begins to affect his
aesthetic judgment. Since the "merely going round" of
birdsong, leaf, and wine reproduces the rhythms of the
cosmos on a terrestrial scale, it provokes pleasure rather
than disgust. If the angel, first apprehended as a "beast
disgorged," has become at last an attitude to be realized,
might not the hero, the "exceptional monster," be similarly
appropriated? The hero, too, is a human invention and his
final elegance our own, did we but know it. Stevens, alluding to the major man poems of "It Must Be Abstract" as
though they had never been far from his thoughts in the
intervening eighteen sections of "Notes," proposes that we
can do all that heroes can; specifically, we can rise superior
to repetition and even take pleasure in it.

One might proceed directly from this proposition to its
contemporary social and political application, as developed in the epilogue to "Notes." The invocation and thirty
poems preceding the epilogue concentrate on the poet's
war—a war that is also a love affair—with reality. In 1942,
the pressure of reality included awareness of a literal war
being fought in Europe. Stevens suggested how the poet's
war depends on the soldier's in a prose note appended to
Parts of a World, where he observes that the poetry of war
proceeds from a "consciousness of fact, but of heroic fact,
of fact on such a scale that the mere consciousness of it
affects the scale of one's thinking and constitutes a participating in the heroic."[34] What the poet takes from the soldier, the consciousness of mostly disagreeable facts, he re-

34. New York: Knopf, 1942, p. 183.

stores to him in a form conducive to heroism. Like
MacCullough listening to the surf, the soldier may experience the encroachment of a "leaner being" as he reads his
book in a barrack. When poetry sticks thus in the blood,
the fictive hero becomes real, incorporated even as sacra-
mental bread is incorporated by the communicant. If
"faithful"—that is, if accurate and suffused with faith in
the idea of man—the poet's speech enhances the soldier's
life, making it less "poor," and eases his dying.

The epilogue of "Notes" attempts in this way to bridge
the gap between pure poetry and contemporary events
along the lines prescribed in "The Noble Rider and the
Sound of Words." Indeed, it goes beyond the lecture in
suggesting that the poet's elite should include, in time of
war, the hypothetical common soldier. Those acquainted
with the kind of reading material usually found in American army barracks may scout Stevens' soldier as his supre-
mest fiction. But, as Glen MacLeod has shown, this cultivated European "Monsieur" has some basis in fact, being
probably a reminiscence of Eugène Emmanuel Lemercier,
whose *Lettres d'un soldat* inspired Stevens' 1918 sequence
of war poems bearing the same title (*OP* 10–16). In one of
his letters, Lemercier describes how he and his fellow non-
commissioned officers distracted themselves from the discomfort of trench warfare by humming, from memory, the
nine symphonies of Beethoven.[35]

Nevertheless, the epilogue is more a corollary of
"Notes" than its warranted conclusion. That distinction
belongs to Section X, a poem resonant with echoes of the
entire sequence. Here Stevens addresses reality, by nature
"fat" with the plenitude of earth, summer, and night, in a
moment of change. Shaded by the tree of fixity, he finds
this transition from the familiar to the unfamiliar initially
distressing; like the *professeurs* at the Sorbonne, he would
assign the fat girl her place in a purely rationalistic scheme

35. *Wallace Stevens and Company*, p. 58.

of things. But as he contemplates her further, investing her with an inner life of her own, his strict civility gives way to affection. He no longer feels disposed to name her flatly, as the blue woman names the phenomena outside her window. Neither can he forgo naming her altogether, as the professor of "It Must Be Abstract" advises in the case of the sun. Instead, he foresees a time when he will name her as the Canon's sister names her daughters, simply and affectionately. "[M]y green, my fluent mundo" is the lover's distortion of nature, the fiction that contains reality and holds it to itself without fixing it unnaturally.[36]

"Notes toward a Supreme Fiction" thus traces the arc described in Section XXII of "The Man with the Blue Guitar," issuing from the "vivid transparence" of its invocation and returning to the "crystal" of its conclusion. At either terminal is poetry, personified by the Interior Paramour and an exterior paramour enveloped in interiority. Are the intervening lines, over six hundred of them, an absence in reality? The reader knows they are not, knows that the poem acquires in transit the fluent green which irradiates the final crystal. That color stands for all of the "true appearances"—the phrase is only apparently a contradiction in terms—which "Notes" takes from the world and gives back to it, in the universal intercourse.

Regarded from a slightly different angle, "Notes" is a poem that interrogates the self as relentlessly as it does the relation between reality and imagination. Stevens' "A Dish of Peaches in Russia," published three years earlier, anticipates this aspect of "Notes." The speaker of the poem is a man who lives habitually in a state of emotional exile from reality, here represented as his native village in Russia. So intense is his encounter with a dish of peaches that he reverts briefly to his disenfranchised "Russian" self and its

36. A sentence in Stevens' lecture "The Figure of the Youth as Virile Poet" (1943) helps to explicate both the "mundo" of this poem and the "fat girl": "It is the *mundo* of the imagination in which the imaginative man delights and not the gaunt world of the reason" (*NA* 57–58).

idiom. During the course of the poem, the speaker alternates between two personae: the "medium man" he had once been and the self-conscious, abstracted person he now is. The latter twice interrupts the sensuous description of the peaches to ask "Who speaks?"—a question that reflects his estrangement from his pre-exilic self. Comprehending at last the nature of his profoundly disturbing and delightful experience, the speaker marvels, "I did not know / That such ferocities could tear / One self from another, as these peaches do."

"Notes toward a Supreme Fiction" is in this sense a ferocious poem. From the self that enjoys angels, it tears the self that prefers evenings without them; from the self that requires a surrogate divinity, it tears the self that feels good without a thinker of the first idea. While it gives each of these its due, it necessarily presents a more vivid picture of medium man than it does of his abstract counterpart, the heroic idea of man. That idea, realized mythically as major man and elaborated in other poems of the thirties and forties, is the subject of the next chapter.

· 7 ·

Major Man

"It Must Be Human": thus did Stevens further qualify his surrogate object of belief in 1954, a dozen years after publishing "Notes toward a Supreme Fiction" (L 863–64). Though he never wrote an addition to the 1942 poem elaborating this note, it was neither an afterthought nor an extrapolation from the other three. Rather, it is present in "Notes" as an unspoken assumption, one closely linked in Stevens' mind with "It Must Be Abstract." Like the first idea of reality, the idea of man is an abstraction. As symbolized by major man, this idea can magnify us in our own eyes and thereby help us, Stevens believed, to resist the pressure of contemporary reality. Provided major man remains a variable symbol, responsive to our changing notions of nobility, he will continue to be a source of pleasure and will escape the "cemetery of nobilities" that has claimed most of the noble riders in Stevens' Princeton lecture. He will be, in short, the supreme fiction.

Despite its categorical form, Stevens' fourth note is, like the other three, more a requirement of emotion than of logic. The supreme fiction had to be human partly because Stevens had always felt the moral appeal of heroism. One thinks of his two high-school orations, one eulogizing the self-made man, the other referring "in well turned sentences," as the local newspaper reported, "to the heroes, the gods and the scholars."[1] Several years later, we have the journal entry written upon returning from Stephen

1. *Reading Eagle*, 24 June 1897, p. 5, col. 1. Stevens' address was entitled "The Thessalians."

Crane's funeral: "There are few hero-worshippers. There-fore, few heroes" (*SP* 79). This was the young idealist trying to be the hard-boiled reporter; one sees a similar tactic later, in the comic and ironic masks of *Harmonium*.

Beginning in the early thirties with poems like "The Revolutionists Stop for Orangeade" (1931), "Lions in Sweden" (1934), "The American Sublime" (1935), and "Some Friends from Pascagoula" (1935), Stevens began to improvise sounds and images that would lend nobility to life. In *Owl's Clover* (1936), we have seen, these were first enlisted in the creation of an ideal hero, ranging in stature from "man of folk-lore" to "super-animal" (*OP* 63). Within days after *Owl's Clover* appeared, New Directions published an anthology containing Stevens' "A Thought Revolved." This poem consists of four very different sections, describing a full revolution from satire to affirmation to burlesque. Of the two affirmative sections, the one entitled "Mystic Garden & Middling Beast" represents the mode of heroism best suited to the contemporary world. As the persona of the poem, a poet, strolls down a typical city street, he occupies two kinds of space: the physical space of cigar stores, Ryan's lunch, hatters, insurance, and medicines; and the imaginary space belonging to the idea of man. The latter, what Stevens might have called description as place, has become more circumscribed since the time of Virgil; but it still includes, in consciously fictive form, those realms by which men have traditionally enlarged their sphere of existence—heaven, hell, and the garden of paradise. The poet might well celebrate these imaginative achievements in secular but "happy" hymns.

Stevens next took up the theme of the hero in "The Man with the Blue Guitar" (1937). Though this poem professedly deals with "the incessant conjunctions between things as they are and things imagined,"[2] its first three sections focus on the contrast between man as he is and

---

2. From Stevens' statement on the dust jacket (second printing) of *The Man with the Blue Guitar and Other Poems* (New York: Knopf, 1937).

man as he might be in poetry. Commanded by his public
to play a tune beyond them yet themselves, the blue guitarist can manage only a conventional image of the hero,
with "large eye" and "bearded bronze." He then dissects
"man number one" in order to locate the principle of his
vitality, but learns that so to dissect is to murder. Near the
end of the poem, he settles upon the "old fantoche" as an
image of humanity (Section XXX). This precursor of the
man in sagging pantaloons is doubtless "ourselves," inasmuch as he appears to be an employee of the Oxidia Electric Light and Power Company (L 791). But he is "beyond
us" only in the sense that he is a representative figure. To
whom shall we turn if we wish to transcend this comic self?
"The Man with the Blue Guitar" was written at a time
when many people looked to the political leader, the "pa-
gan in a varnished car" of Section X, for a sense of personal
worth. Stevens was unable to share this infatuation; "the
cheap glory of the false hero," he told Renato Poggioli
while glossing this section, ". . . made me sick at heart" (L
789).

Stevens confessed his heart-sickness and need for a hero
worthy of admiration in three poems submitted to the *New
York Times* between November 1937 and the following July:
"United Dames of America," "Country Words," and "Force
of Illusions." The last of these opens with the image of a
butcher squeezing a helpless animal to death. This, says
the speaker, is how certain "winds" gripped and subdued
his own mind one evening, before he fell asleep. He is
conscious, however, of a pressure from within that he
might have exerted against this pressure from without:

> Yet there was a man within me
> Could have risen to the clouds,
> Could have touched these winds,
> Bent and broken them down,
> Could have stood up sharply in the sky.

As yet, the "man within" is only potentially a forceful illusion. Perhaps for this reason Stevens changed the poem's

title in subsequent reprintings to "A Weak Mind in the Mountains."

As the Depression succeeded to the inevitable war, Stevens' longing for a hero reached a new pitch of intensity. In the winter of 1940 he read a passage from one of Henry Adams' letters in the *Kenyon Review* and copied it in his commonplace book under the heading, "Of humanism, heroes. . . ." The quotation reads, "I need badly to find one man in history to admire. I am in near peril of turning Christian, and rolling in the mud in an agony of human mortification."[3] Adams' distress must have struck a responsive chord, for shortly after the conclusion of the war Stevens confessed to Henry Church,

> Personally, I feel terribly in need of encountering [a really powerful character]. The other night I sat in my room in the moonlight thinking about the top men in the world today, people like Truman and Bevin, for example. That I suppose is the source of one's desire for a few really well developed individuals. What is terribly lacking from life today is the well developed individual, the master of life, or the man who by his mere appearance convinces you that a mastery of life is possible. (*L* 518)

Truman was, to be sure, enduring one of his periodic lapses from public favor as this was written. But even on Truman's better days, his and Bevin's low-key style of statesmanship was not calculated to meet the requirements of Stevens' imagination.

Though Stevens' poems about the hero span the entire decade from *Owl's Clover* to "Sketch of the Ultimate Politician" (1947), the best and most explicit of them were written during the war years. Stevens was a war poet, after his fashion, and his fashion changed dramatically from the First World War to the Second. In 1918 he had represented a death on the battlefield naturalistically, as an occurrence

---

3. Stevens transcribed this passage (substituting "the agony" for "an agony") from R. P. Blackmur's "Henry Adams: Three Late Moments," *Kenyon Review* 2 (1940): 26, into *Sur Plusieurs Beaux Sujects*, Cahier II, p. 1.

"absolute and without memorial" ("The Death of a Soldier"). By 1945, he had come to think a soldier's death
more significant, could its meaning only be interpreted:

> There are potential seemings turbulent
> In the death of a soldier, like the utmost will,
>
> The more than human commonplace of blood,
> The breath that gushes upward and is gone,
>
> And another breath emerging out of death,
> That speaks for him such seemings as death gives.
> ("Description without Place," III)

Though one might not expect to find an allusion to war
in a poem about the nature of poetry, this was more the
rule than the exception in Stevens' work by 1945. The pattern had been established in his 1940 memorandum regarding the Henry Church Chair of Poetry, a document
that collected his miscellaneous notions about the supreme
fiction and the hero into a rudimentary theory of poetry.
But it was one thing to couch that theory in a poem, quite
another to reduce it to a memorandum. Hence Stevens
briefly assumes the poet's cape in his memorandum when
he notes that the subject matter of poetry is "what comes
to mind when one says of the month of August . . .

⌈'Thou art not August, unless I make thee so'" (L 377).

It is unlikely that anything very definite came to
Church's mind upon reading this line of verse, especially
since Stevens had lifted it from one of his own poems still
in manuscript. That poem, "Asides on the Oboe," first
equates hero and supreme fiction and relates both of them
to the war. After the opening ultimatum—

> The prologues are over. It is a question, now,
> Of final belief. So, say that final belief
> Must be in a fiction. It is time to choose—

Stevens goes on, in Section I, to dismiss both the gods and
actual heroes of the past as objects of final belief. Only the

"philosophers' man," the hero abstractly considered, can still engage our intellect and emotions. Here he anticipates an "aside" that might be played on a skeptical oboe:

> If you say on the hautboy man is not enough,
> Can never stand as god, is ever wrong
> In the end, however naked, tall, there is still
> The impossible possible philosophers' man,
> The man who has had the time to think enough,
> The central man, the human globe, responsive
> As a mirror with a voice, the man of glass,
> Who in a million diamonds sums us up.

We may balk at replacing the gods, obsolete though they may be, with a mere human. Yet we collectively entertain an idealized concept of man which sums up what is best in us. The imagery of glass and diamonds attending this "central man" in the poem suggests his brilliant purity and distinguishes him from "the metal heroes that time granulates." Like glass, too, he is a medium of perception rather than the thing perceived. As in "Mystic Garden & Middling Beast," he constitutes our heroic description or "poem" of the world:

> He is the transparence of the place in which
> He is and in his poems we find peace.
> He sets this peddler's pie and cries in summer,
> The glass man, cold and numbered, dewily cries,
> "Thou art not August unless I make thee so."
> Clandestine steps upon imagined stairs
> Climb through the night, because his cuckoos call.

The central man's poem of August becomes the month itself. Hence this "mirror with a voice" not only reflects and expresses our human nature as it is, but also dramatizes the mastery we long to achieve.

For Walt Whitman, the Civil War had seemed to prove that democracy could produce citizens of heroic stature. Stevens, we have noted, likewise felt that the war then going on in Europe might recall men to a sense of their own dignity, that consciousness of "heroic fact" might precipitate a "participating in the heroic." Section III of "Asides on the Oboe" suggests how such participation might be effected:

> One year, death and war prevented the jasmine scent
> And the jasmine islands were bloody martyrdoms.
> How was it then with the central man? Did we
> Find peace? We found the sum of men. We found,
> If we found the central evil, the central good.
> We buried the fallen without jasmine crowns.
> There was nothing he did not suffer, no; nor we.
>
> It was not as if the jasmine ever returned.
> But we and the diamond globe at last were one.
> We had always been partly one. It was as we came
> To see him, that we were wholly one, as we heard
> Him chanting for those buried in their blood,
> In the jasmine haunted forests, that we knew
> The glass man, without external reference.

Although war dispels the "jasmine scent" of religious illusion and discredits the gods as "external reference," it may also move us to embrace the idea of the hero as our supreme good.

Stevens has little company among modern poets in giving serious attention to the hero. William Carlos Williams spoke for many writers of the early twentieth century when he rejoiced that "noble has been / changed to no bull" ("A Poem for Norman MacLeod"). In the age of the anti-hero, Stevens could not help but be defensive about his interest. "I throw knives at the hero," he told Church in 1942 (L 409). This self-consciousness combined with intense fascination to produce some of his more evasive poems. The evasiveness was also purposeful. After telling one correspondent that evasiveness helps to support a fictive figure, he went on to explain, "The long and short of it is that we have to fix abstract objectives and then to conceal the abstract figures in actual appearance. A hero won't do, but we like him much better when he doesn't look it and, of course, it is only when he doesn't look it that we can believe in him" (L 489). Stevens was facing a difficulty not unknown to theologians: he had to speak eloquently of the ineffable. The credible hero must be neither too abstract nor too concrete, neither too remote nor too familiar.

He addressed this challenge in several wartime examinations of the hero. Besides "Notes toward a Supreme Fiction," three poems are especially important and might have shared the rubric "It Must Be Human" with the major man poems of "Notes": "Montrachet-le-Jardin" (1942), "Examination of the Hero in a Time of War" (1942), and "Chocorua to Its Neighbor" (1943). Three lesser pieces, one of them written after the war, add significant details to the hero's portrait: "Gigantomachia" (1943), "Paisant Chronicle" (1945), and "The Pastor Caballero" (1946). Most of these successfully negotiate the dilemma mentioned above by exploiting the resources of rhetoric and by avoiding obvious internal contradictions. Only when the poems are compared point by point do the contradictions and evasions manifest themselves. Yet the contradictions tell us much about Stevens' difficulty, even ambivalence, in projecting a fictive hero. For this reason, I treat these seven poems as though they were a single discursive poem setting forth the hero's origin, his nature, and his role.

Mystery envelops the hero's origin in all seven poems. They follow "Asides on the Oboe" in relating his birth to the war; thus "the great arms / Of the armies, the solid men, make big the fable" ("Chocorua," XXIV). But how the soldier as empirical fact produces the hero as hypothetical projection is left deliberately vague. We know only that he is one of war's "sudden sublimations," that he is

> to combat what his exaltations
> Are to the unaccountable prophet or
> What any fury to its noble centre.
> ("Examination," III)

The hero, in short, arises spontaneously and unaccountably. Yet, just as the prophet prepares himself for the visitations he cannot produce at will, we must ready ourselves mentally and emotionally for the hero. In "Montrachet" it is thought, "our singular skeleton," that summons forth the hero. In "Notes" he springs "from reason, / Lighted at midnight by the studious eye" ("Abstract," IX). In "Chocorua" it is our desire for heroism that brings him into being: "He rose because men wanted him to be" (XIV).

Like the heroes of mythology, Stevens' hero enjoys an ambiguous nature. Since he is "part desire and part the sense / Of what men are" ("Chocorua," XVI), he is at once human and superhuman, substantial and insubstantial, common and extraordinary. Our desire creates the part of him that is more than humanly capable, the part that

> seems
> To stand taller than a person stands, has
> A wider brow, large and less human
> Eyes and bruted ears: the man-like body
> Of a primitive. He walks with a defter
> And lither stride. His arms are heavy
> And his breast is greatness. All his speeches
> Are prodigies in longer phrases.
> His thoughts begotten at clear sources,
> Apparently in air, fall from him
> Like chantering from an abundant
> Poet, as if he thought gladly, being
> Compelled thereto by an innate music.
> ("Examination," IX)

The hero not only delivers prodigious speeches; he is himself a prodigy of speech. In Stevens' 1948 lecture, "Imagination as Value," he records Pascal's complaint against public figures who establish their authority by virtue of elaborate costume. Stevens takes the opposite view: if style of dress fosters civil order, then style is a "potent good" (*NA* 133–34). He had likewise associated sartorial with literary style in "The Pastor Caballero," published two years previously. Of the cavalier's "hat" in this poem, Stevens asserts that

> The flare
> In the sweeping brim becomes the origin

Of a human evocation, so disclosed
That, nameless, it creates an affectionate name,

Derived from adjectives of deepest mine.

Desire, then, moves us to clothe the hero in superlatives. But since he is also part the sense of what men are, there are limits to his superiority. It is fitting, to paraphrase "Chocorua," XV, that he be larger than life and free of our faults; yet beyond a minimal transcendence he begins to seem exclusively a phenomenon of rhetoric and so raises the doubt expressed at the end of "Examination," X:

> Can we live on dry descriptions,
> Feel everything starving except the belly
> And nourish ourselves on crumbs of whimsy?

Romantic intoning, Stevens maintains in "Notes," cannot be the origin of major man ("Abstract," IX). Rather than try to sustain ourselves on wishful thinking and grandiose descriptions, we should strive "To project the naked man in a state of fact" ("Montrachet"). Although Stevens once calls the hero "the eccentric" ("Examination," IV), he more characteristically describes him as "the self of selves,"

> Not father, but bare brother, megalfrere,
> Or by whatever boorish name a man
> Might call the common self, interior fons.
> ("Chocorua," IV, XXI)

Is the hero therefore the common man, plain and simple? Stevens invites that conclusion in Section V of "Examination," where he sets forth what appear to be major and minor premises:

> The common man is the common hero.
> The common hero is the hero.

He does not finish this syllogism, and most of his poems of the hero militate against its logical conclusion. The hero is the common self, but not the common man. He is born, not of woman, but of thought and feeling. He is the ideal being whom the merely human MacCullough of "Notes" apprehends in the sound of the ocean surf ("Abstract," VIII). Stevens hedges occasionally, and wants his hero to be substantial as well as insubstantial. "It is part of his conception," he affirms in one place, "That he be not conceived, being real" ("Examination," XIII). In "Chocorua," too, he asserts that

> The substance of his body seemed
> Both substance and non-substance, luminous flesh
> Or shapely fire: fire from an underworld,
> Of less degree than flame and lesser shine.   (VII)

But he typically associates the hero with a crystalline imagery to suggest his ideal purity and pure ideality. Indeed, Stevens would prefer not to assign him any image whatsoever. "How could there be an image," he asks in "Examination," XII,

> an outline,
> A design, a marble soiled by pigeons?
> The hero is a feeling, a man seen
> As if the eye was an emotion,
> As if in seeing we saw our feeling
> In the object seen and saved that mystic
> Against the sight, the penetrating,
> Pure eye. Instead of allegory,
> We have and are the man, capable
> Of his brave quickenings, the human
> Accelerations that seem inhuman.

This passage and the similar one in "Notes" ("Abstract," IX) echo the Old Testament injunction against graven images, though not quite to the same purpose. A fixed image of the hero would tempt us not to idolatry, but to disbelief. Moreover, we demand that the hero be minutely responsive to changes in our notions of heroism. Stevens' very language stresses a fluid ideal: the hero is a "quickening" or "acceleration" rather than a design or a marble.

Yet the hero may be fugitive to a fault. By the conclusion of each of the four major poems of the hero, he has vanished along with the feeling that created him. What role might so evanescent a creature be expected to fulfill? His labors are less—or other—than Herculean, to judge from "Examination," XV, and "Paisant Chronicle." According to the former poem, the hero spends his day studying wallpaper and lemons; according the latter, he may be found at a café table, before a dish of country cheese and a pineapple. Stevens uses these rather banal illustrations to distinguish major man from what Sidney Hook calls the "event-making" hero.[4] His hero will neither alter the course of history nor save us from our enemies. He will not even save us from our daily routine. He may, however, help us to see the ordinary in an extraordinary way, since "where he was, there is an enkindling, where / He is, the air changes and grows fresh to breathe" ("Chocorua," XXII). What is more, he may help us to view ourselves differently. Just as the poet in "Notes" who imagines an angel can, in a sense, do "all that angels can" ("Pleasure," VIII, IX), so the man who conceives the idea of the hero discovers his own heroism. The soldiers of "Gigantomachia" lack strength and courage until convinced that a "braver being" informs their number; thereupon each becomes a giant, his sense of his own stature so enhanced that the moon seems by comparison to stretch a mere twenty feet. In his most rhapsodic moments, Stevens implies that the heroic perspective may shrink time as well as space. The "drastic community" first envisioned in "Mr. Burnshaw and the Statue" (1936, OP 51) seems all but achieved in these compelling lines from "Montrachet":

> Fear never the brute clouds nor winter-stop
> And let the water-belly of ocean roar,
> Nor feel the x malisons of other men,
>
> Since in the hero-land to which we go,
> A little nearer by each multitude,
> To which we come as into bezeled plain,

4. *The Hero in History: Studies in Limitation and Possibility* (New York: John Day, 1943), p. 154.

The poison in the blood will have been purged,
An inner miracle and sun-sacrament,
One of the major miracles, that fall

As apples fall, without astronomy,
One of the sacraments between two breaths,
Magical only for the change they make.

The hero who emerges from Stevens' poems of the forties is, then, a creature of contradictions. He is man and
more than man, physical and ideal, a doer of ordinary
deeds and a prophet who can make his prophecies come
true. One who has read only the passages abstracted
above, concerning the hero's origin, nature, and role,
might reasonably wonder how these poems of the hero
survive their anomalous subject matter. That the poems
not only survive but flourish is a tribute to Stevens' artistry
and artfulness. In his best poems of the hero, the context
justifies any number of contradictory assertions. "Notes
toward a Supreme Fiction," as the title suggests, pretends
to nothing like a systematic or exhaustive treatment of its
subject. "Montrachet-le-Jardin" is an avowedly speculative
poem. The poet declares at the outset that if, and only if,
there are things worth loving beyond the sensuous world,
he will love them. He then intuits some such thing in
"night's undeciphered murmuring" and goes on to guess
at its nature. The very ambiguity and vagueness of that
undeciphered thing, the hero, permit anything to be said
of it. In "Examination of the Hero in a Time of War," the
poet presides over several examiners, each of whom views
the hero differently. Though the poet occasionally passes
judgment on these viewpoints—"Chopiniana," he sniffs at
the improvisation of Section IV—he is usually content to
let them stand, contradictions and all.

The most daring poem of the four is "Chocorua to Its
Neighbor," which apparently sprouted from Section XXI of
"The Man with the Blue Guitar." Chocorua, actually a
mountain in New Hampshire, had symbolized the human
race in the 1937 piece, and Stevens had proposed that its

"shadow" might serve as a substitute for the gods. In "Chocorua to Its Neighbor" the shadow has become the idea of the hero. Stevens scorns subterfuge in "Chocorua," preferring to emphasize the hero's contradictions rather than gloss them over. Thus the hero is

Both substance	and non-substance (VII);
not man	yet . . . nothing else (VIII);
Without existence,	existing everywhere (VIII),
beyond [men]	yet of themselves (XV);
an eminence,	But of nothing (XX);
that will disappear	. . . and yet remain (XX);
metaphysical metaphor, / But	. . . Physical if the eye is quick enough (XXII);
a space	That is an instant nature (XXIII);
fortelleze,	though . . . Hard to perceive and harder still to touch (XXIV).

Like an algebraic equation in which all of the terms finally cancel, "Chocorua" is composed of mutually exclusive predications and unimaginable images. One cannot object that it is too specific for belief. But the poem differs from an equation in one crucial respect: though the rhetoric cancels, the hero abides as a kind of emotional resonance and way of seeing the world. Thus the hero of "Chocorua to Its Neighbor" is a fiction in Vaihinger's sense of the word; he enters into our self-estimate only to drop out of the final reckoning. Yet, for Stevens at least, he made all the difference in the final reckoning.

From the very first, Stevens' major man has provoked comparison with another hero of more than human stature: Nietzsche's overman. Stevens invites the comparison in "Montrachet-le-Jardin," where he calls his hero "superman," using the term George Bernard Shaw had popularized as the English rendering of *Übermensch*.[5] Several

5. Shaw's *Man and Superman* was published in 1903. Thomas Common also used the word "Superman" in his translation of *Thus Spake Zarathustra* for the *Complete Works of Friedrich Nietzsche* (1909), while Alexander Tille

months after the poem was published, Stevens received a letter from Henry Church in which Church managed to call Erasmus both a sixteenth-century Socrates and "the archtype [*sic*] of the Renaissance Biermensch" ("beer-drinker").[6] Church, who was then reading *The Birth of Tragedy*, admitted that his judgment of Erasmus owed something to Nietzsche's estimate of Socrates. Though Church did not mention major man in his letter, Stevens wrote in reply that he had not read Nietzsche since his youth, and that his interest in the hero had nothing to do with the *Biermensch* (*L* 409). Again in 1945, when José Rodríguez Feo pressed him to identify the major men of his recent poems,[7] Stevens avowed that they were not "Nietzschean shadows" (*L* 485). In each case, he anticipated and moved to forestall the attribution of influence, possibly before it had occurred to his correspondent.

Stevens' major man did in fact have something to do with the overman, and it will repay the effort to consider that something more closely. Nowhere else in Stevens does one have an intellectual influence whose sources and extent can be specified with as much certainty; hence this episode suggests how he may have absorbed other influences. Merely to gloss Stevens' poems with passages from Nietzsche would of course be an exercise in futility. One wants to know why Stevens found Nietzsche's ideas attractive at just this moment in his career, and how he modified them to suit his own purposes.

Stevens was actively interested in Nietzsche during two widely separated periods—the years before and during World War I, and the last years of World War II. Before 1918, his allusions to Nietzsche presuppose little direct ac-

---

had preferred "Beyond-Man" for his rendering of the same work in 1896. I follow Nietzsche scholar and translator Walter Kaufmann in using "overman," to distinguish Nietzsche's *Übermensch* both from Shaw's ideal and from the hero Stevens occasionally called "super-man."

6. Letter of 8 June 1942.

7. Letter of 13 Jan.

quaintance with the philosopher's writings. In 1906, for example, he wrote in his journal, "We go slumming in a quarter, we help starving Asiatics—true; but we do not pursue the ideal of the Universal Superman—at least not today. But we may the day after tomorrow" (*SP* 162). In 1913, I have noted, he used a Nietzschean epithet to express his ambivalent feelings toward his hometown, the Reading he deemed "too, too human."

These allusions are probably phrases caught from the wind, and serve to remind us that Nietzsche was much in the air during the first decades of this century.[8] His impact on England and America was remarkable, despite the handicap of poor translations and expensive editions. His work achieved notoriety even before it appeared in English, thanks to Max Nordau's *Degeneration*, a virulent and widely read attack on "decadence" which first appeared during the Oscar Wilde trials and placed Nietzsche, among others, in Wilde's company. That Nietzsche's work received its first serious critical attention in the pages of the *Savoy*, second only to the *Yellow Book* as a medium of decadence, did nothing to dispel its aura of mauve morality.[9] But if Nietzsche recruited his first English admirers from the ranks of the aesthetes, they soon learned to discriminate between Pater and the philosopher of the overman. Many, like Yeats, rejoiced in the difference. Nietzsche's energy, hardness, and discipline promised to deliver them from the deliquescent passivity of aestheticism. Before long, nearly every platoon within the anti-Victorian camp had its official version of Nietzsche with which to confound the opposition. Socialists conveniently ignored Nietzsche's

8. This account of Nietzsche's early reputation in England, and to some extent in America, is indebted to David S. Thatcher's *Nietzsche in England 1890–1914* (Toronto: University of Toronto Press, 1970). Patrick Bridgwater's *Nietzsche in Anglosaxony* (Leicester: Leicester University Press, 1972) covers much the same ground, with specific application to Stevens on pp. 191–201.

9. Havelock Ellis, "Friedrich Nietzsche," *Savoy*, no. 2 (Apr. 1896), pp. 79–94; no. 3 (July 1896), pp. 68–81; no. 4 (Aug. 1896), pp. 57–63.

diatribes against socialism, Darwinians his rejection of Darwin, feminists his slurs against womanhood. Nietzsche's stoutest defenders, in fact, staffed an ostensibly Fabian journal, the *New Age*.

In America, Nietzsche's work quickly became a weapon in the anti-puritan arsenal, especially when supplemented with snatches of Freud. The puritan, the argument ran, was merely exercising his will to power and desire for pleasure according to pathological rules of his own. There was, too, growing disenchantment with democracy in the first decades of this century, and independent spirits welcomed Nietzsche as an antidote to "leveling." Both the puritan-baiters and the intellectual elitists found a spokesman in H. L. Mencken, whose *The Philosophy of Friedrich Nietzsche* (1908) was one of the first American introductions to the overman and whose essays in the *Smart Set* and the *American Mercury* did much to foster the popular image of Nietzsche as a scourge of the "booboisie."[10]

Stevens' journal entry concerning the "Universal Superman" suggests that in 1906 he was more familiar with Shaw's Nietzsche than with Mencken's Nietzsche or even Nietzsche's Nietzsche, for he seems to regard the overman as a socialistic experiment on a vast scale. As early as 1915, however, he may have picked up *Thus Spake Zarathustra*, for his ring of naked men chanting their devotion to the sun in "Sunday Morning" recalls Zarathustra's recurrent vision of "warmer souths" where the gods dance ashamed of all clothes.[11] Around 1917, Stevens later told Henry Church, he looked into *Zarathustra* and three other volumes—*The Genealogy of Morals*, *The Case of Wagner*, and *The*

10. Frederick J. Hoffman, *The Twenties: American Writing in the Postwar Decade*, rev. ed. (New York: Free Press, 1962), pp. 344–45.

11. *Complete Works*, XI: 174–75, 240. Hereafter, I cite the Levy edition parenthetically in my text, with volume and page numbers following the abbreviation *CW*. The volumes cited include Part I of *Human, All-Too-Human* (vi), *Thus Spake Zarathustra* (xi), *Beyond Good and Evil* (xii), *The Genealogy of Morals* (xiii), and Part II of *The Will to Power* (xv).

Dawn of Day.[12] Though he may have read these in German—he had taken six semesters of the language at Harvard and would remark to Church upon the difference between reading Nietzsche in the original and reading him in translation (*L* 462)—he need not have taken the trouble, since English translations of all four works had been available since 1903.

Several passages in "Lettres d'un Soldat" (1918) may reflect his reading of *Thus Spake Zarathustra*. Section II (reprinted as "Anecdotal Revery" in *OP* 12–13) brings to mind the backward-looking "small people" whom Zarathustra views as stumbling blocks (*CW* xi.204–5). Section V, entitled "The Surprises of the Superhuman" when it was salvaged for the second edition of *Harmonium*, contrasts the bourgeois concept of justice with that suitable to "Übermenschlichkeit." Section VII, later called "Negation," recalls Zarathustra's dialogue with the last pope, in which he too compares God to a bungling potter (*CW* xi.318).[13]

Nietzsche was no longer a novelty when Stevens resumed interest in him two dozen years later. By the end of the thirties, Nietzsche's overman had attained an innocuous immortality in a series of American comic books, while his own reputation had suffered a fate scarcely less comic, in its way. During World War I the English government had spied on the *New Age* staff and had expelled one of their number, Oscar Levy, while the American Department of Justice had charged Mencken with being an agent of "the German monster, Nietzsky."[14] Socialists of the twenties and communists of the early thirties were wont to season their rhetoric with Nietzschean phrases. This was never

12. Letter of 5 Jan. 1943.
13. This comparison also appears in two other texts with which Stevens was familiar: Jeremiah 18 and Edward Fitzgerald's translation of the *Rubáiyát of Omar Khayyám*, Stanzas 82–90.
14. Mencken recalls his encounter with the Department of Justice in the introduction to his translation of *The Antichrist*. (New York: Knopf, 1920), p. 15.

very appropriate, considering Nietzsche's opinion of the "utopians," but it became even less so after 1935, when Elisabeth Förster-Nietzsche told Hitler that he was her brother's overman.[15] By 1940, the few souls who had failed to grasp Nietzsche's role in World War II could turn to a professor at the Boston College Law School for enlightenment; the gist of his lecture to a Catholic women's group on April 24 became a headline in that day's *Boston Evening Transcript*: HITLER WAR URGE BLAMED ON INSANE PHILOSOPHER.[16]

The intellectual climate of the forties did not favor disinterested study of Nietzsche, and this alone would account for Stevens' reluctance to admit an influence from that quarter. Until 1943, moreover, Nietzsche was but a dim memory from his earlier reading. Always scrupulous about intellectual and stylistic contamination, Stevens would probably have preferred to leave the memory unrefurbished, especially since he regarded Nietzsche's thought as a "distorting" influence (*L* 431–32). But Church wrote him few letters between the spring of 1942 and the fall of 1946 that did not mention Nietzsche. Church had turned to the philosopher at first for his own edification, then with a view to writing a play about a businessman who chances upon Nietzsche's ideas and tries to put them into practice.[17] Church abandoned the play a few months later for the "anecdotal" study which would occupy most of his remaining years. His working title—"Nietzsche Primer or a Dillettante [*sic*] looks at Nietzsche"[18]—suggests both the nature of that study and his qualifications for writing it.

Though Church's reading never resulted in anything so tangible as a play or monograph, his letters did pique his

---

15. Eric Bentley, *A Century of Hero-Worship*, 2nd ed. (Boston: Beacon, 1957), p. 255.
16. Page 11, cols. 7–8.
17. Letter from Church to Stevens, 28 July 1942.
18. Letter from Church to Stevens, 28 Nov. 1942.

friend's interest. In September 1942, Stevens ordered the complete Oscar Levy edition of Nietzsche's works from the London bookseller Hugh Rees.[19] He waited until December for word from Rees before contacting a bookseller in New York, who sold him copies of the four works he had seen a quarter of a century earlier plus Daniel Halévy's *The Life of Friedrich Nietzsche* and Frau Förster-Nietzsche's *Young Nietzsche*.[20] Stevens apparently made slow headway through these. He gave up on *The Genealogy of Morals* before finishing it, to Church's disappointment.[21] When Church praised *Human, All-Too-Human*, he tried once again to secure copies of the Levy edition, first from booksellers in New York, then from Rees, who eventually provided him with at least four more volumes over the next ten years.[22]

While waiting to hear from Rees, Stevens visited the Theological Seminary and the Watkinson Library in Hartford to examine their holdings. It was possibly at one of these institutions that he read, early in 1944, the first part of *Human, All-Too-Human* (L 462). Though he professed little enthusiasm for the book, at least in translation, his poetry registered one of its themes almost immediately. Nietzsche introduces his discussion of religious faith in

19. Letter from Stevens to Church, 8 Sept. 1942.
20. Letter from Stevens to Church, 5 Jan. 1943.
21. Letter from Church to Stevens, 5 Aug. 1943.
22. The Levy edition was renumbered after several volumes had appeared, making it difficult to determine which titles Stevens owned. In a letter to Church of 17 June 1944, he mentions receiving Volumes IV (either Part I of *Thoughts Out of Season* or *Thus Spake Zarathustra*) and VI (Part I of *Human, All-Too-Human* or *On the Future of Our Educational Institutions*). An invoice from Rees of 11 June 1953 records the sale of Volumes I (Part I of *Thoughts Out of Season* or *The Birth of Tragedy*) and V (Part II of *Thoughts Out of Season* or *Beyond Good and Evil*). This invoice was laid in Part I of *Thoughts Out of Season* (identified on the half-title page as Volume I of the *Complete Works*, hence probably the Volume I of the invoice), the sole volume of Nietzsche remaining in Stevens' library when it was acquired by the Huntington Library in 1975. The other volumes were doubtless among the books Mrs. Stevens sold around 1958 to a bookseller who kept no record of the titles purchased.

this volume by suggesting that men use religion to mitigate the effects of evil and so reduce their suffering. Since a narcotic cannot remove the cause of pain, Nietzsche is moved to exclaim,

> How greatly we should like to exchange the false assertions of the priests, that there is a god who desires good from us, a guardian and witness of every action, every moment, every thought, who loves us and seeks our welfare in all misfortune, —how greatly we would like to exchange these ideas for truths which would be just as healing, pacifying and beneficial as those errors! (*CW* vi.112)

Four months after telling Church he had read *Human, All-Too-Human*, Stevens had completed "Esthétique du Mal," whose third section echoes Nietzsche's sentiment:

> The fault lies with an over-human god,
> Who by sympathy has made himself a man
> And is not to be distinguished, when we cry
>
> Because we suffer, our oldest parent, peer
> Of the populace of the heart, the reddest lord,
> Who has gone before us in experience.
>
> If only he would not pity us so much,
> Weaken our fate, relieve us of woe both great
> And small, a constant fellow of destiny,
>
> A too, too human god, self-pity's kin
> And uncourageous genesis . . . It seems
> As if the health of the world might be enough.

Stevens expressed the same idea more obliquely in a poem published at the same time as "Esthétique," and few could miss the Nietzschean allusion in its title—"Less and Less Human, O Savage Spirit."

After 1944 Stevens' references to Nietzsche became more random and less important. He may have reread *Thus Spake Zarathustra*, for its two major subjects, the over-man and eternal recurrence, appear in "Description without Place" (1945). Section IV places Nietzsche's distorting mind with Lenin's; each sees his peculiar obsessions reflected in a pool of water, with Nietzsche studying "The eccentric souvenirs of human shapes . . . In perpetual revolution, round and round." In "The Dove in the Belly" (1946), Stevens used the Hebrew musical term "Selah," an unusual word he may have remembered from the wanderer's song in *Zarathustra* (CW xi.374–79).[23] Again in a 1948 letter to Rodríguez Feo, he expressed his autumnal mood with an allusion to Nietzsche: "How this oozing away hurts notwithstanding the pumpkins and the glaciale of frost and the onslaught of books and pictures and music and people. It is finished, Zarathustra says; and one goes to the Canoe Club and has a couple of Martinis and a pork chop and looks down the spaces of the river and participates in the disintegration, the decomposition, the rapt finale" (*L* 621). Whatever Nietzsche would have thought of the Canoe Club and its cuisine, he would have appreciated the rest of the letter, which excoriates a world in which the weak affect to be strong and the strong keep silence, in which group living has all but eliminated men of character.

Stevens therefore read Nietzsche at various periods in his life and turned some of his reading into poetry. But what of the hero? By the time he began rereading Nietzsche early in 1943, he had already written "Montrachet-le-Jardin," "Examination of the Hero in a Time of War," "Notes toward a Supreme Fiction," and possibly "Chocorua to Its Neighbor." At best, he only half-remembered the overman from his earlier reading. Yet there are affinities between major man and the overman, and these appear not only in the nature of the hero projected but also in the logic of his projection. The heroes are similar because they were shaped by similar needs and aspirations. As Stevens told Hi Simons in 1941, "where a man's attitude coincides with your own attitude, or accentuates your own attitude, you get a great deal from him

23. The word "Selah" also appears in *The Book of Psalms* (New York: American Bible Society, 1900) which Stevens purchased in 1900; it survived his Bible purge of 1907 (see *L* 102) and may be the copy he was "digging into" in 1909 (*L* 141).

without any effort. This, in fact, is one of the things that makes literature possible" (*L* 391).

Nietzsche, like Stevens, had graduated from religious disillusion to hero-worship. He believed that man had projected his sense of power onto a fictitious being whom he called God, and had then defined himself by his weakness. Eventually, even his God became too human—too much a reflection of weak human nature—and in Jesus he finally died of a human weakness, pity. Upon losing his faith in God, man lost faith in all that God represented; he lost faith, in effect, in his own better nature. In the throes of the ensuing "great loathing" or nausea, man is tempted to nihilism, to denial of all values. Recovery from nausea lies in realizing that God had been simply the most effective of man's "views of utility"; there are other such perspectives which, though fictitious, sustain one's sense of mastery over the world. Hence Nietzsche insisted that certain illusions are more valuable and life-promoting than the truths sought by the dialectician; the will to ignorance may in fact serve the will to power. In keeping with his esteem for fictions, he considered art both a vital activity and a seduction to life. "Art is with us," he asserted in a famous aphorism, "in order that we may not perish through truth" (*CW* xv.264).

Nietzsche's willful ignorance extended preëminently to his own creations, as one soon discovers when trying to extract a consistent notion of the overman from his work. Like Stevens, he felt a profound need of the hero he created; he prayed for "[a] glimpse of a man that justifies the existence of man, a glimpse of an incarnate human happiness that realises and redeems, for the sake of which one may hold fast to *the belief in man!*" (*CW* xiii.44). Like Stevens, too, he demanded that his surrogate god be everything God had been, yet entirely credible. To this end he cloaked the overman in some of his more poetic prose. In the following paragraphs, I divest the overman of his poetry, the better to compare him with major man. I consider his origin, nature, and role according to the scheme used for Stevens' hero.

Nietzsche anticipated Stevens in regarding war as the breeding ground of heroes. His own apocalyptic experience of the will to power came while he was serving as an ambulance-man in the Franco-Prussian War; upon witnessing an awesome cavalry charge, he became convinced that the desire to overpower was the motive force of life itself.[24] Some of the least palatable passages in his work extol the value of war in reaffirming manliness and preparing the way for the overman. Yet if war favors the creation of the overman, it does not produce him automatically. Indeed there seemed to be no sure historical route to the hero. Though Nietzsche ridiculed the notion of inevitable linear progress and thought the millennium merely a displaced Christian heaven, he derived little comfort from the Darwinian theory of evolution. Mankind seemed not to be progressing as a species, though higher types did occur fortuitously. On the contrary, the process of natural selection—perhaps because it is no longer natural but cultivated—seemed to militate against the higher type, creating instead a race of mediocre and fragmentary beings.

In *Thus Spake Zarathustra*, Nietzsche replaced the theories of inevitable progress and natural selection with his doctrine of eternal recurrence. The great wheel of being revolves eternally, now bringing the higher type of man to the fore, now the lower; the overman is the "great noontide" of being, not its sunrise or sunset. Though Zarathustra is at first despondent at the prospect of eternal recurrence, he ultimately learns to affirm life despite its recurrent suffering and reversions to the lower type of man. Nietzsche saw nothing deterministic in the cycle of being. He often hinted that eugenics and even political power might be enlisted in the breeding of higher men. First and foremost, however, the overman is a creation of

24. Bentley, p. 100.

will. To will is to create, Nietzsche believed, but in creating the gods man had overstepped the limits of his will. The overman, he rather arbitrarily determined, is man's supreme creation of will within the realm of possibility.

A specific war in Europe similarly moved Stevens to reflect seriously upon the hero. Though less acquainted than Nietzsche with actual combat, he laid more stress on its negative side; thus in "Asides on the Oboe" he called it the central evil as well as the central good. He was more interested in the metaphorical battle which the mind continually wages against outmoded conventions. The mind, as he put it in "Man and Bottle" (1940),

> has to content the reason concerning war,
> It has to persuade that war is part of itself,
> A manner of thinking, a mode
> Of destroying, as the mind destroys,
>
> An aversion, as the world is averted
> From an old delusion, an old affair with the sun,
> An impossible aberration with the moon,
> A grossness of peace.

Unlike Nietzsche, Stevens had no philosophical quarrel with the historical theories of the socialists or the Darwinians. He too ridiculed the millennium as a misplaced heaven ("A Duck for Dinner," OP 65) and represented time as emerging from the waste of the past and moving into the waste of the future ("Mr. Burnshaw and the Statue," OP 49). However, when it came to proposing an alternative model of human history he could sound very socialistic. Men were gathering for a "mighty flight of men" and the poet was to point their way ("Mr. Burnshaw," OP 51; "A Duck for Dinner," OP 64). Again in "Montrachet-le-Jardin" he spoke of "the hero-land to which we go," a hope which suggests Shaw's race of supermen rather than Nietzsche's random overmen. As for Darwin, Stevens conceded in 1955 that we live in Darwin's world, not Plato's, and we may as well make the best of it (OP 246). He nevertheless combined his belief in long-term progress with an acceptance of short-term recurrence. In "Notes," we have seen, he at first protests a robin's repetitious song, then accepts it as

> One of the vast repetitions final in
> Themselves and, therefore, good, the going round
>
> And round and round, the merely going round,
> Until merely going round is a final good,
> The way wine comes at a table in a wood.
>
> ("Pleasure," IX)

Nietzsche could scarcely have found a better rhythmic equivalent of his eternal recurrence than these rime-ridden, vertiginous lines. They whirl Stevens beyond acquiescence to approval and finally to his conjecture that the hero may be "he that of repetition is most master."

One of the more intriguing resemblances between Stevens and Nietzsche involves their ideas of creative will. Stevens prepared for writing his lecture "The Noble Rider and the Sound of Words" (1941) by reading I. A. Richards' *Coleridge on Imagination* and there encountered Coleridge's classic distinction, which he paraphrased as follows: "Fancy is an activity of the mind which puts things together of choice, *not* the will, as a principle of the mind's being, striving to realize itself in knowing itself" (*NA* 10).[25] Nietzsche had seconded Coleridge's notion of the will as the agent of creative imagination when he made Zarathustra tell his disciples,

> . . . I taught you: "The Will is a creator."
> All "It was" is a fragment, a riddle, a fearful chance—until the creating Will saith thereto: "But thus would I have it."—
> Until the creating Will saith thereto: "But thus do I will it! Thus shall I will it!" (*CW* xi.170)

Stevens echoed Coleridge and Nietzsche when he tried to capture the essence of poetry in the verse "Thou are not August unless I make thee so" and again when he

---

25. Extensive markings in Stevens' copy of *Coleridge on Imagination* (London: Kegan Paul, 1934) testify to his close reading of the book. Besides citing and quoting Richards in "The Noble Rider," Stevens occasionally picks up a phrase from Coleridge by way of Richards—e.g., "Plato's dear, gorgeous nonsense" (*NA* 3).

mounted his "figure of capable imagination" upon a horse "all will" ("Mrs. Alfred Uruguay," 1940).

Typically, however, Nietzsche defined the creative will so as to include an important nuance: he regarded the will as an impulse simultaneously to create and to dominate— often to dominate by creating powerful fictions. That Stevens inclined toward the Nietzschean view of imagination can be seen in Section XIX of "The Man with the Blue Guitar." Of the "monster" which confronts the poet in that poem, Stevens later wrote, "[the monster is] nature, which I desire to reduce: master, subjugate, acquire complete control over and use freely for my own purpose, as poet" (L 790). For Stevens, imagination was a quasi-biological drive. He concedes in "Mountains Covered with Cats" (1946) that the imagination cannot propagate itself and is in this respect "without the will to power / And impotent." But the poem goes on to speculate that even Freud, in the clairvoyance of eternity, would grant a measure of potency to things which remain unique precisely by remaining unprolific.

Had Stevens been asked to choose between Freud and Nietzsche, he would not have had to consider long. Though familiar with the Freudian cliché that art is sublimated sexual energy, he preferred to believe with Nietzsche—and Freud's colleague Alfred Adler—that sex and art are in turn manifestations of egotism. "There is not the slightest doubt," he wrote in 1936, "that egotism is at the bottom of what a good many poets do. . . . The truth is that egotism is at the bottom of everything everybody does, and that, if some really acute observer made as much of egotism as Freud has made of sex, people would forget a good deal about sex and find the explanation for everything in egotism" (L 305–6). About the time Stevens was working on "The Noble Rider and the Sound of Words," and therefore most preoccupied with Coleridge and Freud, he wrote "Poem with Rhythms" (1941), which represents the mind as a hand located between the candle of imagination and the wall of reality. "It must be," Stevens says as he contemplates the shadow-hand projected onto the wall,

> that the hand
> Has a will to grow larger on the wall,
> To grow larger and heavier and stronger than
> The wall; and that the mind
> Turns to its own figurations and declares,
> *"This image, this love, I compose myself*
> *Of these. In these, I come forth outwardly.*
> *In these, I wear a vital cleanliness,*
> *Not as in air, bright-blue-resembling air,*
> *But as in the powerful mirror of my wish and will."*

For both Stevens and Nietzsche, then, the hero was a product of history and creative will. While they appealed to different models of human history, they agreed that men create heroes—as well as gods and poems—in order to dominate reality.

On turning from the origin of Nietzsche's overman to his nature, one discovers some of the same contradictions that beset Stevens' idea of the hero. The overman is by definition a superior and as yet nonexistent being; only when man overcomes himself will he arrive at the overman. With some inconsistency, Nietzsche accepted the Darwinian hypothesis that man had evolved from lower primates, and he assumed evolution would eventually produce a creature as superior to modern man as modern man is to the ape. Though little can be known of this overman, since he is as yet in the womb of time, we have Nietzsche's word for it that he will be cold, hard, unpitying, and contemptuous of the "herd." Like Zarathustra, he will be a mountain-dweller and a solitary. For all his transcendence, however, the overman will not be an ethereal being. In *The Birth of Tragedy*, Nietzsche had idealized the figure of the "wise and enthusiastic satyr." Unlike the Socratic dialectician, for whom everything must be intelligible to be good, the satyr is part of nature and utters its chthonic wisdom by instinct. Nietzsche wished to retain this Dionysian virtue in his overman, so insisted that he be *Überthier* as well as *Übermensch*, superbeast as well as superman (*CW* xv.405). Though Nietzsche tended to hypostatize his overman and even to speak of the racial mixtures favorable to his nurture, he was painfully aware that the overman was as yet a shadowy fiction and would probably remain so for many millennia. On one occasion, Zarathustra admits almost despite himself that overmen, like gods, are merely poets' parables (*CW* xi.153).

Stevens was far more tolerant than Nietzsche of the general run of humanity. Though he clothed his hero in the imagery of sun and mountains and ice, he also insisted that major man be grounded in the common man and not exceed him by too much. Whereas Nietzsche had considered the study of "average man" the most disagreeable of the philosopher's duties (*CW* xii.38–39), Stevens admonishes the ephebe in "Notes toward a Supreme Fiction" to fashion the final elegance of the hero from the most pathetic and disoriented minim of humanity. At best, the poet should "meditate the highest man, not / The highest supposed in him and over" ("Examination," XIV). Perhaps Stevens' Depression-era skirmish with the Marxists informed his subsequent ideal of the hero, making it more democratic than it would otherwise have been. But if the Marxists belatedly forced him to respect the common man, they budged him not an inch from his contempt for "theoretical people" ("A Duck for Dinner," *OP* 65). His hero continued to resemble Dionysus more than Socrates. In 1936 he had called reason a "fatuous fire" and had proposed that men install some "super-animal" in the chair of fate ("A Duck for Dinner," *OP* 63; cf. *L* 371). In 1942, Stevens' hero still looked rather like Nietzsche's "blond beast," with his

> wider brow, large and less human
> Eyes and bruted ears: the man-like body
> Of a primitive.
>
> ("Examination," IX)

Like the overman, too, Stevens' hero remained a possibility, a fiction. Only in the poem of the hero, and in one's elevation of spirit upon reading the poem, does he live and have his being.

In assigning a role to the overman, Nietzsche was as anxious as Stevens to distinguish his hero from the "event-making" man. The overman is his own reason for being; his value lies, not in any effects he might produce, but in his very superiority to ordinary men and their affairs. It was Napoleon who justified his victories, not the victories that justified Napoleon (*CW* xv.313–14). Nietzsche's insistence on the overman's autonomy was part of his general critique of goal and purpose, whether these appeared as ideals, desiderata, teleology, final cause, or apocalyptic history. As traditionally interpreted, goal and purpose had conduced to man's moral immaturity by relieving him of his duty to choose his own values and goals. When these external value systems collapsed, he was naturally tempted to nihilistic denial of all value. Nietzsche called for an "experimental morality" akin to modern existentialism: man must create his own values, he must be a moral legislator rather than a moral scientist. The overman, as a created value, enabled Nietzsche to admit purposiveness by the back door after he had driven it from the front. To the extent that one participates in the overman's strength and mastery, one can endure and even exult in the death of God and the prospect of eternal recurrence. How was this participation to be effected? "If anyone long and obstinately desires to *appear* something," Nietzsche believed, "he finds it difficult at last to *be* anything else. The profession of almost every individual, even of the artist, begins with hypocrisy, with an imitating from without, with a copying of the effective" (*CW* vi.70). Whether or not the overman is a feasible ideal for mankind, it stood Nietzsche in good stead. It was both the product of his will to power and a means to greater assurance—some would say delusion—of potency. So we might infer, at least, from one of his cryptic notebook entries: "*Greatest elevation* of man's *consciousness of strength,* as that which creates superman" (*CW* xv.425).

Stevens likewise posited the hero as value at a time when other values were suspect. Where Nietzsche had to contend with the pessimism of Schopenhauer, Stevens had to cope with Freud and the logical positivists. He answered Freud's attack on illusion, specifically religious illusion, in "The Noble Rider and the Sound of Words" and again in "Imagination as Value" (*NA* 14–15, 139). As he was preparing the latter, he chanced upon a philosophic donnybrook in the London *New Statesman and Nation.* A contributor who signed himself "Oxonian" had reported to the journal that postwar Oxford undergraduates, denied recourse to traditional values by A. J. Ayer's *Language, Truth and Logic* (1936), were in peril of losing their souls to fascism.[26] The ensuing melee, carried on chiefly in the correspondence section, involved Ayer himself, C. E. M. Joad, and others. It also moved Stevens to dip into Ayer's book, where he found metaphysical statements placed on a par with poetic statements. Values, Ayer seemed to say, are imaginary (see *NA* 137–38). Yet Stevens was not particularly alarmed at this proposition. Three years later, in fact, he would lecture on the poetry of various philosophical concepts, including Nietzsche's eternal recurrence ("A Collect of Philosophy," *OP* 194). He could face Ayer with equanimity because, like Nietzsche, he believed that men must create their own values and those values will necessarily be fictive. Imagination is consequently a moral faculty of some importance. It is, as Stevens contends in "Imagination as Value," "the power of the mind over the possibilities of things; but if this constitutes a certain single characteristic, it is the source not of a certain single value but of as many values as reside in the possibilities of things" (*NA* 136).

26. "A Visit to Oxford," 26 June 1948, pp. 518–19.

The hero was one such value, one of those propositions about life that make life what it is. Stevens shared Nietzsche's conviction that one can imagine an ethical ideal, then appropriate it psychologically. In "The Figure of the Youth as Virile Poet" (1943), he asserts that the poet "shares the transformation, not to say apotheosis, accomplished by the poem" and follows Bergson in comparing this apotheosis to the aspirations of the saints (*NA* 49–51). The reader, to the extent that he is moved by the sound of the poet's words to suspend his disbelief, inhabits "A hero's world in which he is the hero" ("Montrachet-le-Jardin"). Considering major man either aesthetically, as a product of the imagination, or morally, as a means to enhance the quality of life, one must concede that he is the most daring and ambitious of Stevens' personae, the cynosure of his mythology of self.

This is not to say that he is the most convincing of Stevens' mythic figures. Most of us read the major man poems as we read Yeats's *The Tower* or Eliot's *Four Quartets*—for the superlative poetry and not for the informing mythology. We attend with varying degrees of indulgence or irritation to those passages which recall the Coué formula of "conscious autosuggestion" so popular in the twenties: "Every day in every way I am getting better and better." When we doubt that we are getting better or nobler, we are relieved to find Stevens telling Henry Church that he liked Rhine wine, blue grapes, good cheese, endive, and books as much as supreme fiction (*L* 431). In a prophet, this seems a redeeming weakness. But for Stevens it was simply another mode of belief, the mode appropriate to medium man. What he said of life after death in "Flyer's Fall" (1945) might also be said of life before death: it is a "dimension in which / We believe without belief, beyond belief."

· 8 ·

The Intensest Rendezvous

To celebrate the publication of Stevens' *Collected Poems* on October 1, 1954, Alfred A. Knopf gave a party at the Harmonie Club in New York. Among the guests he invited was John Crowe Ransom. Unable to attend, Ransom sent his regrets, adding,

> I have the extremest liking for his verse, and it is a fact that I think it is valuable not only for its poetic quality but for its ideas: for me he is arguing on behalf of a secular culture based on Nobility, and I think that is the best culture that we are going to have, and a practicable one at the same time; though his critics have never mentioned this, it is very plain if one reads the poems, and it will become plainer, indeed it will become compulsive, when the *Collected Poems* are issued all in one volume.[1]

Knopf, alert to the commercial value of this sentiment, apparently passed it on to Stevens' editor, Herbert Weinstock, who asked Stevens if they might use all or part of it to publicize the book. Stevens demurred, though he admitted that Ransom had "[hit] the bull's eye" and that he was delighted by the comment.[2] "To use it for publicity," he said, "might well subject what is closest to me to distortion."

From remarks Stevens made to Weinstock and later to Robert Pack and Ransom himself, it appears that he feared several kinds of distortion. He did not want to be identified with a group that had adopted the word "nobility" as its

1. Quoted in letter from Herbert Weinstock to Stevens, 20 Sept. 1954.
2. Letter to Weinstock, 21 Sept.

shibboleth a few years previously (L 880).[3] Neither did he want to be classed with the secular humanists or social humanitarians, "the healers who speak (and take up collections) on Sundays in parlors at the Waldorf, and so on."[4] Besides the prospect of being associated with a particular school or creed, however noble, Stevens disliked having his poetic achievement defined once and for all. "The trouble is," he told Ransom, "that once one is strongly defined, no other definition is ever possible, in spite of daily change" (L 880n).

Stevens' last point was well taken. Had he published his *Collected Poems* in 1947 rather than 1954, Ransom's note might have appeared on the dust jacket without seriously misrepresenting the contents of the volume. In 1947, Stevens' entire career seemed, in retrospect, to have been directed toward the creation of major man as the embodiment of his supreme fiction. Few readers could have guessed, then, that he would virtually ignore the hero after *Transport to Summer*. But how could it have been otherwise? Major man was born, not only of Stevens' need for heroes and his preoccupation with a supreme fiction, but also of his meditations on the war; he required flesh-and-blood soldiers, as he said in "Chocorua to Its Neighbor," to "make big the fable" (Section XXIV).

Yet Stevens might well have abandoned his heroic fable around 1945 even if there had been no surrender that year. In January and February 1945, José Rodríguez Feo was pressing him to be more specific regarding the major men of his recent poems.[5] Who were they? Was Stevens' intention at all mythological? Stevens, though he was aware that

---

3. Again in the letter to Weinstock of 21 Sept., Stevens mentions a "school which was so much resented a few years ago." Though a number of "schools" come to mind—the Nietzscheans and New Humanists of the early century, various fascist literary groups of the thirties and forties, even Ransom's Agrarians—I cannot positively identify the school to which Stevens alludes.

4. Letter to Weinstock, 21 Sept.

5. Letters from Rodríguez Feo to Stevens, 13 Jan. and 13 Feb.

nothing could be more fatal to the supreme fiction than to state it "definitely and incautiously" (*L* 863), nevertheless felt obliged to respond to these questions. He did so in "Paisant Chronicle," where he prosily asserts that the major men

> are characters beyond
> Reality, composed thereof. They are
> The fictive man created out of men.
> They are men but artificial men. They are
> Nothing in which it is not possible
> To believe, more than the casual hero, more
> Than Tartuffe as myth, the most Molière,
> The easy projection long prohibited.

This projection of the hero is indeed too easy. Though Stevens apologized to Rodríguez Feo for the residual ambiguity of his definition (*L* 489), he had in effect turned major man to stone, the "marble soiled by pigeons" of "Examination of the Hero in a Time of War," XII. In poems like "The Pastor Caballero" (1946) and "Sketch of the Ultimate Politician" (1947), which regard the hero out of the corner of the eye rather than directly, Stevens' wartime ideal recovers some of its original fluidity. But as a suggestive image of the supreme fiction, major man perished in 1945 of terminal definition.

The supreme fiction lived on, abstract and still changeable, as the "central poem" of the late forties and early fifties. Beginning in 1947, Stevens delivered a series of lectures—"Three Academic Pieces" (1947), "Effects of Analogy" (1948), "Imagination as Value" (1948), and "The Relations between Poetry and Painting" (1951)—that recur to this poem of poems, though the idea had been with him at least since he proposed "THE GRAND POEM: PRELIMINARY MINUTIAE" as his preferred title for *Harmonium* (*L* 237). To his autumnal speculations, he brought the experience of his long career as a poet. Experience had taught him, for example, that there are certain proprieties to be observed in the realm of image and analogy. He speaks of several of these in "Effects of Analogy," among them the quality he calls "appositeness." For the poet or reader with a lively sense of the apposite, it will seem as if "in the vast association of ideas there existed for every object its appointed objectification" (*NA* 114). Stevens developed this insight a year later in "Study of Images II," which asserts that "pearly women" surpass witches as emblems of the moon and witches in turn excel the brown "ice-bear." It is as if, Stevens concludes, "the centre of images had its / Congenial mannequins, alert to please,"

> . . . as if the disparate halves
> Of things were waiting in a [betrothal] known
> To none, awaiting espousal to the sound
>
> Of right joining, a music of ideas, the burning
> And breeding and bearing birth of harmony,
> The final relation, the marriage of the rest.

Stevens concedes in "Imagination as Value" that "it would be the merest improvisation to say of any image of the world, even though it was an image with which a vast accumulation of imaginations had been content, that it was the chief image" (*NA* 151–52). Yet this did not deter him from improvising such an image in "A Golden Woman in a Silver Mirror," which first appeared with "Study of Images II." The golden woman is an image whose capacity for representing several kinds of reality—the sun, the moon, and a woman named Belle—suggests that it may be the center of images or a near approach to that center. The silver mirror is the perceiving mind, which both reflects and—unlike the "unreflecting" leaves in nature—reflects upon this symbol. One assumes that the golden woman and her sorority will vanish when death shatters the human mirror; but Stevens conjectures that this "king's queen" may reside apart from human thought. If so, it would be at once the "mother" of poetry, that from which it issues, and its "glittering crown," that to which it returns. "A Golden Woman in a Silver Mirror" is Section XXII of "The Man with the Blue Guitar" in yet another guise.

Stevens was familiar with Baudelaire's notion that there

exists "an unascertained and fundamental aesthetic, or order" of which poetry and the other arts are manifestations (*NA* 160). In a tribute to critic Paul Rosenfeld, he dressed Baudelaire's idea in the German word for "creation" and a phrase from Mallarmé to characterize the world in which Rosenfeld might have lived: "Perhaps there existed for him an ideal *Schöpfung*, a world composed of music, but which did not whirl round in music alone; or of painting, but which did not expand in color and form alone; or of poetry, but which did not limit itself to the *explication orphique* of the poet" (*OP* 262).[6] Occasionally, there appears a poet-philosopher—Coleridge comes readily to mind—who becomes fascinated with the ideal *Schöpfung* to the detriment of his own *explication orphique*. Stevens, who shared Coleridge's philosophic turn of mind, was determined to write poems rather than treatises. He maintains in "A Collect of Philosophy" (1951) that while both philosopher and poet seek an integral vision of the world, each demands something different of his integration:

> The philosopher searches for an integration for its own sake, as, for example, Plato's idea that knowledge is recollection or that the soul is a harmony; the poet searches for an integration that shall be not so much sufficient in itself as sufficient for some quality that it possesses, such as its insight, its evocative power or its appearance in the eye of the imagination. The philosopher intends his integration to be fateful; the poet intends his to be effective. (*OP* 196–97)

When successful, the philosopher's integration explains why things are as they are; it is comprehensive, inevitable, and determinate. The poet's integration, by contrast, should be a prologue to what is possible, teasing one into making new discoveries or seeing new relationships

---

6. "L'explication orphique de la Terre . . . est le seul devoir du poète," Stevens wrote in *Sur Plusieurs Beaux Sujects* (Cahier II, p. 10) in 1947, quoting Mallarmé. In a letter of 7 Mar. 1947 to Reading poet Byron Vazakas, he noted that the word "schöpfer" was one used by people "down home" (Yale).

among things. It is therefore ironic that Stevens' sole sustained treatment of the central poem should be one of his least "effective" efforts in every sense of the word. "A Primitive Like an Orb" (1948) does teem with suggestive analogies for the central poem, which is called a "primitive" or archetype; an "orb" or planet; an "essential poem"; a "huge, high harmony"; a "miraculous multiplex of lesser poems"; a "vis"; a "principle"; a "nature"; a "patron of origins"; and a "skeleton of the ether." Heeding his own advice in "A Collect of Philosophy," Stevens tries not so much to define the central poem as to evoke its appearance in the eye of the imagination. But the result is either fustian, the trumped-up rhetoric of "whirroos / And scintillant sizzlings such as children like," or mechanical echoes of successful earlier pieces like "Chocorua to Its Neighbor" and "Notes toward a Supreme Fiction." The hero appears as illustration at the end of Stanza VIII and is called "angelic" in Stanza X. As a version of the supreme fiction, the central poem meets the three criteria set forth in "Notes": it is abstract (Stanzas X, XI), it changes (Stanza XII), and it gives pleasure (Stanza IX). Where "Notes" had concluded with a "That's it" and the image of the fat girl revolving in crystal, "A Primitive" concludes with a "That's it" and the image of a giant "ever changing, living in change."

"A Primitive Like an Orb" is an ineffective poem because it strains to be effective. Conversely, "Looking across the Fields and Watching the Birds Fly" (1952) sets out to satirize a fateful integration but ends by demonstrating its poetic effectiveness. As the poem opens, we discover the philosophical Mr. Homburg on one of his visits to Concord, at "the edge of things" and presumably at the periphery of common sense. On these aberrant occasions he is wont to insist that "The spirit comes from the body of the world. . . ." This is not quite Crispin's thesis that "his soil is man's intelligence," however, for Concord is still awash in Emerson's Oversoul. Mr. Homburg's world is a "pensive nature,"

. . . Too much like thinking to be less than thought,
Obscurest parent, obscurest patriarch,
A daily majesty of meditation,

That comes and goes in silences of its own.

Stevens at first maintains his distance from Mr. Homburg, dismissing his theory as another of his "more irritating minor ideas" and dubbing his cosmos "a mechanical / And slightly detestable *operandum*." But as the poem proceeds he warms to Mr. Homburg's integration and invests it with a highly seductive rhetoric of its own. Only at the end does he introduce a "new scholar" to remind us that, however effective this integration may be, it is none the less fateful, leaving little scope for spontaneous thought or creativity. In Mr. Homburg's scheme of things, human thought is merely a function of nature's mechanical "thinking" and the poet's verse an automatic and predictable response to natural stimuli, like the dove's clockwork cooing in "Song of Fixed Accord," published with "Looking across the Fields" in the *Hudson Review*.

Mr. Homburg and the new scholar speak for Stevens' ambivalence. The philosopher in him still subscribed to the view he had recorded in his commonplace book in the thirties. "For myself," he had written then, "the indefinite, the impersonal, atmospheres and oceans and, above all, the principle of order are precisely what I love; and I don't see why, for a philosopher, they should not be the ultimate inamorata."[7] Rejecting the premise "that the universe is explicable only in terms of humanity," he hankered after an order beyond anthropomorphism, an order Mr. Homburg believes to be

free

From man's ghost, larger and yet a little like,
Without his literature and without his gods . . .

7. *Sur Plusieurs Beaux Sujects*, Cahier I, p. 7.

This order is more than a little like man's ghost. Mr. Homburg is one of those German Romantics who, as Santayana remarked, "imagine that all reality might be a transcendental self and a romantic dreamer like themselves; nay, that it might be just their own transcendental self and their own romantic dreams extended indefinitely."[8] Yet Mr. Homburg's integration—and Stevens'—is sufficiently impersonal and fateful that the "new scholar" or poet feels the need of "a human that can be accounted for."

One can read much of Stevens' late work as an effort to account for the human, to mythologize the fateful aesthetic of the universe and so make his poetic and philosophic eyes see one. This enterprise, which recalls his earlier attempt to give human form to the supreme fiction, had to begin with a mundane question of poetic representation: what does a fateful order look like? how shall it be shown to the reader? A dozen poems in *The Auroras of Autumn* (1950) and "The Rock" section of the *Collected Poems* (1954) represent aesthetic, the fateful order, as an autumn landscape. Though Stevens asserts that the absence of imagination must itself be imagined, he can barely summon the strength in the fall. "It is as if," he says in "The Plain Sense of Things" (1952),

> We had come to an end of the imagination,
> Inanimate in an inert savoir.
>
> It is difficult even to choose the adjective
> For this blank cold, this sadness without cause.

"In a Bad Time" (1948) suggests the peril of this passive stance. The man who beholds the order of the northern sky may be possessed by it: "For him cold's glacial beauty is his fate." Unless he can break the spell of this fateful beauty by a strenuous exercise of imagination, it will bind him as effectively as any Arthurian enchantress. In "Puella

8. *Winds of Doctrine*, p. 195.

Parvula" (1949), Stevens suggests that as a first step imagination must subdue mere thinking, for thought is susceptible to the terror of aesthetic. Once the mind has been reduced from "wild bitch" to little girl, the imagination can proceed as "dauntless master" to create a mythic "human tale."

"Puella Parvula" promises a *summarium in excelsis* which had in fact appeared a year earlier; surely the Latin phrase does not overstate the importance of "The Auroras of Autumn" (1948) among Stevens' later poems. In the first six sections of the poem, he confronts the aurora borealis (from which he takes his title) as he would an immense stage, "a theatre floating through the clouds" (Section VI). His alter ego, the "scholar" who witnesses the celestial spectacle, feels the inadequacy of his "one candle" before the "arctic effulgence." He lacks the imaginative means to accommodate it mythologically. "What company, / In masks," he cries out in desperation, "can choir it with the naked wind?" (Section IV). Halfway through the poem, the "company" and its props have included a great serpent and a cabin deserted on a beach, a gentle mother and a strong father. Of these, the father had seemed most capable of choiring it with the naked wind. Where the others merely change, he is master and measurer of change (Section IV). But the father's attempt to stage-manage an elaborate pageant, with storytellers, musicians, dancers, and imposing sets, had resulted only in a "loud, disordered mooch" (Section V).

After the father exits with his fantastical troupe, the scholar of one candle wonders whether the auroras might not be the production of another stage manager, like the father but infinitely more capable:

> Is there an imagination that sits enthroned
> As grim as it is benevolent, the just
> And the unjust, which in the midst of summer stops
>
> To imagine winter? When the leaves are dead,
> Does it take its place in the north and enfold itself,

Goat-leaper, crystalled and luminous, sitting

In highest night? And do these heavens adorn
And proclaim it, the white creator of black, jetted
By extinguishings, even of planets as may be,

Even of earth, even of sight, in snow,
Except as needed by way of majesty,
In the sky, as crown and diamond cabala?

(Section VII)

Supposing there were such an imagination and that it were responsible for the tragedy writ large in the heavens, it would not be itself an actor in that tragedy, compelled to "leap by chance in its own dark." Yet it is not exempt from its own nature. Inconstant,

It must change from destiny to slight caprice.
And thus its jetted tragedy, its stele

And shape and mournful making move to find
What must unmake it and, at last, what can,
Say, a flippant communication under the moon.

Imagination disarms its own tragedy by introducing an element of the capricious, the non-fateful. Its "flippant communication" thus marks the turning point in the poem, from the tragic rhetoric of the first six sections to the "idiom of an innocent earth" which prevails in the last three sections. For every tragic reading of the human condition, imagination offers another and less portentous reading. It might be the scholar of one candle whose oversolemn declarations (here emphasized by italics) the imagination interrupts in Section IX:

This drama that we live—We lay sticky with sleep.
This sense of the activity of fate—

The rendezvous, when she came alone,
By her coming became a freedom of the two,
An isolation which only the two could share.

By its first rejoinder, the imagination suggests that most of us live "as Danes in Denmark all day long," largely oblivious of life's drama. The second reply turns a rendezvous with fate into a rendezvous with freedom, anticipating Stevens' strategy three years later in "Final Soliloquy of the Interior Paramour" (1951). Finally, this superior imagination refuses to endorse the image of disaster—"Shall we be found hanging in the trees next spring?"—which the bare trees and wind seem inevitably to conjure up. Disaster, if it comes at all, will come "Almost as part of innocence, almost, / Almost as the tenderest and the truest part."

The last section of "Auroras" proclaims what might be called, by analogy with "Credences of Summer," the credences of autumn: the world is neither comic nor tragic but innocent. To be sure, it is populated by unhappy as well as happy people, the "full of fate" as well as the "full of fortune." Hence Stevens' scholar of one candle, now a fully enlightened rabbi, cannot rise to the optimistic heights of Emerson's Orphic poet, who in the closing paragraphs of *Nature* had dismissed evil as an optical illusion. But he is commissioned to preach a doctrine very like the traditional doctrine of Providence—that there is a "never-failing genius" who contemplates the larger economy of existence and is capable of making adjustments when things get out of balance. More than capable, this supreme fiction is compassionate, regarding humanity "As if he lived all lives, that he might know." In this respect he—or it—differs from Ananke, the "unmerciful pontifex" of "The Greenest Continent" (1936, *OP* 60). But neither is he a major man; where the hero of "Chocorua to Its Neighbor," XXI, had been fraternal and immanent—

> Not father, but bare brother, megalfrere,
> Or by whatever boorish name a man
> Might call the common self—

the imagination that sits enthroned in the heavens is paternal and transcendent, like Mr. Homburg's "obscurest patriarch."

In the course of "The Auroras of Autumn," Stevens moves from a fateful aesthetic to a temporarily effective mythology (the mother and father) and finally to a mythological vision not far short of theology. Fortified by this vision, he can regard the convulsive world of time, the "hall harridan" of the final stanza, with equanimity. "Auroras" is typical of the late poetry not only in its rhetorical strategy, the mythologizing of aesthetic, but also in its choice of mythologies. In the early poetry, Stevens had cultivated a variety of outlandish poses, appearing as aesthete, dandy, and clown or projecting such figures onto the stage of his imagination. These dramatis personae constitute what Joseph Riddel has rightly called "a self (or many faces and gestures of a self) in emergence."[9] Together with the hero of his middle period, they enabled him to surpass or extend his limited experience as the son of a lawyer, later a lawyer himself, living in comfortable middle-class surroundings in Pennsylvania, New York, and Connecticut. To write his exotic poetry—and that was the only kind he could write at first—he required exotic poses and perspectives. In the late poetry, he turns from the exotic to the homely, from dandified clowns and masterful heroes to figures resembling his own parents and, as in a glass darkly, the God of his boyhood and youth.

Stevens' late mythology has, then, a pervasively "parental" character; in fact, he often regards God as simply "our oldest parent" ("Esthétique du Mal," III). Yet it would not do to confound the divine parent, who remained always a fiction for Stevens, with the parents he had known and the parent he was. Taking our cue, therefore, from the sequence of personae in "The Auroras of Autumn," we will consider first the earthly mothers and fathers in the late poetry, then their celestial exponent.

The father and mother of "Auroras" appear in poems

9. *The Clairvoyant Eye: The Poetry and Poetics of Wallace Stevens* (Baton Rouge: Louisiana State University Press, 1965), p. 272.

written over the entire course of Stevens' career, but with greater frequency in the late poetry. His diction is one index, albeit crude, of his preoccupation. As the following table suggests, nearly two-thirds of the poems in which he uses "parent" words appeared after 1940, during the last third of his career.[10] The columns on the right indicate the number of poems in which the key words appear:

	after 1913	*after 1940*
parent(s)	12	10
parental	3	3
parentage	1	1
mother(s)	30	16
motherly	1	0
maternal	4	2
father(s)	18	14
paternal	1	1
pater	1	0
patriarch(s)	6	3
totals:	77	50

These words appear in similar contexts and have similar connotations from first to last. The mother is muse, nurse, nature, and moon. In one atypical poem, she appears as "Madame La Fleurie" (1951), the witch who devours the poet and his works. Usually, as Stevens asserts in "Auroras," III, the mother's face is the "purpose" of the poem; that is, the poem is written so as to put a familiar and agreeable face on an unfamiliar and possibly frightening reality. Thus Stevens represents death as the mother of beauty in "Sunday Morning" and mother as the beauty of death in "The Owl in the Sarcophagus" (1947). The father of the poems either complements the mother—he is sun to her moon, strength to her gentleness, imagination to her reality—or duplicates her role as nature and native

10. In determining the number of poems in which Stevens uses these words, I have relied on Thomas F. Walsh's *Concordance to the Poetry of Wallace Stevens* (University Park: Pennsylvania State University Press, 1963).

land and image of death (see "Lulu Morose," *OP* 27; "The Irish Cliffs of Moher"; and "The Owl in the Sarcophagus," I). He is sometimes bearded, like Garrett Barcalow Stevens in the photograph his son favored (*L* 454, 455).

Both mother and father are fateful figures, in their way, since they prolong their physical and spiritual lives in their offspring. The mother in "The Owl in the Sarcophagus" cries out to the living, "Keep you, keep you, I am gone, oh keep you as / My memory . . ." (Section I). The philosopher in "The Role of the Idea in Poetry" philosophizes because he is "Determined thereto, perhaps by his father's ghost" (*OP* 93), while Aeneas in "Recitation after Dinner" carries Anchises on his back, "His life made double by his father's life" (*OP* 87). These and similar poems suggest that, as Stevens puts it in "Things of August" (1949), "The sentiment of the fatal is a part / Of filial love" (Section IV). But to love one's parents is to embrace one's destiny, not as a set of irksome conditions imposed by an impersonal order, but as a legacy imbued with affection.

Stevens came to a new appreciation of that legacy and its place in his mythology of self while pursuing his genealogical study during the forties. I have recounted elsewhere the story of his attempt to reconstruct his family's past, an effort that cost him a good deal of time and—since he employed several professional genealogists—money.[11] He succeeded in tracing his mother's family back to the original European emigrant, a Huguenot exile named Clothilde Zeller. Some of Clothilde's descendants claimed she was a Valois, a member of the French royal family; but Stevens, in the spirit of disinterested inquiry that characterized his research, disputed their claim. The evidence suggested that Clothilde was a German of common stock, and Stevens was content to be part of this "old and rugged

11. "To Realize the Past: Wallace Stevens' Genealogical Study," *American Literature* 52 (1981): 607–27. For further discussion of this subject, see Brazeau, pp. 265–88, and Thomas F. Lombardi, "Wallace Stevens and the Haunts of Unimportant Ghosts," *Wallace Stevens Journal* 7 (1983): 46–53.

Pennsylvania Dutch family" regardless of its social standing.[12]

On his father's side, he assumed that he was solidly Holland Dutch; but when he pursued the Stevens and Barcalow lines, sometimes retracing the course of his father's study seventy years previously, he came to a couple of surprising conclusions. The first Stevens in America, whatever his national origin, had emigrated from Prussia. The Barcalow ancestor, as Garrett Barcalow Stevens had doubtless begun to suspect in 1871, was a Scot who had married into the Dutch Hogeland family. Stevens resisted the idea that he carried Scottish blood in his veins until he visited a Delaware branch of the family in 1946. Thereafter, convinced beyond a reasonable doubt, he was as proud of his Scottish ancestry as he was of the German and Dutch.

Considering Stevens' previous indifference to family history and tradition—an indifference, we have seen, that helped to smooth the course of love when he was courting Elsie—one wonders what precipitated his genealogical interest in 1941, just as he was reaching the peak of his poetic powers. Several factors apparently combined to get him going: simple nostalgia for the past, Elsie's concurrent passion for the study of her own family, and—probably most important—the fear that his own generation of Stevenses might pass away without leaving to the next generation a record of their past.[13] His brothers Garrett and John had died in 1937 and 1940, respectively, and his sister Elizabeth followed in 1943.

Whatever Stevens' motives, he had by the end of 1943 some tangible results to show for his effort: a detailed report on the Stevens line, handsomely bound in two volumes, plus two portfolios of photographs representing people and places named in the report. He subsequently

12. Letter to John A. Zellers, 28 June 1948.
13. Stevens' niece, Jane MacFarland Wilson, believes that her uncle's genealogical interest was sparked by his reunion with his sister Elizabeth and the younger generation of the family at his brother John's funeral in 1940; see Brazeau, p. 266.

assembled reports on other lines of descent and collected a small trove of family heirlooms. In 1944 he joined the Saint Nicholas Society of New York, whose members can trace themselves to a native or resident of the city or state of New York prior to 1785. To his chagrin, he was never able to qualify for membership in the Holland Society, whose members must go back in the direct male line to a resident of the Dutch colonies in America before 1675.

Not a clubman by temperament, Stevens sought to join these groups from much the same motive that led him to prepare a scholarly genealogy and enshrine it in an attractive binding. "My object in joining these societies," he told the genealogist who prepared the report, "is not vanity, but the desire to make a record, or, rather, to take advantage of a repository of the family line. Then too, I think that such societies serve to keep alive something that is worth keeping alive."[14] Though he admitted that he was "not particularly keen about dinners, which are the life of such organizations,"[15] he attended regularly at the Saint Nicholas Society dinners and seems to have appreciated this ritual recurrence to a tradition. He wrote "Tradition," a poem whose title he later changed to "Recitation after Dinner" (OP 86–88), for the centenary Paas or Easter Monday Festival of the Saint Nicholas Society in 1945. He probably wrote "A Ceremony" (OP 151–53), a brief interlude also concerning the nature of tradition, for a similar occasion.

More significant for the reader of Stevens' poetry are the intangible results of his genealogical study. Surrounded after 1941 by reminders of his family's past, he lived a life of "extraordinary references"—a life framed not only, as in the poem of that title, by Indian-fighters, but also by pioneers, soldiers, farmers, and tradesmen.[16] He

14. Letter to Lila James Roney, 25 Nov. 1942.
15. Letter to Emma Stevens Jobbins, 11 Dec. 1944.
16. Although "Extraordinary References" (1946) is set in the Tulpe-hocken, which was settled by the Zeller family, the name Jacomyntje is from the Stevens line, where it appears several times.

told Victor Hammer, then teaching at a college in Lexington, that Kentucky exerted a strong hold on his imagination because many of his ancestors had passed through the state a century and a half previously (*L* 607). When Norman Holmes Pearson invited him to give the Bergen Lecture at Yale in 1948, he gladly assented, noting that he was a member of the Bergen family.[17] World War II reminded him of battles fought centuries earlier. The old-time soldier in "Examination of the Hero in a Time of War" (1942) uses the Pennsylvania Dutch polyglot when he proclaims his belief that "The Got whome we serve is able to deliver / Us" (Section II). In "Dutch Graves in Bucks County" (1943), modern armies go about their noisy business with little regard for battles fought long ago by the soldiers buried in Bucks County, most likely in the Dutch cemetery at Feasterville. Because freedom is "like a man who kills himself / Each night" and cannot be passed from one generation to the next, the Dutchmen must "Know that the past is not part of the present." But since each generation is involved in the same quest for freedom, Stevens can address these old soldiers as "semblables" and conclude that the modern "divergence" from the past is not so dramatic as to prevent their understanding the present.

"Dutch Graves" only begins to suggest the relation of the past to the present, as Stevens understood it. He came to regard himself as both physically and spiritually the product of his ancestry. He attributed his robust physical constitution to the Barcalows and Hogelands, who had "built up" the weaker Stevens line.[18] Except for some of the more colorful women, he considered his Dutch forebears to be persons of solid character, not particularly brilliant but capable of great "moral excitement" due to their Dutch Reformed religion.[19] To ancestors like Clothilde Zeller and Kitty Conover Barcalow, he believed that he

17. Letter to Pearson, 10 Dec. 1947 (Yale).
18. Letter to Jobbins, 11 Dec. 1944.
19. Letter to Floyd R. Du Bois, 30 Jan. 1942.

owed whatever of fire and imagination he possessed.[20] Clothilde had reputedly killed four Indians with an axe, one after another, as they tried to come in through a window during a raid on her homestead, Fort Zeller; Kitty became a heroine of the American Revolution when, as a girl of fifteen, she drove the family cow into a swamp to prevent it from falling into enemy hands.[21]

Though Stevens had dismissed the importance of family background as a young man, saying, "Our spirits are what we will them to be, not what they happen to be" (*SP* 209), he later came to regard fate as a matter of temperament and temperament as a matter of heredity. Apologizing to his daughter for his occasional fits of moodiness, he wrote in 1942, "My own stubbornnesses and taciturn eras are straight out of Holland and I cannot change them any more than I can take off my skin" (*L* 422). The whole episode of which this letter is part serves to demonstrate his assertion, for he found himself adopting toward his daughter's experiment in independence the same stance his father had taken toward his own brief journalistic career. A couple of years later, he would oppose Holly's marriage to John Hanchak even more strenuously than Garrett Stevens had opposed his marriage to Elsie. Remembering the past, he was none the less condemned to repeat it.

Along with physique and temperament, Stevens believed that he had inherited certain of his poetic preoccupations. His "reality-imagination complex" was, he asserted in 1953, uniquely his own (*L* 792). But it was also a latter-day version of complementary instincts which had informed his ancestors' lives—their belief in God and their attachment to the soil. Although his Dutch ancestors defi-

---

20. Letters to Mary Owen Steinmetz, 27 May 1943; and Roney, 15 Sept. 1943.

21. Stevens relates the Clothilde Zeller story to Steinmetz in a letter of 1 Sept. 1944; he tells Agnes Storer in a letter of 4 May 1945 that he had long been familiar with the Kitty Conover story and may have heard it from his father.

nitely believed in heaven, as Stevens once reminded Henry Church (*L* 430), he particularly associated religious feeling with the Pennsylvania Germans on his mother's side of the family, who had come to America seeking freedom of worship. "Pennsylvania Germans," Stevens told Barbara Church in 1954, "have visions during their work with the greatest regularity. These are the things that invited them to the New World and sustained them there. How curious it is that we don't have chapels in factories or insurance offices" (*L* 843).

Stevens pondered this curiosity at some length in a 1948 essay, "About One of Marianne Moore's Poems" (*NA* 93–103). In the second section of the essay, which seems at first to digress from his discussion of Moore's "He 'Digesteth Harde Yron,'" Stevens recalls three vignettes from a genealogical holiday he and Elsie had taken in 1946, partly to visit places associated with the Zeller family. He describes a cartouche over the door of Fort Zeller, signifying that the house and those who lived in it were consecrated to the glory of God. "Their reality," Stevens points out, "consisted of both the visible and the invisible." He then describes the "stout old Lutheran" whose life is so intimately bound up with the church at Stouchsburg, where Clothilde Zeller's death was recorded, that his reality might be said to be the building and adjoining graveyard themselves. Finally, Stevens recalls his visit to the Trinity Tulpehocken Reformed Church, to which his great-great-grandfather Franz Zeller and his family had belonged. His description of the graveyard, with its limestone wall, cedars, and grazing sheep, is a short prose-poem evoking a sense of bleakness and desolation. This is the reality of the modern skeptic, the insurance executive who would not be altogether at ease with a chapel in his office. Yet he is sufficiently imbued with *nostalgie du divin*, the topic of one of his letters about the time he wrote this essay (*L* 596), to experience the absence of something. "There could not be," Stevens remarks in summary, "any effective diversion from the reality that time and experience had created here, the desolation that penetrated one like something final."

Stevens' elegy in a country churchyard proves not to be a digression after all, for he goes on to commend Moore's ability to master the most intractable realities in her poetry, an ability that rivals the ostrich's assimilation of hard iron. Her poems are like the books he had seen at the Morgan Library, which suddenly lent color and life to his bleak experience of the Pennsylvania graveyard. Citing the philosopher H. D. Lewis, Stevens concludes that poetry must assume the function once served by religion, of mediating "a reality not ourselves," a reality "adequate to the profound necessities of life today or for that matter any day" (NA 99, 102).

If poetry is the medium, what reality shall it mediate? Stevens' maternal grandfather, very much alive as a kind of hereditary instinct, offers one answer to this question in "The Bed of Old John Zeller" (1944). Unable to rest in the disorderly "bed" of his grandson's freethinking mind, John Zeller compels him to seek a "structure of ideas" analogous to the old theistic world-view. He personifies the impulse that moved Stevens to project a supreme fiction or central poem in the forties and fifties. Not to accede to this impulse, Stevens implies in "Outside of Wedlock" (1942), would amount to betrayal of his ancestors (OP 76–77).[22] But in "The Bed of Old John Zeller" he rejects this as the "easy" solution. "It is more difficult," he maintains,

> to evade
> That habit of wishing and to accept the structure
> Of things as the structure of ideas.

In late poems like "The Course of a Particular" (1951), Stevens manages at least briefly to evade the habit of wishing. Hearing the cry of leaves swept by the wind, he refuses to make anything but literal sense of the sound, insisting that it

22. The Benjamin who appears in this poem is probably Benjamin Stevens, Wallace Stevens' grandfather. Blandenah—or Blandina, as the

is not a cry of divine attention,
Nor the smoke-drift of puffed-out heroes, nor human cry.
It is the cry of leaves that do not transcend themselves,

In the absence of fantasia, without meaning more
Than they are in the final finding of the ear, in the thing
Itself, until, at last, the cry concerns no one at all.

(OP 96–97)

Yet the course of this particular is ultimately a course of thought. Stevens is not, here, the snow man of an early poem, who has no choice but to see nothing that is not there and the nothing that is (CP 10). Rather, fully conscious of the meanings he might ascribe to the cry of the leaves, he deliberately rejects each of them. On another day, he might listen to the cry of the leaves as Professor Eucalyptus of "An Ordinary Evening in New Haven" (1949) listens to the sound of the rain in the spout, ready to seize "The description that makes it divinity" (Section XIV). With that description, the ear's "final finding" would yield to the demands of imagination and the course of a particular come full circle.

Stevens saw no reason to isolate any moment in the imagination-reality cycle and cling to it alone; "both of these things project themselves endlessly," he said in 1951, "and I want them to do just that" (L 710). Especially during the fall and winter of 1948–49, however, he began to feel that modern art and literature had tipped the scale toward imagination. His response to a Jean Arp sculpture is typical of this period:

> The piece called Dream of An Owl is . . . full of the disintegration of reality in the imagination. No doubt Arp is tightly aesthetic and no doubt his conceptions occur to him in moments of aesthetic intensity. But he lacks force. His imagination lacks strength. His feelings are incapable of violence. (L 628)

Thirty-five years previously, Stevens might have endorsed Arp's aesthetic program as an expression of the same spirit

---

name is spelled in "Analysis of a Theme" (1945)—was the name of at least three women in the Stevens line.

that animated the 1913 Armory Show. By the late forties, he was looking to artists like Tal Coat to redress the balance in favor of realism. From Coat he purchased in 1949 the painting he described as follows:

> It is a still life in which the objects are a reddish brown Venetian glass dish, containing a sprig of green, on a table, on which there are various water bottles, a terrine of lettuce, a glass of dark red wine and a napkin. Note the absence of mandolins, oranges, apples, copies of Le Journal and similar fashionable commodities. All of the objects have solidity, burliness, aggressiveness. (L 654)

For Stevens, the Venetian glass dish became the "angel" so neglected by the fashionable or merely aesthetic artists of his day: reality. The water bottles, terrine of lettuce, glass of wine, and napkins became the befitting entourage of reality, a group of peasants. Indeed, in Stevens' poem based on the painting, "Angel Surrounded by Paysans" (1950), the angel tells the countrymen that he is one of them, a *paysan*.

It pleased Stevens to think that Coat's still life, so full of the solidity, burliness, and aggressiveness he valued, was the work of a Breton peasant (L 654). The more he learned about the Pennsylvania farmers and craftsmen in his own past, the more he sought the trademark of the peasant in other writers' work, as a token of authenticity. On receiving a copy of Henri Pourrat's L'Exorciste in 1954, he told Barbara Church that he preferred Pourrat's simple country people to the "Parisians" who populated much French literature of the day (L 832). In letters to Pourrat himself, Stevens typically praised the French author for his attachment to Auvergne. "You are truly a prodigy of love for your native land," he wrote Pourrat in 1952, "and a tireless recorder of her life, past and present."[23] Among contemporary American poets, Stevens singled out John Crowe Ransom as the "instinct and expression" of his native Ten-

23. Letter of 14 Feb. L'Exorciste is one of four Pourrat books at the University of Massachusetts Library, all inscribed to Stevens by the author.

nessee and its people (*OP* 260). Speaking of Ransom's enterprise in a homage he contributed to the *Sewanee Review* on the occasion of Ransom's sixtieth birthday, Stevens said,

> One turns with something like ferocity toward a land that one loves, to which one is really and essentially native, to demand that it surrender, reveal, that in itself which one loves. This is a vital affair, not an affair of the heart (as it may be in one's first poems), but an affair of the whole being (as in one's last poems), a fundamental affair of life, or, rather, an affair of fundamental life; so that one's cry of O Jerusalem becomes little by little a cry to something a little nearer and nearer until at last one cries out to a living name, a living place, a living thing, and in crying out confesses openly all the bitter secretions of experience. (*OP* 260)

Whether or not this passage describes Ransom's achievement, it does suggest one of Stevens' late aspirations—the desire to approach the Jerusalem of his native land. But which native land? A resident of Hartford for most of his adult life, he could pass as a Connecticut Yankee. "It is not that I am a native," he said in a script written for a Voice of America radio broadcast series, "but that I feel like one" (1955, *OP* 296). He speaks in the same place of the "true mythology of the region," forged in Connecticut's colonial past and inherited by its twentieth-century inhabitants. It was possibly this notion that inspired "A Mythology Reflects Its Region," a poem Stevens wrote about the same time as the radio script. To be "true," according to the poem, a regional mythology must partake of the character of its human maker, projected larger than life yet deriving palpably from "the substance of his region, / Wood of his forests and stone out of his fields / Or from under his mountains" (*OP* 118).

Deep down, however, Stevens belonged to the wood and stone of Pennsylvania rather than Connecticut. The New England state provided him with settings for poems like "Of Hartford in a Purple Light" (1939) and "An Ordinary Evening in New Haven"; it officially honored him when he won the National Book Award in 1955; but it could not supplant in his affections the region he always called home. In the quest for his ancestors, he could not overlook the "parent before thought," the fatherland which, he suggests in "The Irish Cliffs of Moher" (1952), is also first father. Eastern Pennsylvania was the stage on which he reconstructed much of his past, and he managed to visit Reading at least three times during the years 1943 through 1946, despite the difficulties of travel for a man who did not drive an automobile and disliked staying in a hotel or with relatives. Hence it is not surprising that he used Pennsylvania place names more frequently in the late poetry than any time previously.

Sometimes, the place name has a purely casual interest to anyone but Stevens, though the reader may benefit from learning that Mount Neversink of "Late Hymn from the Myrrh-Mountain" (1946) is often shrouded in mist rising from the Schuylkill River, that Ephrata of "Memorandum" (1947, *OP* 89) resounds with katydids in summer, and that the Swatara River of "Metaphor as Degeneration" (1949) is known for its Stygian hue. In other poems, the name of a place serves, like the name of an ancestor, to suggest the presence of the past in the present as a kind of fate. "A Completely New Set of Objects" (1946), for example, recalls a festive scene re-enacted each summer when Stevens was a boy.[24] Emerging from darkness, the canoes on the Schuylkill River seem at first to be products of an alien and original genesis. But in the shadows cast by the Chinese lanterns, one comes to recognize the faces of friends. It is as though the whole scene existed simply to gratify an ancestral longing for these very shapes and shadows. One has discovered, not a new world, but the "verdure" or enduring vitality of those patriarchs buried "Under Tini-

---

24. Donald R. Shenton describes this festival in "The Reading That Stevens Remembered," *Historical Review of Berks County* 24 (1959): 108.

cum or small Cohansey." This last phrase is justified by more than its euphony, for Stevens had sought information regarding his father's side of the family in these cemeteries.[25] The disclosure sought in "Thinking of a Relation between the Images of Metaphors" (1946) is of somewhat the same order, if one brings to the Perkiomen Creek a sense of its meaning for Stevens. "This creek," he told a genealogist, "when I was a boy, was famous for its bass. It almost amounts to a genealogical fact that all his life long my father used to fish in Perkiomen for bass, and this can only mean that he did it as a boy" (*SP* 5). Like old John Zeller in "Two Versions of the Same Poem," published a few months before "Thinking of a Relation," the fisherman awaits a revelation he is fated to seek, if not necessarily to find.

In another category of poems using Pennsylvania place names, the place epitomizes the peasant's agreement with his native reality. Thus "Credences of Summer" represents the Oley Valley in which some of his Zeller ancestors had settled as "A land too ripe for enigmas, too serene" (Section IV). So complete and sufficient is this reality that the "singer" or poet must avert his eyes before he can celebrate it in words (Section VII). To be truly the *paysan*, he would have to speak the language of the landscape, the "Pure rhetoric of a language without words" (Section IV). This is the strategy of the countryman in the 1950 poem of that title, who walks in silence beside the Swatara River, which flows through Lebanon County to the Susquehanna River and thence into Chesapeake Bay. But neither its source ("cap") nor its destination ("cape") interests the countryman. He is intent on simply "being there," perfectly attuned to the creek's distinctive character.

Absorbed in the Swatara as a physical entity, the countryman is presumably indifferent to that aspect of the creek

25. Stevens had suggested to May E. Enders that she check records in the Presbyterian churches of Tinicum, Pa., and Cohansey, N.J., in letters of 3 Dec. 1945 and 29 Mar. 1946.

which most engages the writer of the poem—its linguistic reality. For Stevens as poet, the Swatara is a phenomenon of sound, in this case the darkly sinuous sound of its Indian name. The Indian name in turn suggests the Anglo-Saxon adjective "swarthy," which he uses five times in counterpoint with the word "Swatara." In effect, the poem marks the distance between Stevens and the countryman he aspired to be in some of his late work. To be sure, the regional writer is always something of a contradiction, and for much the same reason that the medium man–poet seems a contradiction: writing entails a degree of self-consciousness which qualifies his regional identity. Stevens recognized this in Ransom's case when he said, apropos of feelings aroused by the sight of familiar local objects,

> There are men who are not content merely to acknowledge these emotions. There are men who must understand them, who isolate them in order to understand them. Once they understand them it may be said that they cease to be natives. They become outsiders. Yet it is certain that, at will, they become insiders again. In ceasing to be natives they have become insiders and outsiders at once. And where this happens to a man whose life is that of the thinker, the poet, the philosopher, the teacher, and in a broad generalized sense, the artist, while his activity may appear to be that of the outsider, the insider remains as the base of his character, the essential person, something fixed, the play of his thoughts, that on which he lavishes his sense of the prodigious and the legendary, the material of his imagination. (*OP* 260–61)

Here Stevens formulates what might be called the literary principle of indeterminacy. Just as the physicist must forgo measuring the momentum of an atomic particle when he tries to locate its position, so the writer must temporarily suspend his feeling for a region in order to isolate its source. Inevitably, both scientist and writer interfere with the phenomena they observe. Yet Stevens maintains that the poet's identity as "insider" can remain the base of his character and the material of his imagination. To write convincingly about life, he told José Rodríguez Feo, one must write not as a student or artist but as "a good barbarian, a true Cuban, or a true Pennsylvania Dutchman" (L 624). On another occasion he observed to Henry Church, "*Il faut être paysan d'être poète*" (L 461). Taken together, these remarks say it all: Stevens was a Pennsylvania Dutchman who wrote always of his native region, but always in the language of the outsider.

Consequently, what he called his "unique and solitary home" in "The Poem That Took the Place of a Mountain" (1952) was not the land of his boyhood, exactly, but a *paysage imaginaire* derived from it. "The real is only the base," he asserted in an adage, adding, "But it is the base" (*OP* 160). Unlike those *fin de siècle* heroes Axël and Des Esseintes, he never sought to create an autonomous, self-sufficient world of imagination. As long as human nature is what it is, he maintains in Section V of "An Ordinary Evening in New Haven," it will continue to find satisfaction in two different realms: half of the self adheres to "common earth" while the other half searches for majesty in "moonlit extensions" of reality. Stevens' *Collected Poems* explores all ramifications of the self, ranging freely between the sphere of the *paysan* and that of the visionary. On a smaller scale, long sequences like "An Ordinary Evening" allowed Stevens the latitude in which to develop and resolve his contrary theses; hence this endlessly elaborating form was perhaps his most congenial medium. He also wrote a handful of poems during his lifetime which, though relatively brief, suggest the full scope of his vision. One thinks of "Anecdote of the Jar" and "The Idea of Order at Key West" from the earlier work, "To an Old Philosopher in Rome" and "The World as Meditation" from the later. Preëminent among Stevens' synoptic shorter pieces, however, is the poem that lent its title to the final section of the *Collected Poems*—"The Rock" (1950).

"The Rock" is a rock-like poem, monolithic and superficially simple but, on closer scrutiny, dense to the point of being nearly impenetrable. Though its three sections proceed logically from one to another, their logic is seen more clearly when they are read in reverse order. In Section III, Stevens identifies the controlling image of the poem as "the gray particular of man's life" or, as he later put it in an interview with a Yale divinity student, "simply the sphere of the world."[26] Inert in itself, the rock serves man as the step to all of his imaginative ascents and descents; though virtually colorless itself, it reflects the green-blue of his rhapsodies and the red of his dreams. Thus as material cause, "The starting point of the human and the end," the rock partakes of its transformations.

In Section II, Stevens examines more closely the relation between the rock and its imaginative transformations. Assuming that the rock's barrenness is a condition which must be "cured," how shall one proceed? To cover it with "leaves," such as the leaves of poetry, might distract us from the rock for a time, but this would be a merely cosmetic cure. A truly efficacious cure would arise from the rock itself or—what amounts to the same thing, since the rock is a fact of human experience—from ourselves. Yet the leaves, if they seem inconsequential when considered one by one, might amount in sum to a curative fiction or icon. Two years previously, Stevens had speculated that there might be a theory of the world based on "a coordination of the poetic aspects of the world" (L 590). Here, he hypothesizes that this central poem might accomplish in the metaphysical realm a feat that would be impossible in the organic realm: if this and if that, the leaves might bud and bloom and bear fruit as though they were actually rooted in the rock as ground. Man, inasmuch as he has created this prolific poem, shares its fertility, his body "quickened" and his mind "in root." "This is the cure," Stevens concludes,

26. Signe Culbertson, "One Angry Day-Son," *In Context* 3, no. 3 (1955): 13.

Of leaves and of the ground and of ourselves.
His words are both the icon and the man.

This miraculous cure takes place, if indeed it does take place, "In the predicate that there is nothing else." What else might there be? The alternative cure, not mentioned here, is the same to which Professor Eucalyptus had alluded when he sought "God in the object itself, without much choice" ("An Ordinary Evening," XIV). Though Stevens proceeds in Sections II and III as if there were no God beyond the object, the gray particular, he had in fact admitted another assumption—and that a "vital assumption"—in Section I. This section opens in a state of imaginative barrenness or abstraction. The poet—there is no reason to think he is not Stevens—is unable to take possession of either his past experience or his poems. The family home, a moment of passion, his strummings on the blue guitar seem alike unrealized and remote. It is as though he had never had a role in the drama of his own existence. His life seems rather to have been the work of an anonymous stage manager, produced

In the sun's design of its own happiness,

As if nothingness contained a métier,
A vital assumption, an impermanence
In its permanent cold, an illusion so desired

That the green leaves came and covered the high rock,
That the lilacs came and bloomed, like a blindness cleaned,
Exclaiming bright sight, as it was satisfied,

In a birth of sight. The blooming and the musk
Were being alive, an incessant being alive,
A particular of being, that gross universe.

The assumption elaborated in these lines is vital not only in the sense of "being alive" but also in the sense of being essential to the cure hypothesized in Section II. Section II begins with leaves; once the leaves are there, one can project a cure of the rock in terms of a purely human mythology. Section I takes the cure one step further back, by suggesting why there should be leaves rather than nothing at all. It is at this point, J. Hillis Miller has shown in a provocative essay, that "The Rock" forces the reader to confront the uncanny, indeterminable element which lies just below the surface of language and, indeed, of life.[27] Who or what "desires" change and is "satisfied" when change takes the form of leaves? The syntax obscures the agent or agents of these verbs; the sun and nothingness, though candidates for first cause, seem to be suggestive illustrations of something else. That something is never named and remains a kind of surd in the poem. But since it sponsors the "pearled chaplet of spring," the "magnum wreath of summer," and "time's autumn snood," it has much in common with a vital assumption discussed earlier in this chapter—the imagination that presides over seasonal change in Section VII of "The Auroras of Autumn."

Poems like "Auroras" and "The Rock" suggest that Stevens found in this cosmic imagination a serviceable myth to account for orderly change in the physical universe as well as the poetic. Couched always in a carefully hedging style, the myth is never mistaken for non-mythic reality of the kind theists ascribe to their gods. Nevertheless, a poem like "A Child Asleep in Its Own Life" (1954, OP 106) suggests that Stevens found emotional as well as intellectual solace in playing child to this austere parent. He had always believed, Eliot notwithstanding, that the poetry does matter; and he came increasingly to believe that it matters more than the individual poet. Herein lies a surprising affinity between Stevens and the poet he considered his "dead opposite" (L 677): much as Eliot effaced himself before the Supreme Being, Stevens effaced himself before supreme imagination.[28] Several readers have observed that

27. "Stevens' Rock and Criticism as Cure," *Georgia Review* 30 (1976): 5–31; 330–48.

28. This may help to explain a paradox Roy Harvey Pearce points out in *The Continuity of American Poetry* (Princeton: Princeton University Press, 1961)—that Stevens' later poems, as befits their culminating position in

his personal cure of the rock took on distinctly theological overtones when he exchanged the vocabulary of the hero and the central poem for phrases like the "central mind," the "External Master," and the "great Omnium" (*CP* 524; *OP* 105, 102, 106).[29]

The late poetry renders plausible an episode that took place near the end of Stevens' life. In 1952 he told Thomas McGreevy, half-facetiously, that he wished he had more time to make up his mind about God (*L* 763). His wish was granted several years later, under circumstances he would not have chosen but which rendered the question of belief more urgent. On April 22, 1955, he entered Saint Francis Hospital in Hartford for exploratory surgery and spent most of the next two months convalescing away from home and office. Whether or not he suspected he was dying of cancer—he was not told, on the advice of his physician—he had been forcibly reminded of his mortality. Thus he may have been more than usually susceptible to the example and influence of the Roman Catholic priest and nuns who attended him at the hospital. It was as though he had stepped bodily into his own 1952 poem, "To an Old Philosopher in Rome." He told Father Arthur P. Hanley, then the chaplain at Saint Francis, that he had been thinking of converting to Catholicism for a long time. Father Hanley affirms that he instructed Stevens in the Catholic faith and, sometime between his readmission to the hospital on July 21 and his death on August 2, baptized him and administered the sacrament of Communion.[30]

---

the Adamic strain of American poetry, preach a "universal egocentrism," yet are at the same time his least "personal" poems (pp. 393, 413). In the Culbertson interview cited above, Stevens speaks of the poem as less the creation of an individual poet than an "external force" or "demi-urge" of the age (p. 12).

29. See, for example, Morris, p. 112, and James Benziger, *Images of Eternity: Studies in the Poetry of Religious Vision from Wordsworth to T. S. Eliot* (Carbondale: Southern Illinois University Press, 1962), pp. 240–43.

30. The information in this and the previous sentence comes from my conversation with Father Hanley on 5 June 1981 and his letter of 14 June 1981. According to Father Hanley, the archbishop of the Archdiocese of

Assuming that Stevens did convert to Catholicism, what precisely did it mean to him? I suspect that by his "conversion" he did not so much subscribe to an orthodox creed as endorse its value, in the manner of Santayana. Though his choice of denomination was dictated partly by the circumstances of his final illness, it accorded with his habit of visiting Saint Patrick's Cathedral in New York to meditate or, as he put it in 1902, to feel "how the glittering altar worked on [his] senses stimulating and consoling them" (*SP* 104). Readers who regard Stevens as fundamentally an aesthete and dandy will see a certain fitness in his turn to Rome, since he thereby placed himself in the company of celebrated Decadents like Barbey d'Aurevilly, Huysmans, Beardsley, Wilde, Dowson, and Lionel Johnson.[31] Be that as it may, his Catholic profession in effect drew the line between his adult accommodation with religion and what William James would have termed the "dead" hypotheses of his boyhood faith.

Even if it were possible to reconstruct the substance of Stevens' final belief, we should probably not have a faith very different from—or even more specific than—the one he professes in "Final Soliloquy of the Interior Paramour," a moving poem that might serve as an appropriate coda to this study of his mythology of self. Before turning to "Final Soliloquy," however, we might briefly review that mythology with the help of another piece, "Conversation with Three Women of New England" (1954, *OP* 108–9).

This genial *envoi* recalls Stevens' attempt, a decade pre-

Hartford requested that Stevens' baptism not be recorded or made public lest people think that Saint Francis Hospital actively sought to convert non-Catholic patients. The Reverend Thomas J. Lynch, chancellor of the Archdiocese, confirms that there is no record of Stevens' baptism at the hospital, the Avery Nursing Home, or the parishes in which these are located.

31. James Baird sees another kind of predisposition to Catholicism in Stevens' poetry; he maintains in *The Dome and the Rock: Structure in the Poetry of Wallace Stevens* (Baltimore: Johns Hopkins Press, 1968), pp. 305–7, that the poetry reveals an affinity for the structures—architectural, liturgical, and imaginative—of the Church of Rome.

viously, to represent the creative ferment that eventuated in a Picasso painting (see Chapter Three). Like Picasso's "half-a-dozen men at once conversing together," Stevens' three women are animae or modes of the self. Though purely internal, they determine how the external world will be seen, since "The mode of the person becomes the mode of the world, / For that person, and, sometimes, for the world itself." Stevens addresses each of his animae in turn, identifying her peculiar "mode." The first is an idealist in quest of life's "single source and minimum patriarch" at the center of the world or thought. To her we may attribute Stevens' preoccupation with a universal aesthetic, a preoccupation that led him to the myth of Ananke in the thirties, to the supreme fiction and the central poem in the forties and fifties.

The second anima, by contrast, urges us to scale our mental artifacts—be they gods, heroes, or fictions—to the dimensions of man and nature as we normally experience them. For her, the world is a place of concrete particulars rather than "capital things of the mind"; she speaks for the Stevens who posed as aesthete in the early poetry, medium man during the middle phase, and *paysan* in the late poetry.

The third anima takes a position somewhere between and to one side of her sister selves. Man, she contends, is defined neither by God nor by his world but by himself. He may pursue this strategy as a self-made man in the manner of Garrett Stevens, as a dandy, or as the creator of major man.

These three women carry on an animated conversation throughout Stevens' career. One discourses brilliantly of Plato and Santayana, another of Pater and Pourrat, another of Baudelaire and Nietzsche. Each remains her staunch New England self even as she betrays exotic influences. To which does Stevens give the final nod? Though the third anima offers a persuasively synthetic view, she does not have quite the last word in the conversation. This is reserved for their host, who, civil to the last, asks whether it might not be

> enough to have seen
> And felt and known the differences we have seen
> And felt and known in the colors in which we live,
> In the excellences of the air we breathe,
> The bouquet of being—enough to realize
> That the sense of being changes as we talk,
> That talk shifts the cycle of the scenes of kings?

As one might expect of a "conversation," this poem celebrates the pure good of talk. Conversation is the vehicle by which one passes through various modes of being, as one would tour the Continent or savor a mixed bouquet of flowers. Why choose among them, when choice would impoverish experience?

Only an ungrateful reader would wish away this bouquet of being, for with it would go much of Stevens' *Collected Poems*. Yet this "enough" is almost too much. Thinking of Yeats's breath-taking descent into the foul rag-and-bone shop of the heart, one would like, for once, to catch Stevens out of this after-dinner mood, when he is so full of himself and so full of his selves. One turns with something like relief to "Final Soliloquy of the Interior Paramour," where one finds, not Yeats's squalor perhaps, but poverty of a sort. The poem's title is not a stage direction, as in the similar early poem, "To the One of Fictive Music" (1922). The soliloquy, if a speech delivered by two persons can be termed such, consists of a mere six words: "God and the imagination are one." But what remarkable words these are, even though they have been prepared by poems like "The Auroras of Autumn" and "The Rock." The "We say" which precedes this proposition, like the "Or so they said" which follows a synopsis of the Christian gospel in "Notes toward a Supreme Fiction" ("Pleasure," III), signals its status as myth rather than empirical fact or logical deduction; but it is a myth to live by, one that identifies the world imagined with the Goodness Personified of religion.

For the soliloquy to have its full effect, it must be spoken from a stage that has been properly set. In an address to the Poetry Society of America about the same time he wrote "Final Soliloquy," Stevens said that the genius of poetry chooses "as her only apt locale in a final sense the love and thought of the poet, where everything she does is right and reasonable" (*OP* 243). Therefore poetry, he goes on to say, "is to be found beneath the poet's word and deep within the reader's eye in those chambers in which the genius of poetry sits alone with her candle in a moving solitude." The opening lines of "Final Soliloquy" recreate this chamber and its special atmosphere:

> Light the first light of evening, as in a room
> In which we rest and, for small reason, think
> The world imagined is the ultimate good.
>
> This is, therefore, the intensest rendezvous.
> It is in that thought that we collect ourselves,
> Out of all the indifferences, into one thing:
>
> Within a single thing, a single shawl
> Wrapped tightly round us, since we are poor, a warmth,
> A light, a power, the miraculous influence.

If there is value in a colloquy which continues indefinitely to shift the cycle of the scenes of kings, there is value, too, in simplifying the décor and recollecting one's selves momentarily into one thing. Only then can the poet speak a soliloquy that will be not merely an act of appreciation but what Stevens called, in his Poetry Society address, "an act of conscience." The single shawl is the poet's refuge from his "indifferences"—from the apathy, distraction, even empathy which impede self-recollection.

Stevens' choice of pronoun should not be overlooked, for it gives the poem its profoundly intimate character. Helen Vendler captures what one would expect to be the

emotional tenor of a soliloquy when, apropos of "An Ordinary Evening in New Haven," XX, she says, "The naked
being isolated in a chamber, perceiving the world as debris
of life and mind, is a true enough picture of Stevens as the
composer of this canto and of large tracts of this poem."[32]
It is also a true enough picture of the autumnal Stevens as
she represents him in her study of his longer poems. But
it is not quite the Stevens we encounter in "Final Soliloquy." Here, abjuring the naked and solitary "I," he adopts
a "we" that reflects his sense of communion with the spirit
of poetry—a spirit, as I suggested in Chapter Two, that
includes not only his own creative anima but also his sense
of his audience. This rendezvous, the intensest, precipi-
tates another, more inclusive rendezvous when he and his
muse recall the larger imagination to which they belong.
So to remember is to forget themselves:

> Here, now, we forget each other and ourselves.
> We feel the obscurity of an order, a whole,
> A knowledge, that which arranged the rendezvous[,]
>
> Within its vital boundary, in the mind.
> We say God and the imagination are one . . .
> How high that highest candle lights the dark.
>
> Out of this same light, out of the central mind,
> We make a dwelling in the evening air,
> In which being there together is enough.

Stevens senses, in this lucid integrity, both the fatality
and the freedom of his position. Though passive in the
embrace of that which arranged the rendezvous, he actively collaborates in the making of his dwelling. Aesthetic
and mythology are for a moment congruent. When the
"candle" flares, brighter and still brighter, his spirit soars
with it. How high that highest candle lights the dark! From
this exhilaration, which has little in it of religious awe and
less of personal pride, he modulates to a feeling of quiet

32. *On Extended Wings*, p. 287.

satisfaction. It is as though the world had been destroyed and created anew, the light once again divided from darkness. If this is poverty, it is the poverty of the Book of Genesis, with whose Creator Stevens could affirm, on the seventh day of his poetic enterprise, it is good, it suffices, it is enough.

Index of Works by Wallace Stevens

Page numbers in italics indicate fuller discussions of the works.

General Index

Compositor:	Graphic Composition
Text:	10/12 Palatino
Display:	Palatino
Printer:	Braun-Brumfield, Inc.
Binder:	Braun-Brumfield, Inc.